Global Intellectual Property Rights

Global Intellectual Property Rights

Knowledge, Access and Development

Edited by

Peter Drahos
and

Ruth Mayne

First published 2002 by
PALGRAVE MACMILLAN
Houndmills, Basingstoke, Hampshire RG21 6XS and
175 Fifth Avenue, New York, N.Y. 10010
Companies and representatives throughout the world

PALGRAVE MACMILLAN is the global academic imprint of the Palgrave
Macmillan division of St. Martin's Press, LLC and of Palgrave Macmillan Ltd.
Macmillan® is a registered trademark in the United States, United Kingdom
and other countries. Palgrave is a registered trademark in the European
Union and other countries.

ISBN 0–333–99027–7 hardback
ISBN 0–333–99028–5 paperback

This book is printed on paper suitable for recycling and
made from fully managed and sustained forest sources.

A catalogue record for this book is available
from the British Library.

Library of Congress Cataloging-in-Publication Data
    Global intellectual property rights : knowledge, access, and development /
    edited by Peter Drahos and Ruth Mayne.
        p. cm.
    Includes bibliographical references and index.
    ISBN 0–333–99027–7 (hardback) – ISBN 0–333–99028–5 (pbk.)
        1. Intellectual property (International law) I. Drahos, Peter, 1955–
    II. Mayne, Ruth. III. Oxfam GB.
    K1401 .G58 2002
    341.7'58–dc21   2002074831

10   9   8   7   6   5   4   3   2   1
11   10   09   08   07   06   05   04   03   02

Printed and bound in Great Britain by
Antony Rowe Ltd, Chippenham, Wiltshire

This book is based on a collection of papers for a seminar organised and
supported by Oxfam International. Oxfam GB is a member of Oxfam
International and is associated with the publication of the papers as a contribution to informed debate on issues of global equity. Opinions expressed
in the papers are the responsibility of the individual authors and not necessarily those of Oxfam GB or any institutions or organisations with which
authors are affiliated.

Contents

Notes on the Contributors

Kumariah Balasubramaniam is Pharmaceutical Adviser to Consumer International's Health and Pharmaceutical Programme in Asia and the Pacific. He has worked extensively in the area of consumer access to essential drugs. He has a PhD in clinical pharmacology and was Senior Pharmaceutical Adviser in the Technology Division of UNCTAD in Geneva between 1978 and 1983.

Michael Blakeney is Herchel Smith Professor of Intellectual Property Law at Queen Mary Intellectual Property Research Institute, London. He has published widely on intellectual property law. His books include *Legal Aspects of the Transfer of Technology to Developing Countries* (Oxford: ESC, 1989), and *Trade Related Aspects of Intellectual Property: A Concise Guide to the TRIPS Agreement* (London: Sweet & Maxwell, 1996).

Carlos M. Correa is Director of the Master's Programme on Science and Technology, Policy and Management, at the University of Buenos Aires. He is an influential writer on intellectual property issues, particularly as they affect developing countries. His most recent publications include *Integrating Public Health Concerns into Patent Legislation in Developing Countries* (South Centre, 2000), *Intellectual Property Rights, the WTO and Developing Countries: The TRIPS Agreement and Policy Options* (London: Zed/TWN, 2000).

Peter Drahos is Professor in the Research School of Social Sciences at the Australian National University. He has degrees in law, politics and philosophy. His publications include *A Philosophy of Intellectual Property* (Dartmouth, 1996) and, with John Braithwaite, *Global Business Regulation* (Cambridge University Press, 2000).

Martin Khor is the Director of Third World Network, which brings together several development and environment NGOs in the developing world. Martin is an economist who took his degree at Cambridge University. He is the author of several books, the latest being *Globalisation and the South*, and has been a consultant for several UN agencies.

Gary Lea is Lecturer in IP Law at Queen Mary, University of London. Gary has taught and researched in intellectual property since 1992. His interests lie in the development and exploitation of IP in the IT and telecoms sector.

James Love is Director of Ralph Nader's Consumer Project on Technology, USA. He is an influential economist who has worked on the trade-related aspects of intellectual property since 1994, and on IP issues relating to medicines, information technology and technology transfer since 1990.

Stuart Macdonald is Professor in the Management School at Sheffield University, UK. He has worked for 20 years in many countries as an academic researcher concerned with intellectual property issues. He has advised governments, patent offices and large corporations on patent issues. His research has been supported by research councils and authorities in many countries, including the European Commission, the Economic and Social Research Council in the UK and several government departments.

Ruth Mayne is a policy adviser on trade, investment and economics at Oxfam GB and currently specialises in intellectual property issues. She is a trained economist, has worked in development for over 20 years, and has written on a range of subjects and is co-editor of *Regulating International Business*.

Sol Picciotto is Professor at Lancaster University Law School, specialising in international economic and business law and regulation. He was a founding editor of *Capital & Class* and of *Social and Legal Studies*, is the author of *International Business Taxation*, as well as numerous articles, and has edited books including *Regulating International Business*.

Willem Pretorius is a barrister. He has had extensive experience in competition policy and law in Africa.

Suman Sahai is Convenor of the Gene Campaign, India and has a PhD in genetics. The Gene Campaign is a grassroots research and advocacy group which has 35 Core Groups in 17 states. These serve as centres for public education, awareness generation and advocacy on issues of intellectual property rights, national legislation, biological resources, indigenous knowledge and farmers' rights.

Alan Story has been lecturer in intellectual property law at Kent Law School in Canterbury, Kent, UK since 1999. He is co-chair of WIPOUT (www.wipout.net), the Intellectual Property Counter Essay Contest, and is a member of the TRIPS Action Network. He has written on a range of intellectual property and property theory issues.

John Sulston (FRS) is co-founder of the Human Genome Project, Cambridge. Until recently, he was director of the Sanger Centre, where one-third of the human genome is being unravelled. Prior to this he worked at the Salk Institute for Biological Studies and then at MRC Laboratory of Molecular Biology, where he helped to produce and sequence one of the earliest animal genome maps of the nematode. He was elected to the Royal Society in 1989, and was knighted in the UK's New Year's Honours List in 2000.

Preface

This book arose out of the considerable and growing controversy surrounding the new global system of intellectual property rules that govern rights over knowledge. With the shift to the new knowledge economy these rules are becoming the focus of one of the most intense struggles to reform globalisation. The outcome will determine who will control the major new technologies of the twenty-first century.

Against this backdrop, Oxfam International and a group of UK-based academics organised an international seminar in Brussels in March 2001 that brought together key policy makers, academics, scientists, developing country trade negotiators and NGOs. The papers in this volume reflect this diversity of training, perspective and experience. One of the aims of the seminar (and of this book) was to achieve a better policy understanding of the issues through a synthesis of the views of those NGOs at the cutting edge of the global campaigning and debates that have accompanied the globalisation of intellectual property and the views of leading academic experts.

The seminar focused on the Agreement on Trade-Related Aspects of Intellectual Property Rights (TRIPS) – a key international instrument governing rights over knowledge – and sought to generate critical debate about possible reforms to these rules. Many of the seminar papers, on which this book is based, point out that while intellectual property protection can play a useful role in stimulating investment and innovation, the current system does not adequately balance this with the broader public interest in allowing the maximum number of people to use and benefit from new knowledge, particularly those living in poor countries.

To date, much of the controversy over global intellectual property rules has focused on TRIPS but concern is also growing about the way in which bilateral trade and investment agreements are being used to ratchet up intellectual property standards. Together these rules will ultimately affect the lives of billions of people, yet they are being introduced with minimal public debate. TRIPS was, for example, pushed through by a handful of rich countries under the influence of a heavy corporate lobby without the informed participation of many developing countries.

The problem for poor countries and people is that the extended monopolies granted by these rules allow powerful Northern-based companies to extend control over markets and raise the price of vital technology goods. Critics argue that the upshot for poorer countries will be their further exclusion from access to medicines, seeds and educational materials. Nowhere has this been more graphically illustrated than in the inability of African governments to afford patented HIV/AIDS medicines. In developing countries, which are mainly net importers of modern technology, the main effects of TRIPS will be higher prices for protected technologies and goods (for example, patented medicines and seeds) as well as restricted scope for imitating and adapting new technologies.

More broadly, the application of global intellectual property rules raises at least three wider issues that go to the heart of public discontent about globalisation. First, they raise stark questions about human rights. The Universal Declaration of Human Rights establishes the rights to adequate health provision, food and education, along with the right to share in the benefits of scientific progress, as basic human rights. These rights have primacy as a matter of international law, but there is growing evidence that in some areas they are being made subordinate to the investment priorities of corporate intellectual property owners.

Secondly, there is growing disquiet about the way the rules are removing broad scientific knowledge, particularly in genetics, medicines and plant sciences, from the intellectual commons. Not only does this reduce people's control and access to vital resources, it skews research in favour of those who can pay and inhibits the free exchange of knowledge on which technological progress depends.

And finally the rules raise serious questions about the democratic functioning of the World Trade Organization (WTO). The TRIPS Agreement was negotiated within the multilateral forum of the WTO – a body that should reflect the public interest of all its members. Yet since its inception, rich-country and corporate bias has weighed heavily in both the design and implementation of TRIPS. It is a striking anomaly that an organisation charged with developing rules for free trade is providing a legal framework for the development and enforcement of global information monopolies.

It is not surprising that as the rules begin to bite there are growing demands for public debate. The chapters in this book, most of which were papers given at the Brussels seminar, seek to contribute to that debate. This book is not an argument against intellectual property protection, but rather against the one-size-fits-all approach of TRIPS and some other trade agreements that block sustainable development and create avoidable suffering. It is a call for a more flexible set of rules which differentiates between countries at different levels of development, different sectors and products, particularly those that play a vital social role. It is also a call for a more democratic system of standard-setting that places intellectual property regulation within a framework of human rights objectives, including the right to development.

We thank the speakers, as well as the authors of additional contributions. We also thank the co-sponsors of the seminar including the International Business Regulation Forum,* Action Aid, Consumer International, Médecins Sans Frontières, WWF International, Center for International Environmental Law, Berne Declaration, Consumer Unity and Trust Society Centre for International Trade, Economics and Environment, International Cooperation for Development and Solidarity, and Institute for Agriculture and Trade Policy. We are grateful to those who helped with the seminar including Ruchi Tripathi, Ellen t'Hoen, Cecilia Oh, Matthew Stilwell, Bob Van Dillen, Kristin Dawkins, Sol Picciotto, Geoff Tansey and Alan Story. We are also grateful to the EC and government officials who took the time to speak at and participate in the seminar, particularly Pascal Lamy, the EC Trade Commissioner, and Mr Defraigne, Head of Cabinet of Commissioner Lamy and Francisco Cannabrava, Second Secretary, Permanent Mission of Brazil to the United Nations and the World Trade Organization in Geneva. Special thanks, too, to those in Oxfam GB who helped organise the seminar – particularly Anni Long and Claire Godfrey. Peter Drahos also thanks Julie Ayling for her invaluable assistance with the editing process.

PETER DRAHOS
RUTH MAYNE

---

* The International Business Regulation Forum is an informal group of UK-based academics and NGOs that seeks to build new alliances and explore constructive and innovative approaches aimed at developing an effective international regulatory framework for investment.

List of Abbreviations

AIDS	acquired immune deficiency syndrome
CAFC	US Court of Appeals of the Federal Circuit
CAS	Central Advisory Service
CBD	Convention on Biological Diversity
CFCs	chlorofluorocarbons
CGIAR	Consultative Group on International Agricultural Research
CGRFA	Commission on Genetic Resources for Food and Agriculture
COP	Conference of Parties (to CBD)
DSU	Dispute Settlement Understanding
DSB	Dispute Settlement Board
EC	European Commission
ECJ	European Court of Justice
EDV	Essentially Derived Variety
EPC	European Patent Convention
EU	European Union
FAO	Food and Agriculture Organization
FDI	Foreign Direct Investment
GATS	General Agreement on Trade in Services
GATT	General Agreement on Tariffs and Trade
GDP	gross domestic product
GNP	gross national product
GRAIN	Genetic Resources Action International
GRULAC	Group of Countries of Latin America and the Caribbean
GURT	gene use restricting technology
HAI	Health Action International
HGP	Human Genome Project
HIV	human immune deficiency virus
IDMA	Indian Drug Manufacturers Association
IIPA	International Intellectual Property Alliance
ILO	International Labour Organization of the UN
IMF	International Monetary Fund
IPRs	intellectual property rights
ISAAA	International Service for the Acquisition of Agri-biotech Applications

ISNAR	International Service for National Agriculture Research
ISO	International Standards Organization
MEA	Multilateral Environment Agreement
MFN	most favoured nation
MNCs	multinational drug companies
MSF	Médecins Sans Frontières
MTA	Material Transfer Agreement
NAFTA	North American Free Trade Agreement
NAROs	national agricultural research organisations
NCE	new chemical entity
NCI	National Cancer Institute
NICs	newly industrialized countries
NGOs	non-governmental organisations
NPCI	New Commercial Policy Instrument
OAU	Organization of African Unity
OECD	Organization for Economic Cooperation and Development
PBRs	plant breeders' rights
PhRMA	Pharmaceutical Research and Manufacturers of America
PMA	Pharmaceutical Manufacturers Association (South Africa)
PVP	plant variety protection
RAFI	Rural Advancement Foundation International
R&D	research and development
RMI	rights management information
SNP	single nucleotide polymorphism
SRIs	software-related inventions
TRIPS	Agreement on Trade-Related Aspects of Intellectual Property Rights
TWN	Third World Network
UCC	Universal Copyright Convention
UNAIDS	Joint United Nations Programme on HIV/AIDS
UNDP	United Nations Development Programme
UNCTAD	United Nations Conference on Trade and Development
UNHCR	United Nations Commission on Human Rights
UNIDO	United Nations Industrial Development Organization
UPOV	International Union for the Protection of New Varieties
USTR	United States Trade Representative
WCT	WIPO Copyright Treaty 1996
WHO	World Health Organization
WIPO	World Intellectual Property Organization
WPPT	WIPO Performances and Phonograms Treaty
WRI	World Resources Institute

1
Introduction

Peter Drahos

Intellectual property rights have gone global. States around the globe are converging upon the same set of intellectual property standards in areas of law such as copyright, patents, trademarks and industrial designs, as well as upon the remedies available for the enforcement of these rights. Moreover, in many cases states are shifting to higher standards than previously prevailed in their domestic law – longer terms of protection, fewer exceptions to the scope of rights and sometimes new rights. The case for the globalisation of standards in some areas of regulation seems clear cut. Not many would argue the case for patchily applied or lower standards of aircraft safety or nuclear power station regulation. Is the case for the globalisation of higher standards of intellectual property, standards which affect access to things like medicines, books and information technology, persuasive in the way that it seems to be for aircraft safety or nuclear power station operation? The chapters in this volume suggest that the case for the globalisation of intellectual property rights is anything but persuasive. More disturbingly, the chapters in Part II suggest that global intellectual property rules may well be an obstacle to development.

Under the Agreement on Trade-Related Aspects of Intellectual Property Rights (TRIPS), the 144 Members of the World Trade Organization (WTO) are obliged to give effect to a set of basic minimum principles and rules covering copyright, trademarks, geographical indications, industrial designs, patents, layout-designs of integrated circuits, protection of undisclosed information and the enforcement of intellectual property rights. The states in the world are in different stages of economic development. They are also profoundly unequal. Judging how unequal depends on the indicators one uses (the World Bank has more than 500 indicators in its development databases), but on any set of indicators that includes income, health and education a picture of great economic inequality emerges (see Chapter 6 by Balasubramaniam in this volume).[1] In poor countries up to 50 per cent of children under 5 are malnourished, while in rich countries the figure is less than 5 per cent. Gaps in income have doubled in the last forty years with the top twenty wealthiest countries now having an average income thirty-seven times that of the twenty poorest. The poor not only continue to be with us, but their numbers in Sub-Saharan Africa, Latin America, South Asia, Central Asia and some post-Communist European states are rising. In parts of Africa, the AIDS epidemic has created a hell in which gains in life-expectancy of the last century are about to be lost.

Is there, bearing in mind these deep inequalities, a case for globalising intellectual property rights? For example, both the US and Rwanda are members of the WTO. Does it make sense to oblige both the US and Rwanda, which is a least-developed country member of the WTO, to enact a patent law that allowed for the patenting of pharmaceutical products?[2] The US has the world's largest pharmaceutical company (Pfizer), a sophisticated research pharmaceutical industry and a massive research infrastructure which includes 3676 scientists and engineers in R&D per million people.[3] Rwanda does not have a research pharmaceutical industry and only 35 scientists and engineers in R&D per million people. On the face of it there may be a case for a pharmaceutical product patenting rule in the US, but almost certainly not in Rwanda. Rwanda by enacting such a rule is not likely to trigger a wave of indigenous pharmaceutical innovation or foreign investment from pharmaceutical companies. Such innovation and investment depend on many other factors aside from patent rules. Even if Rwanda enacted a 40-year patent term, for instance (TRIPS requires 20 years as a minimum), one suspects that Pfizer would not begin to invest heavily in Rwanda. Here we have the makings of a case for states being allowed to have some discretion in setting the level of intellectual property protection in the case of pharmaceuticals.

If national sovereignty over the rules that regulate innovation in information is important to development goals such as health, why have developing states ceded so much of that sovereignty? Has it been through choice or coercion? The chapters in Part III of this volume indicate that coercion has been the key mechanism in explaining the spread of intellectual property norms. Given all this, what should be done about intellectual property rights and TRIPS in particular? The chapters in Part IV address this issue.

What is development about?

A recent World Bank report says that development is about 'improving the quality of people's lives, expanding their ability to shape their own futures.'[4] Those involved in development no longer think of it simply in terms of increasing household income. Development is about achieving a group of objectives for poor people including better educational and job opportunities, greater gender equality, better health and nutrition, the protection of the environment, natural resources and biodiversity.[5] Drawing on 50 years of development experience a three-pronged strategy for development based on the promotion of opportunity, facilitating empowerment and enhancing security has been proposed.[6]

Fundamental to achieving these objectives is international cooperation amongst states. Global markets, global private actors in the form of transnational corporations (TNCs), global environmental problems and global security problems mean that no one state, rich or poor, can operate in isolation. Financial regulators know from experience that if a financial crisis begins in the US, Europe or Asia it must be tackled by them working together as an international group, otherwise they risk the meltdown of the world's financial system. Globalisation is slowly bringing about the need for states to recognise reciprocal duties of care and cooperation.

It is now clear that major development problems such as lack of market access for developing countries' exports, ill health and lack of education in developing countries 'can be solved only with cooperation from high-income countries'.[7] Two of the areas identified for international action aimed at poverty reduction are directly related to the globalisation of intellectual property rights: the provision of international public goods and increasing the participation of poor states in global decision-making fora.

Development, intellectual property and public goods

A number of the chapters in this volume draw attention to the fact that in the past developed countries set intellectual property standards to suit their own stage of economic development (see Chapters 6, 11, 12 and 14 by K. Balasubramaniam, W. Pretorius, M. Khor and S. Picciotto). Roughly speaking, all countries at some point used the strategy of freeriding. A freerider is a person who takes the benefit of an economic activity without contributing to the costs needed to generate that benefit. In the case of intellectual property the freerider takes the benefit of information for which the costs of discovery/creation have been met by the producer. The producer does not lose the information (for this reason information is described as a public good), but rather faces competition from the freerider who gains use of it as well. The purpose of creating intellectual property rights is to provide an incentive for producers to invest in the production of information by giving them a means (the intellectual property right) of preventing freeriding. A freerider is not a bad person in economic theory. On the contrary, the freerider performs an important economic function by diffusing information. The diffusion of information is fundamental to allowing competitive markets to work. The more producers, for example, who know how to make a therapeutic drug the better from society's point of view because those producers will have to compete on price in order to sell it. Freeriding is only economically inefficient if it reaches levels that deter producers from investing in the cost of discovering information in the first place. Intellectual property rights are a form of government regulation of the market. When governments should intervene in information markets is a complex empirical question. There is, it might be said, a disturbing modern tendency to overintervene to protect or strengthen business monopolies based on intellectual property rights. Importantly, all intellectual property rights are designed in ways that prevent the intellectual property owner from having an absolute grip on the information (for example, limited terms, limited rights, the need to re-register, and so on). The whole point of this government regulation is to ensure that the information is diffused into the intellectual commons where other producers and creators can make use of it. (Chapter 3 by Carlos Correa discusses some of the pro-competitive features that are built into intellectual property rights.) Because intellectual property is a form of government regulation it is open to problems such as regulatory capture. TRIPS in essence is the outcome of the international regulatory capture of the WTO process by concentrated producer interests in the form of pharmaceutical, film and software TNCs all holding large intellectual property portfolios and therefore with much to gain from government intervention.

Freeriding has been rampant throughout economic history. Over the centuries states have either not participated in the intellectual property system (for example, Switzerland had no patent law until 1888) or they have done so, but in ways that favoured their own producers (for example, by not recognising the rights of foreign intellectual property owners). These freeriding strategies continued throughout the twentieth century. Intellectual property rights were narrowly defined, seen as exceptions rather than the norm and the infrastructure for their enforcement both within states and amongst states was poor to non-existent. This has almost certainly been a very good thing. Stuart Macdonald's argument (see Chapter 2) that the patent system is fundamentally anti-innovation applies to most forms of intellectual property. We do not want, for example, a copyright regime that is so tight that it deters the kind of entrepreneurship that led to an innovative business model such as Napster. The act of creation depends heavily on the free flow of ideas and the exchange of information. Chapter 4 by John Sulston, describing the human genome project, shows just how dependent large modern scientific projects are on an international community of scientists exchanging information with each other. The creative process does not work well under the red tape of intellectual property rights systems. Indeed, intellectual property rights can, as John Sulston reveals in Chapter 4, have a destabilising effect on creative processes within groups.

Certain large scientific projects can only be tackled by scientists working together as an international community and with public funding. The human genome project is a case in point. The foundational nature of the information that emerges from such projects is too important for present and future generations to be locked up by intellectual property rights. It has to remain a public good, a part of an intellectual common from which no researcher is barred.

Many developing countries achieved sovereignty after World War II. When it came to the regulation of intellectual property and their development they followed the same sorts of freeriding strategy that developed countries had. Developed states with their large stocks of technology and scientific knowledge had generated, in effect, public goods that could be accessed by developing countries if they acquired the relevant scientific capacity (as in the case of the Indian pharmaceutical industry) or could be transferred to developing countries as a public good (as in the case of the provision of new higher yielding seed varieties).

The globalisation of intellectual property rights has seen access to information made more costly and difficult (the need to search for owners, negotiate licences, and so on). This in turn has meant that development based on access to public goods using strategies of freeriding and diffusion have been circumscribed. Chapter 8 by Alan Story dealing with copyright and education and Chapter 9 by Gary Lea dealing with copyright, patents and information technology illustrate this. Gary Lea's chapter also points out that developing countries have been unsuccessful in obtaining international rules on technology transfer.

The transfer of international public goods to developing countries has been made more difficult by the expansion of intellectual property rights systems. Privately held patents over biological materials and research tools have made it much harder for international public research to provide public goods to developing countries. Michael Blakeney, in Chapter 7 on the impact of intellectual property on international agricultural research, reveals a growing problem of private goods driving out public ones.

The globalisation of intellectual property rights is not a substitute for international public goods related to development for two reasons. First, intellectual property rights primarily act as incentives for TNCs to produce products for wealthy Western consumers. If the poor want more patent-based R&D for malaria they will have to hope that it overtakes obesity and impotence as a problem in Western societies. Secondly, the poor in developing countries cannot afford to pay TNCs the prices they demand for their intellectual property products (see Chapter 9 by Kumariah Balasubramaniam). No amount of clever price discrimination by these TNCs will see their products made affordable to the 2.8 billion people who live on $2 a day and 1.2 billion who live on less than a $1 a day. Pharmaceutical markets made competitive by generic manufacturers are the best long run guarantee of access to medicines for the poor.

There is one other deep discordance between the globalisation of intellectual property rights and the present development policy agenda. Developing countries need income. Yet one clear effect of TRIPS will be trade gains for developed countries at the expense of developing countries.[8] One especially troubling feature of TRIPS is that it sets up a flow of revenue from the less developed to the more developed, thereby contributing to a global *structural* inequality in the world. At the same time TRIPS does not address the exploitation of the intangible assets of developing countries (which means they continue to suffer problems such as biopiracy – the unauthorised use of indigenous knowledge and biological materials by TNCs). It is hard not to conclude that through the rules of intellectual property the rich have found new ways to rob the poor.

Resisting information feudalism

A major theme running through the present policy development agenda is the empowerment of the poor: '[p]oor people and poor countries should have greater voice in international forums'.[9] The globalisation of intellectual property is an example of the way in which the deeds of globalisation do not match this policy aspiration. When TRIPS was being negotiated no African country was a player in any of the key negotiating groups that shaped its final contents (see Chapter 10 by Peter Drahos). When South Africa went down the path of passing legislation aimed at obtaining cheaper pharmaceutical products to deal with the AIDS crisis the response from the international pharmaceutical industry was litigation and from US and EU officials pressure and harassment to change this law (see Chapters 11 and 15 by Willem Pretorius and Ruth Mayne).

The reality of standard-setting for developing countries is that they operate within an intellectual property paradigm dominated by the US and EU and international business. Developing countries are encircled in the intellectual property standard-setting process. TRIPS sets high minimum standards. Bilaterally the bar on intellectual property standards is being raised even higher.[10] Within the interstices of this paradigm there are steps that developing countries can take. Chapters 3, 5 and 14 by Carlos Correa, James Love and Sol Picciotto discuss the use of compulsory licences, the adjustments that can be made in intellectual property law to encourage the diffusion of information and principles of interpretation that might be used to secure better outcomes under TRIPS in terms of social welfare. However, they also reveal that in this global intellectual property paradigm developing countries face the prospect of having to pursue development strategies through lawyers' games.

There is no shortage of policy proposals by developing countries on what to do about TRIPS and the intellectual property paradigm more generally (see Chapter 12 by Martin Khor). Chapter 13 by Suman Sahai on 'India's Plant Variety Protection and Farmers' Rights Legislation' demonstrates that intellectual property laws that pay heed to the assets of the poor can be drafted and passed. It also reveals the importance of the democratic process in the design of welfare-enhancing intellectual property laws. The model law drafted by the Organization of African Unity in consultation with community groups and NGOs is another example of the way in which intellectual property principles can be fashioned to serve local communities and farmers.[11]

Developing countries do not lack an understanding of intellectual property. In the 1950s and 1960s India and Brazil developed critiques of Western patent regimes and African states pushed for the recognition of folklore as a proper subject matter of copyright protection. It is precisely because developing countries have shown they have the capacity to develop models that threaten the hegemony of current Anglo-American–German intellectual property models that their efforts have been crushed. Nowhere is this clearer than in the use of the trade regime to extend Western models of intellectual property law that are deeply discordant with development policies and strategies. US and EU trade negotiators listen to the concentrated voices of organised international business, not the voices of the poor, because those concentrated voices whisper Siren-like of trade gains to be won and losses to avoid. Hard tactics are used by US and EU negotiators to drive hard bargains with developing countries on intellectual property bilaterally and multilaterally.

Developing countries can resist the globalisation of intellectual property by forging alliances with NGOs. There are now thousands of national and international NGOs working on intellectual property issues as they arise in the food, agriculture, seed, health and biotechnology sectors. Other NGOs work on intellectual property issues as they affect education, software programming, libraries, privacy and free speech. These many weaker actors offer the possibility of a new global politics of intellectual property. Putting together a coalition of weak actors to counter the sovereignty of business over the rules of information requires vision and energy. The last chapter in this volume, by Ruth Mayne, which describes the way in which NGOs forced the US, the EU and big business into a dialogue over intellectual property and health in the context of the health crisis in developing countries, suggests the possibility of such a global politics. It was this politics which achieved a significant victory in the form of the *Declaration on the TRIPS Agreement and Public Health* at the WTO Ministerial Conference in November 2001. Such a politics offers the best chance of gaining global intellectual property standards that genuinely promote welfare.

Notes

1. The facts in this paragraph come from the World Bank's *World Development Report 2000/2001: Attacking Poverty* (OUP: New York, 2001).
2. As a least-developed country Rwanda does get the benefit of a ten-year transitional period under TRIPS before it has to apply most TRIPS standards. Para. 7 of the *Declaration on the TRIPS Agreement and Public Health* (Doha, WTO Ministerial, November 2001) extends the time of implementation for least-developed countries to 1 January 2016 on some aspects of product patents. A least-developed country may, however, bilaterally agree to implement these standards before that date.
3. *World Development Report 2000/2001: Attacking Poverty* (OUP, New York, 2001), p. 311.
4. World Bank, *The Quality of Growth* (New York: OUP, 2000), p. xxiii.
5. See Deepa Narayan *et al.*, *Voices of the Poor: Can Anyone Hear Us?*, World Bank (New York: OUP, 2000), ch. 2.

6. *World Development Report 2000/2001: Attacking Poverty* (OUP, New York, 2001), pp. 6–7.
7. *Ibid.*, p. 188.
8. See, for example, K.E. Maskus, 'Intellectual Property Rights and Economic Development' (2000) *Case Western Journal of International Law*, vol. 32, pp. 471, 493.
9. *World Development Report 2000/2001: Attacking Poverty* (New York: OUP, 2001), p. 12. See also, Deepa Narayan *et al.*, *Voices of the Poor*, ch. 7.
10. See P. Drahos, 'BITS and BIPS: Bilateralism in Intellectual Property' (2001) *Journal of World Intellectual Property*, vol. 4, p. 791.
11. See, *The OAU's Model Law: The Protection of the Rights of Local Communities, Farmers and Breeders, and for the Regulation of Access to Biological Resources*, Organization of African Unity, Scientific, Technical Research and Research Commission, Professor J.A. Ekpere, Project Coordinator, PMB 2359 (Lagos, Nigeria, November 2000).

Part I

Innovation and Diffusion of Technology

2
Exploring the Hidden Costs of Patents

Stuart Macdonald

Introduction

The popular conception of the patent system is one of mad inventors with ludicrous inventions and equally absurd expectations that the product of their years of pottering in the garden shed will change the world. Precisely the same system is the bulwark of strategy in some of the world's most powerful companies, and is fundamental to the way the drugs of modern medicine are discovered and developed. Can the one instrument serve such diverse purposes (see Thurow, 1997)? Certainly those for whom the patent system is of critical strategic importance think so for they frequently declare that it benefits the independent inventor and the small firm. They insist that the patent system encourages the innovation by the weak as well as the strong, and that society is much the richer for this innovation.

This chapter considers just who does benefit from the patent system and then turns to the other side of the coin: the costs of the patent system. Most discussion of the system seems not so much to deny the existence of costs as to ignore them. Yet, the costs would seem to be considerable and their distribution as uneven as that of the benefits. Those who reap most benefits from the patent system are not those who incur most costs, and while benefits are finely focused, costs are much more widely distributed. The greatest cost of all would seem to be borne by society as a whole in terms of damage done to innovation, which is curious given that the fundamental purpose of the patent system is to encourage innovation for the benefit of society as a whole.

The conventional view of patents

The patent is the instrument of the intellectual property system best known and most closely associated with innovation. The patent is the outcome of a bargain between the inventor and society by which society grants the inventor certain rights to his or her invention in return for the inventor's disclosure of whatever it is he or she has invented (see Taylor and Silberston, 1973). Without these rights, it is conventionally argued, the inventor would be unable to reveal his or her invention for fear that others would steal it. Consequently, the inventor would have little incentive to invent, and society would forgo the invention and all its benefits. Thus, the patent system neatly offers the inventor the opportunity to reap some reward from his or her invention, and provides society with an invention it would not otherwise have had. Everyone benefits, or so it is said.

The patent system bestows its benefits by giving intangible resources – the information of invention – the legal status of property. It is hardly surprising that this mixture of law and wealth should attract the attention of lawyers and economists. These two groups have long dominated discussion of the patent system with the consequence that discussion rapidly descends to sub-paragraphs of legislation and the minutiae of economic theory. This is daunting stuff for those from other fields and there are many other fields with an interest in innovation: in the sciences, any branch of engineering; in the arts and humanities, anything to do with creativity; and in the social sciences, any of a wide range of subjects from management studies to technology policy, from sociology to politics. Indeed, it is hard to think of an area in which innovation (broadly defined as change) is not a major interest, and innovation, be it remembered, is supposed to be the whole purpose of the patent system. It is innovation – not invention – that society wants, and it is for innovation that society has devised the patent system.

Engrossed in the niceties of the patent system, lawyers and economists have compiled a voluminous literature that excludes those not of their persuasions, no matter how great their interest in innovation. The consequence is twofold: their own perception of the patent system has remained untainted by the influence of other fields, and the perception of the patent system outside economics and the law has been sullied by neither. Indeed, the complications and implications of the system pass virtually unnoticed in the world at large, masked by the simple assumption that the patent stimulates innovation, and – equally innocent – that something would surely be done about the system if it did not.

The patent system is taken on trust, vaguely perceived as beneficial and, if not beneficial, at least benign. The patent system is the province of the unworldly, themselves the butt of good-natured jokes. The patent system is not a danger, not a threat.

Patents in practice

The patent has a long and dishonourable history, used as much to reward political loyalty as invention. It has provided the means to award profitable monopolies to friends and cronies as much as to entrepreneurs. Enterprise has flourished during periods when the patent system has fallen into neglect, and has overcome even its complete absence. Invention has survived the perversion of the system to fit the requirements of communist ideology, and still survives peculiarities in the regulations of various national patent regimes. In short, the purity of the patent system is a modern construct, perhaps even a product of economists and lawyers casting limelight on to theory and leaving practice in decent obscurity.

The basic patent bargain works only in theory. In practice, both sides cheat. Most obviously, the patent affords protection only when the patentee can afford to enforce his or her rights, which may mean that the poor have no protection at all (see Mansfield *et al.*, 1981). As the journal *Nature* (1929) noted long ago:

> the consideration for which patent rights may be enjoyed is nowadays not so much the introduction of a new invention as the possession of exceptional wealth.

And if society cheats in not providing the protection the inventor has a right to expect from the patent system, the inventor cheats too. Only in theory does the inventor provide society with the information of invention: in practice, he or she discloses the information required by the patent system, not the information required by society to replicate and develop his or her invention.

> A company's patent lawyers can protect the company's proprietary position without giving away too much in the application process. (Labich, 1988, p. 30)

The patent specification is primarily a legal document, not a source of information for innovation. One respondent to a survey of professional engineers who had taken out patents encapsulated the situation nicely, 'I could barely recognise my own invention in legalese' (Mandeville, 1982, p. 12). Basically, the information contained in patent specifications is available only to those who consult them directly, or who pay others more adept at arcane classifications and the language of lawyers to do so (Liebesny, 1972). Moreover, the delay between the filing of an application and the publication of a specification may be far greater than the pace of change in some industries. In high technology – an activity often associated with the patent system – time rapidly erodes the value of information. In addition, the criteria by which patents are granted pay no heed at all to the contribution patent information might make to innovation. Details of inventions which can make no conceivable contribution are frequently published, as are those of patents designed to mislead or obstruct (Schmookler, 1957).

In short, the patent system is ripe for abuse, and has long been abused. It should not be surprising that the patent system is still being abused. The wonder is that anyone should think otherwise, and this chapter will speculate on just why this might be. The chapter will argue that the strong are most able to exploit the patent system and that they have a great deal to gain from this exploitation. The chapter will also argue that this exploitation is hidden – deliberately hidden – from those who bear its costs. Basically, the strong disguise their own interest in the patent system by emphasising society's interests in the system and the benefits for the weak. Thus, the chairman of both Reed Elsevier and the European Round Table, a grouping of European leaders of business, declares that:

> Protecting intellectual property is crucial, not so much for large companies but for small and medium sized enterprises. (Morris Tabaksblat as quoted in Betts and Groom, 2001, p. 1)

Benefits for the weak – some empirical evidence

In theory at least, the system is particularly appropriate for encouraging the invention of small firms and independent inventors. Large organisations are more likely than small to have the internal resources to develop their own inventions, and so can keep the information of invention to themselves. Smaller organisations must generally seek these resources outside and so must reveal all. In practice, though, the protection the patent system affords the weak against the strong is often illusory, and the problems small firms encounter in protecting their inventions through the patent system are widely acknowledged. There is much less questioning of the advantage they and their innovation are claimed to reap from the other part of the patent bargain, the information the patent system makes available. Small firms cannot depend on vast R&D departments to generate the information required for invention; they must look to external sources for this information and one of the richest of these is said (by patent officials) to be patent specifications.

> Patent specifications are a source of valuable technical information, readily available and much of it *free* for the taking. It is a pity that *so few* manufacturers, engineers and scientists seem to be aware of this. So next time you have a technical problem, check to ensure that it has not been solved already. Even if you don't find a ready solution, you may pick up some good ideas for use in your current or future design. [original emphasis] (Australian Patent Office, 1981, p. 2)

> Each patent specification is a detailed disclosure of the invention and it is this aspect of course which is particularly valuable as a rich source of technical information. (Blackman, 1994, p. 47)

Such assertions are in conflict with the evidence. Two postal surveys were carried out in October 1996, one of the 615 UK small firms (employing between 10 and 250) that had been granted at least one patent in the UK or Europe in 1990, and a control group of 2000 small manufacturing firms in the UK. The overall response was just under 35 per cent. Predictably, these small firms look to customers, suppliers and competitors for information about the latest developments in their industry and market (Figures 2.1a and 2.1b). All other likely sources of external information vie with each other in their uselessness for innovation in small firms, which is interesting in that many of these sources take some pride, and expend considerable public resources, in their efforts to provide information to small firms. Most successful in this unenviable competition are government sources and the patent system. Small firms that have patented declare the patent system to be somewhat less useless than do small firms in general, but the positive side is not encouraging for those who feel that the patent system is obviously a major source of information for innovation in small firms: while just 8 per cent of the small firms in the control group think patent information of some importance, only 12 per cent of small firms which patented, and that therefore have some familiarity with at least the protective side of the system, consider patents are of some importance as a source of information for innovation.

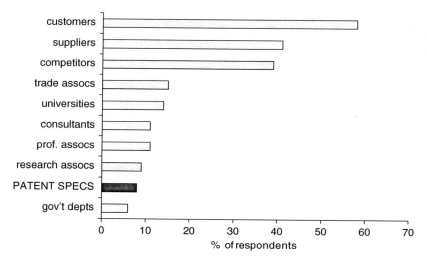

Figure 2.1a   External sources of information rated important for innovation in small firms

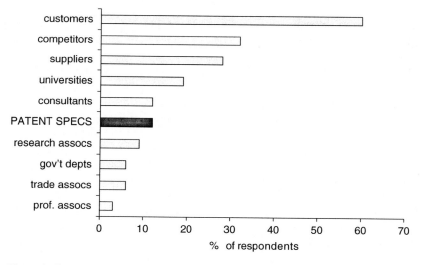

Figure 2.1b   External sources of information rated important for innovation in patenting small firms

It is often argued that the other forms of intellectual property protection – registered designs, copyright and trademarks – being simpler devices, are of more practical use to small firms than patents. This would seem to be questionable. These small firms do not see any form of intellectual property protection as important to their innovation (Figures 2.2a and 2.2b). What is most remarkable is that even those that have patented, and therefore have some knowledge of intellectual property rights, are only slightly more likely to see the other forms of intellectual property protection as benefiting their innovation. In both cases, trademarks and trade secrets are a little more valued than copyright and registered designs, but the difference is marginal and is overwhelmed by the vast majority of small firms considering that all forms of intellectual property protection are of little importance for their innovation.

Most of the firms surveyed because they had been granted a patent in 1990 had since acquired other patents – but not many. On average they had been granted but one other patent, and only 13 per cent had more than ten patents. About half did not apply for patents even on inventions they thought were patentable. Two-thirds had developed their invention since patenting it in 1990, but 87 per cent would have developed the invention even without a patent. Predictably, development is almost exclusively in-house rather than in partnership. Licensing patents to others is not a popular course; 81 per cent of small firms granted a patent in 1990 have not licensed it. Nor has the vast majority licensed patents from anyone else over the last ten years. Not a single firm could boast that it frequently licensed patents from others. Of the few firms that did occasionally license, most gained know-how as part

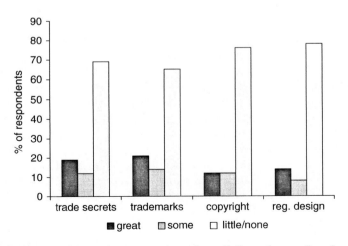

Figure 2.2a Benefits to the innovation of small firms from other forms of intellectual property protection

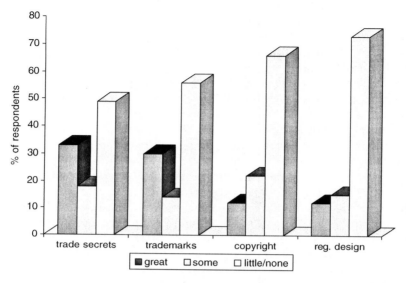

Figure 2.2b   Benefits to the innovation of patenting small firms from other forms of intellectual property protection

of the agreement, but the licence also imposed restrictions on what they could do with the technology. Most common among these restrictions were agreements not to sell outside a geographical area, not to dispute patents, not to sell competing products, and agreements to buy parts from the licensor and to license back improvements.

About half of these small firms regularly conduct patent searches and almost all of these pay a patent attorney to search on their behalf. The most important reason for doing this is to keep track of competitors, but the next most important reasons are to check on potential patent infringements and to prepare patent applications (Figures 2.3a and 2.3b). It has been noted by others that some of the most significant uses to which the patent system is put are demanded by the patent system itself (Australian Patent Office, 1980). When this happens, the patent system is serving not the requirements of innovation, but its own requirements. Even the small firms that search to keep track of competitors are more interested in keeping track of their competitors' patenting than their competitors' technology.

These two surveys paint a somewhat depressing picture of small firms isolated from the external sources of information for innovation that

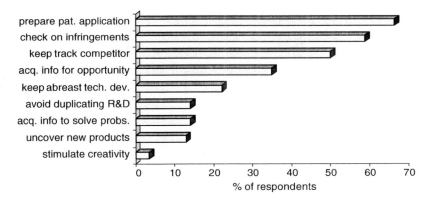

Figure 2.3a   Why patent searches are conducted by small firms

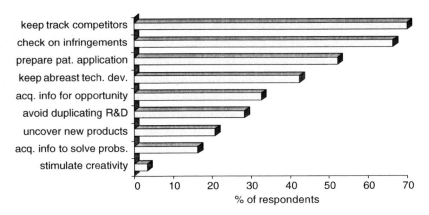

Figure 2.3b   Why patent searches are conducted by patenting small firms

larger firms and firms in rapidly innovating sectors find so important. These small firms seem to rely very heavily on their own resources. There is a range of likely reasons for this, but basically they come down to employees of small firms, and especially senior management, having few resources available to search for information in the outside world and to use the information acquired there. In a small firm, everyone is needed for day-to-day operations, to man the pumps. It should come as no surprise that small firms are highly innovative; their innovation is a necessary response to competition and the fluidity of their markets. Patent protection is little valued and innovation is rife in its absence

(Kahaner, 1983). And among a host of information sources that small firms might use for innovation and rarely do, the patent system is distinctive in being used least of all.

Who does benefit?

It is now more than a decade since Mansfield published his classic table illustrating the importance of the patent system to the innovation of various industries (Table 2.1). The table shows some industries to be very much more reliant on the patent system than others. Basically this is because the invention of these industries is readily codifiable (Levin *et al.*, 1987). This means both that competitors can easily acquire and use the information of invention and that the invention can be thoroughly described in a patent specification. Put another way, the precision of a chemical or pharmaceutical patent specification makes the patent particularly easy to defend and thus enhances the value of the intellectual property (Tapon, 1989). Hardly surprising then that Taylor and Silberston (1973, p. 231) could conclude that the 'pharmaceutical industry stands alone in the extent of its involvement with the patent system'. The pharmaceutical industry has done much to ensure that the patent system meets its own requirements, basically the requirements of large companies, operating with highly codified information on a route to innovation made linear by government regulation and social expectation.

Table 2.1   Inventions that would not have been developed in the absence of patent protection (%)

Pharmaceuticals	60
Chemicals	38
Petroleum	25
Machinery	17
Fabricated metal products	12
Electrical equipment	11
Primary metals	1
Instruments	1
Office equipment	0
Motor vehicles	0
Rubber	0
Textiles	0

Source: Mansfield, 1986.

Set against the benefits society reaps from innovation in those industries where innovation is encouraged by patents must be the monopoly costs these industries insist provide the necessary incentive to innovate. Less obvious is the cost to all those other industries where innovation is not dependent on patent protection, but that must still cope with a patent system that is virtually irrelevant to their requirements. Of course, it can be argued – it is argued – that firms everywhere benefit from the information disclosed and disseminated by the patent system. The argument is much more convincing in theory than in practice. Just as small firms have little use for patent information, large firms in all but those few industries where invention can be neatly encapsulated in a patent specification, attach little value to patent information. It has been calculated that patent information is worth about 0.75 per cent of firms' research and development (R&D) expenditure, and thus an infinitesimal proportion of total innovation costs (Taylor and Silberston, 1973, p. 212). This may help explain why there is such toleration of the poor dissemination of patent information; it is just not worth the spreading.

Invention or innovation?

An invention is a discovery: an innovation is a product or service that is new to the market, or simply new to the adopter (see Schott, 1981). It is important to remember that of the total resources required for innovation, only a small proportion comes from invention; the majority comes from design, production, marketing and the rest of the myriad of activities that contribute to the making of things. This assumes, of course, that every invention contributes something. It does not. Many inventions make no input to any innovation.

> Although most innovations can be traced to some conquest in the realm of either theoretical or practical knowledge that has occurred in the immediate or remote past, there are many which cannot. Innovation is possible without anything we should identify as invention, and invention does not necessarily induce innovation, but produces of itself... no economically relevant effect at all. (Schumpeter, 1939)

This failure to achieve the ultimate goal of successful innovation is often blamed upon what is seen as a rocky road from invention to innovation. Alternative models avoid the notion of a journey, of linearity

(Teece, 1988). These maze models of innovation depict no obvious route from invention to innovation; the journey may start anywhere in the system and may lead anywhere, perhaps to invention more than once, before innovation is reached – if it is ever reached at all. Innovation remains the goal, but getting there is the real challenge: innovation is not simply the last stop on the line (Rothwell, 1992, 1994). In the midst of both linear models and maze models is the patent system – seen as a convenient stretch of fast highway in the former and as a further complication in the latter.

Society may want innovation from its patent system very much indeed, but the patent system is really concerned only with invention (Kingston, 1987). This desire for innovation has produced two arguments in justification of the patent system. Though they are not incompatible, they are seldom presented together (Merges, 1988). Both are rooted in the supposition that invention would not take place if it could be purloined by anyone so inclined. The first argument emphasises development: the patent system gives an incentive to invent because it allows the inventor to reap a reward from his or her invention, either through developing it him- or herself or by selling it to others for them to develop.

Development is the inventor's responsibility, not society's. The second argument is less contingent on development and emphasises information: it is that a bargain has been struck between the inventor and society by which society grants property rights, with which the inventor may do what he or she will in return for giving society the information of his or her invention (Merges, 1988). Society must then use this information to create innovation, and development, with all its uncertainty and irregularity, becomes society's responsibility, not the inventor's. In the first case, society is to get innovation, which is what society really wants: in the second, only information. In the first case, society allows the inventor to make his or her information public: in the second, society demands that he or she make his or her information public. The first case supposes patent information leads directly to innovation and that innovation is society's reward: this is compatible with linear models of innovation. The second fits better with maze models of innovation in that it depicts patent information adding to a social store of information in which information for innovation may be found, and – with the owner's consent – used. In this case, information is society's reward.

Participants in process

While maze models come closer to the reality of innovation than linear models, there are those who prefer to see innovation as the culmination of a linear process. Society generally – and naturally – prefers this simple and direct model of innovation, and the passive role it is required to play. Often, though, this perception is encouraged by the observer's situation, and often it is in his own interest. For example, scientists involved in basic research like to think of their activities as seminal to innovation. And so do the universities and the research laboratories that house the scientists. Similarly, managers who allocate organisational resources for innovation like to feel they are fuelling a process that will produce the innovation they have planned and none of the uncertainties often associated with change; they need to justify resource input in terms of innovation output (see Greiner and Barnes, 1970). And thus it is with public servants anxious to encourage innovation and expected to account for the expenditure of public funds on research in terms of the innovation it will yield (Griliches, 1989). Patent attorneys and those who work for patent offices also have vested interests in the system. More generally, so do those who find the prospect of rampant, uncontrolled and unpredictable innovation disconcerting. For them – and there are many of them – the patent system provides an illusion of certainty in an uncertain world. Amidst the turbulence and tumbrels of even high technology revolution, it is comforting to feel that, even in innovation, there is a proper and established way of doing things:

> the very idea of a patent law is something of an oxymoron: it is a hybrid of two opposing principles, change and order, that live always in tension with each other. (Kass, 1982, p. 43)

To this considerable body of interest in perceiving a linear innovation process must be added those for whom innovation actually is a linear process. There are whole industries whose innovation is strongly influenced, if not actually determined, by what happens in research. In these cases, innovation is indeed a process, almost a routine in which output is basically a product of input. It behoves such industries to spend heavily on research and to protect as best they can not only their innovation, but also the systems on which their innovation, and hence their competitiveness, are dependent. The lengths to which these industries will go to protect the patent system are a measure of how crucial it is to their existence. Their position is not negotiable. Consider the recent unequivocal declaration from the president of one large pharmaceutical group.

> Les produits génériques sont des actes de piraterie qui seront éradiqués comme l'avait été la piraterie au XVII siècle. [Generic

products are acts of piracy which will be eradicated like 17th-century piracy was] (Quoted in Cohen, 2001)

For such industries, the patent system is so compatible with their method of innovation, so integrated with corporate strategy, that it has to be defended at all costs. Attack has been the customary form of defence, the aim being to secure strategic position not simply by maintaining the patent system, but by strengthening it. The size of the pharmaceutical industry, its potential to contribute to public welfare and its experience with R&D make the industry a force to be reckoned with (Miller, 1988; Porter, 1989). It is quite capable of using this power to extort advantage for itself and to impose costs on others.

> We are most interested in a strengthening rather than weakening of the Australian patent law, especially for pharmaceuticals. Substantial weakening might prompt us to drastically shortcut investments in Australia. (Quoted in Mandeville and Bishop, 1982, p. 16)

> The danger is that loss of patents in HIV alone could destroy the global HIV market. The bigger danger is that the broader loss of patents in South Africa could be the thin end of the wedge which smashes patent protection for the industry [worldwide]. And if that happens, then frankly the entire economic base of the pharmaceutical industry is destroyed. (David Ebsworth, Head of Pharmaceuticals in Bayer, as quoted in Pilling, 2001)

Before the strengthening of the patent system, society looked to high technology for a model of how to innovate, not the only or necessarily the best model, but a model that certainly worked. The model was based firmly on the notion that innovation was dependent on the free flow of information. So rapid was the pace of change in semiconductor and IT that the patent system played little part in the transformation. Indeed, the companies that accumulated most patents tended to go out of business, leaving the field to companies much less distracted by patenting (Table 2.2). This could not happen now.

> A weak patent policy did not slow things down in the development of the integrated circuit and microprocessor. In fact, it sped things up. The legal environment of the 1970s allowed Fairchild, Intel and others to get their start, carrying the lesson that strong patents for every industry are not always good. (*Forbes ASAP Supplement*, 1993, p. 62)

Table 2.2 Percentage of total semiconductor patents awarded to firms in the US, 1952–6

	1952	1953	1954	1955	1956
Bell Laboratories	56	51	46	37	27
Established firms	37	40	38	42	53
New firms	7	9	16	21	20

Source: Braun and Macdonald, 1978, p. 68.

The way in which high technology firms innovate now is very different and has been profoundly altered by the patent system (Simon, 1996).

> Software patents are failing to achieve the Constitutional mandate of promoting innovation and indeed are having a chilling effect on innovative activity in our [software] industry. (Shulman, 1995)

Strengthening the system

In the early 1980s, governments turned somewhat desperately to technology to create wealth and employment. As the President of the Pharmaceutical Research and Manufacturers of America (PhRMA), and sometime Commissioner of Patents and Trademarks, noted:

> The shift in the U.S. competitive advantage, away from basic manufacturing and toward high-tech information-based industries such as pharmaceuticals, makes global intellectual property protection an urgent policy priority for the U.S. government and for U.S. industry. (Mossinghoff and Bombelles, 1996, p. 47)

Innovation was the key to competitiveness, but government policy (and corporate strategy for that matter) found difficulty accommodating the undisciplined information flow fundamental to the innovation of a freewheeling Silicon Valley. Policy and strategy were much more comfortable with an interpretation of high technology entrepreneurialism that flaunted the trappings of Silicon Valley in the science park or the European Commission's Esprit Programme (Macdonald, 1987; Marschan-Piekkari *et al.*, forthcoming) while denying the unmanaged and uncontrolled information flow critical to innovation in high technology. The information required for innovation was to be captured and retained, whether in a Fortress Europe defended by the national champions of the electronics industry, or a Fortress America, where alarm at the Japanese and even European threat to competitiveness led to the imposition of national security export controls designed to prevent the loss of high technology information (Macdonald, 1990). At the corporate level, information mercantilism also prevailed with innovation strategy based on the acquisition and retention of information (Macdonald, 1998). Clearly, this climate was hostile to the patent system as an instrument for disseminating information widely so that others can use it, and much more comfortable with the patent system providing a temporary monopoly so that inventors can innovate. The climate was conducive to the strengthening of the patent system.

Pressure to extend the scope of patents was fuelled by the observation that much modern invention did not fit easily within the system's arcane classification. The scope of patents had to be extended if the system were to stimulate the innovation a modern economy requires. The patenting of genetic material is one result, the extension of the patent system to computer software and to business methods in the United States two more. The value of the patent monopoly is related not just to the scope of the patent, but also to the ease with which the patent can be defended. The US Court of Appeals of the Federal Circuit (CAFC) was established in 1982, a response to the need for a specialist body to cope with the growing complexity of some of the new areas into which patents were entering. The Court was also a product of powerful groups looking after their own interests:

> a very small group of large high technology firms and trade associations in the telecommunications, computer and pharmaceutical industries was essentially responsible for the creation of the CAFC. The group believed that a court devoted to patent cases would better represent its interests. (Silverman, 1990, fn. 62)

It is argued that the actions of the CAFC have very much strengthened the US patent system. Between 1982 and 1987, the CAFC upheld 89 per cent of district court decisions that patents were valid: between 30 per cent and 40 per cent had been upheld previously (Silverman, 1990). Penalties for infringement have become very severe:

> Defendants that have been judged guilty of 'wilful and wanton' infringement can be assessed treble damages, interest that accrues while they appeal, and the plaintiff's legal fees. Worse, judges are ordering companies found guilty of infringing to stop selling copycat

products immediately, rather than allowing them to continue business as usual until completion of the appeal. (Perry, 1986)

The result has been to increase the value of an American patent.

This increase in both the scope and the scale of patent protection has
altered the relationship between the conflicting interests inherent in
the system. A weak patent system acknowledges that invention is generally a long way from innovation and of little value in itself: a strong
patent system values invention – patented invention – perhaps even
above innovation. Texas Instruments, for instance, once liberal in its
cross-licensing arrangements with competitors, has become particularly
litigious. Its most profitable product line is now patent royalties. In
some years, the company's licence fees exceed its operating income
(Thurow, 1997). IBM increased its licence income from $30 million in
1990 to nearly $1 billion in 2000 (Rivette and Kline, 2000). Other semi-
conductor companies have converted the cross-licensing which used to
stimulate innovation in the industry into a mechanism for excluding
new entrants and inhibiting innovation (Barton, 1997).

With cases lasting four years plus and running anywhere from
$2 million to $10 million, computer companies are spending as much
time in the courts as they are in the laboratories. (Howes, 1993, p. 7A)

The balance of the system, then, has been tilted in favour of the benefit to society being expected less from the information made available
for innovation, and more from the protection given the inventor to
innovate himself. This shift is evident in a growing tendency in the US
to regard the commercial success of innovations as a major determining
factor in the granting and upholding of patents (Merges, 1988). Thus,
those organisations best equipped to innovate in a fashion compatible
with the patent system, rather than merely to invent, find most value in
the system. These are likely to be large firms. Being well equipped to
innovate themselves, there is little need for these firms to disseminate
their information to society so that society may innovate. In short,
strengthening the patent benefits the large firm whether it innovates
itself or licenses the patent to others: for the weak, able neither to innovate themselves nor to protect their property, strengthening brings no
benefits.

[A]n overemphasis on successful innovation, coupled with reduced
attention to the presence or absence of a true invention, reinforces

only one of the dual policy goals of the patent system: providing incentives to inventors. It ignores the goal of encouraging inventors to disclose technical information. (Merges, 1988, p. 876)

When intellectual property rights are protected, *innovators* are able to recover the costs incurred in research, product development and market development. This cost recovery ... is essential for stimulating the future research and development that is necessary to maintain America's competitive edge. [emphasis added] (Silverman, 1990, fn. 110)

Standing up for the weak

The patent system is much more suited to pharmaceutical and chemical firms than to most others, and these firms gain rather more benefits from the system than others. This would be of no great moment in a world which does not even pretend to be fair were pharmaceutical and chemical firms not disposed to defend their advantageous position by presenting their own innovation as typical of all innovation. Thus, because the pharmaceutical industry spends a fortune on R&D, the industry feels entitled to pontificate on innovation in general and on national competitiveness too.

> Since, today, it takes an average ten years and over $100 million to develop a new drug, only seven or eight years are left for the product to recover its entire investment before manufacturers who made no R&D investment at all are free to copy and compete with it. In the United States, the 1984 Patent Restoration Act has added up to five years of life to a pharmaceutical patent to make up for some of the time lost in the governmental approval process ... If the United States is to avoid further erosion of its competitive position, a new framework for growth must be envisioned ... in which intellectual property rights are protected and in which investment and innovation are encouraged. (Miller, 1988, p. 88)

This is arrant nonsense: the innovation of the pharmaceutical industry is not representative of innovation as a whole and the patent system that is so conducive to pharmaceutical innovation is much less appropriate for other innovation. With something like 22 per cent of the world's patents (Johnston and Carmichael, 1981), the pharmaceutical and chemical industries alone have just about as many patents as all the millions of the world's small firms in all industries put together.

Yet, despite the evidence, the pharmaceutical and chemical industries present themselves as champions of the weak, defenders of the means by which they are able to innovate. This smacks of hypocrisy.

> Indeed, it may fairly be claimed that the provisions of the new law [the Copyright Designs and Patents Act 1988] reflect the interests of the powerful and politically active, not those of society as a whole. (Porter, 1989)

The costs of patents

Discussion of the costs and benefits of the patent system tends to emphasise the benefits. The costs of the patent system are usually ignored altogether, or are presented as trivial. Those most commonly acknowledged are the fees paid to patent offices and to patent attorneys. But there are other costs. There are serious costs. These would seem to be of two sorts:

1. *The costs of illusion (or perhaps disillusion).* The illusion is that the patent system really will deliver the protection and the information it is supposed to deliver. These costs are likely to be heaviest for those who are new to the patent system, and lightest for those who have most experience. The costs of illusion also encompass the costs society incurs in frustrated expectations of innovation.
2. *The costs of distortion.* The patent system is supposed to help meet society's requirements for innovation. Society is not supposed to meet the patent system's requirements, yet this is what happens when resources are diverted from other purposes, including innovation, to satisfy the demands of the patent system. Recall the use of patent information in the small firm survey; it was required not for innovation at all, but to service the patent system. Recall also that the patent system suits the innovation process of a few specialised industries, not the irregularity that is much more typical of innovation generally. In as much as this irregularity is compromised by being tailored to suit the patent system, there is a cost in terms of discouraged innovation.

The costs of illusion

Macroeconomic analysis of the patent system focuses on its net value to society.

> If the system accounts for a net increase in inventions having a value to society exceeding the costs society pays for them, the patent system is justifiable in economic terms. (Markham, 1962, p. 597)

A positive net social value does not require costs and benefits to be evenly distributed, but great benefits for some must entail equally great costs for others. The more stringent the system, the more these benefits would seem to be concentrated among those whose innovation accords with the system, and the greater the costs for those whose innovation does not. Most obviously, the costs of avoiding infringement rise (Moss and Evans, 1987). Any lengthening of the patent term obviously benefits those awarded patents, but less obviously increases both the risk of infringement and the search costs of others seeking to reduce this risk (Gilbert and Shapiro, 1990, p. 112). From this perspective, the information the patent system has accumulated is less a contribution to innovation than an obstacle to innovation. It becomes the responsibility of the patent attorney to help his or her clients avoid such obstacles.

> Corporate patent attorneys have started scrutinizing their companies' patent portfolios and have become more reluctant to give R&D managers the go-ahead on a new idea or business for fear of duplicating a patented product. (Perry, 1986, p. 80)

> Genetics Institute's patent counsel say the strength of the potential patent position is 'a leading factor' in deciding what research to pursue. (Rivette and Kline, 2000, p. 58)

Society's approach to innovation – which is what the patent system exemplifies – has gone very seriously wrong when lawyers decide research priorities, or when property is so valuable because it is protected by patent that industry strategy focuses on defending this property, even at the expense of creating new wealth. A whole vocabulary has developed to describe the role of patents in corporate strategy; amidst patent clustering, patent bracketing, patent walling and patent blitzkrieg there may be little place for innovation. The pharmaceutical industry can be quite ruthless in its defence of what has become critical to its existence (Miller, 1988; Porter, 1989).

Because patent statistics are now taken so seriously, there is pressure on employees in many organisations to create the patents to be counted, and – as in Japanese companies – employees may be offered incentives to patent as much as possible (Shapiro, 1990). A minor industry has developed to tally patents, a practice justified by the observation that patents are one of the few indicators of output from expenditure on innovation. Undeterred by the fact that patents, if they measure anything at all, measure invention rather than innovation (see Rosenberg, 1974; Wyatt, 1977–8; Sciberras, 1986), this minor industry counts patents to compare the technological and competitive strength of companies, industries and whole nations. Share prices rise on news that a patent has been granted, and fall on news that it has been challenged. So secure are profits from pharmaceutical patents that plans are afoot to use them as financial instruments by issuing notes on them to investors (Rivette and Kline, 2000). The wonder is that all this activity can all take place in the complete absence of innovation. Innovation has in many ways been supplanted by the patent, which, in itself, creates no wealth at all.

> I'm convinced that the management of intellectual property is how value added is going to be created at Xerox. And not just here, either. Increasingly, companies that are good at managing IP will win. The ones that aren't will lose. (Richard Thoman as quoted in Rivette and Kline, 2000, p. 54)

The costs of distortion

Whenever resources are diverted from one purpose to another to satisfy the requirements of the patent system, and when the incentive to patent becomes distinct from the incentive to innovate, there is likely to be a cost in terms of discouraged innovation (Takalo and Kanniainen, 1997). Universities, certainly in the UK but elsewhere as well, are anxious to increase their revenue not only because they are expected to cover costs, but also so they can demonstrate demand for their services and, therefore, just how useful these services are. Patenting is seen as an appropriate route to riches, and academics are encouraged to patent whatever can be patented. Resources are diverted from areas with little patenting potential to those with more, and publishing is discouraged if it might interfere with patenting prospects (Feller, 1990). The British Technology Group, which specialises in exploiting university patents, is especially keen to suppress academic discussion.

> Our biggest competitors are not other agencies like ours. They are researchers talking to industry or giving their ideas away at conferences and so on. (Harvey, 1989)

Academics are unlikely to be innovative unless they are free to discuss and exchange ideas. If information flow is being restricted in universities by the requirements of the patent system, then it is unlikely to be flowing freely in other organisations.

The patent system also sets precedent for the appropriation of information by the organisation. The patent system is highly compatible with management methods that focus on the control of information as an organisational resource: with knowledge management, management information systems and the codification of information in IT, for example. There is no place here for personal exchange networks; these are now regarded as organisational property. The Silicon Valleys of the industrial world, and the invisible colleges of the academic, cannot function under such a regime; they wither and die.

Concluding thoughts

Nonsensical as it may sound, the patent system is essentially anti-innovative. This is not just because it assists a very specialised sort of innovation and discourages other sorts. Much more important is that the patent system satisfies the requirements of those who need to feel that innovation is controlled and contained, that innovation is in its place, part of process. Most innovation is not like this at all.

This is not to say that the patent system should be changed. Small business counsellors, enterprise consultants and patent office officials proffer advice on how to use the system better, and on how it might be adapted to offer even better service to users. They argue that, while the fundamentals of the patent system are sound, there is always scope for improvements that would increase the benefits for everyone. For example, there has been much discussion of the merits of rewarding employee inventors (Littler and Pearson, 1979; Orkin, 1984). Such trivial tinkering distracts attention from matters of moment (Polanyi, 1943). The system is inherently imperfect, and fundamental improvement is just not possible. This is why enthusiasm for the system among economists is often so muted.

> If we did not have a patent system, it would be irresponsible, on the basis of our present knowledge of its economic consequences, to recommend instituting one. But since we have had a patent system for a long time, it would be irresponsible, on the basis of our present knowledge, to recommend abolishing it. (Machlup, 1958, p. 80)

In other words, this is as good as it gets.

This does not mean that there is no possibility of increasing the public benefit from the patent system. Appreciating the limitations of the system would achieve this quite simply. Managers of pharmaceutical companies might sleep less soundly at night, but appreciation would not actually reduce the benefits their companies reap from the system, at least not in the short run. It is surely as well that those who bear the costs of the patent system appreciate the nature and extent of these costs. Appreciation in itself would do much to reduce them (see Rothwell, 1983). This appreciation starts with seeing the patent system as it is, and not as others would have us see it. Consider Macaulay's nice observation on the impact of copyright on Dr Johnson's productivity, and consider what such realism might contribute to modern discussion of the relationship between intellectual property and innovation:

> Would it have stimulated his exertions? Would it have once drawn him out of his bed before noon? Would it have once cheered him under a fit of the spleen? Would it have induced him to give us one more allegory, one more life of a poet, one more imitation of Juvenal? (Anon, 1978)

So, does TRIPS (Agreement on Trade-Related Aspects of Intellectual Property Rights) make a difference? Yes it probably does, though perhaps not in the most obvious way. As a fundamental part of the World Trade Organization regime, TRIPS puts intellectual property on a world stage, and the patent system centre stage. This may not be a role that patents can play to everyone's satisfaction. TRIPS is meant to allow the developing world the advantages that use of, and investment in, modern technology can bring, while the developed world secures an adequate return on its research and development. In return for enforcing patent rights, the developing world becomes eligible to join the international high technology community. Like fresh air, sunshine and exercise, the patent system is presented – and accepted – as a good thing. TRIPS follows this custom. Does not Article 7 of TRIPS declare that the protection and enforcement of intellectual property rights should contribute to the promotion of technological innovation and to the transfer and dissemination of technology, to the mutual advantage of producers and users of technological knowledge? Of course, the situation is not quite that simple. Actually, it is not at all simple, which may explain the general tendency to present it as if it were, as if there were no small print.

There is a parallel to be drawn between developing countries and most firms in the developed world. Their interests in the patent system are not dissimilar; they both bear its costs. Just occasionally the patent system will suit their requirements, but more usually it will have little to offer. With limited experience and knowledge of the system, and especially of its complications and ramifications, and with only weak influence, they offer only feeble opposition to the established opinion that the patent system obviously encourages innovation everywhere by protecting and by disseminating information. Consequently, this view prevails.

This situation may be changing. The attitude of the large pharmaceutical firms towards the enforcement of their patents in the developing world has prompted some questioning of the motivation behind TRIPS, and of the implications of the new world patent order. The experience of these companies denying drugs to the poor lest their patent position in the world's richest markets be compromised seems at odds with the promise of TRIPS to operate in a manner conducive to social and economic welfare, balancing rights and obligations. Put briefly and bluntly, TRIPS has forced the developing world to examine the patent system more deeply and thoroughly. This is something that most firms and most governments in the developed world should have done years ago. TRIPS was intended to impress the existing patent order on the whole world: delicious irony if it is TRIPS that initiates the wholesale reassessment of the patent system.

References

Anon (1978) 'Macaulay on copyright', *Journal of Political Economy*, vol. 86, no. 5, back cover.

Australian Patent Office (1980) *Pilot Study of the Users of Patent Information and their Needs* (Canberra, September).

Australian Patent Office (1981) *Patent Literature, a Source of Technical Information* (Canberra: AGPS).

Barton, J. (1997) 'Paradigms of Intellectual Property. Competition Balances in the Information Sector', paper delivered to the OECD workshop, The Economics of the Information Society, London, March.

Betts, P. and B. Groom (2001) 'Industry Urges Faster EU Reform', *Financial Times*, 20 March.

Blackman, M. (1994) 'Taking Patent Information Services to Small and Medium Enterprises', *Intellectual Property in Asia and the Pacific*, vol. 40, pp. 44–67.

Braun, E. and S. Macdonald (1978) *Revolution in Miniature. The History and Impact of Semiconductor Electronics* (Cambridge: Cambridge University Press).

Cohen, D. (2001) 'La propriété intellectuelle, c'est le vol', *Le Monde*, 8–9 April, pp. 1, 13.

Feller, I. (1990) 'Universities as Engines of R&D-based Economic Growth: They Think They Can', *Research Policy*, vol. 19, pp. 335–48.

Forbes ASAP Supplement (1993) 'Patent Plague', p. 62.

Gilbert, R. and C. Shapiro (1990) 'Optimal Patent Length and Breadth', *Rand Journal of Economics*, vol. 21, no. 1, pp. 106–12.

Greiner, L. and L. Barnes (1970) 'Organization Change and Development', in G. Dalton and P. Lawrence (eds), *Organizational Change and Development* (Homewood, Illinois, Irwin-Dorsey), pp. 1–12.

Griliches, Z. (1989) 'Patents: Recent Trends and Puzzles', *Brookings Papers: Microeconomics*, pp. 291–319.

Harvey, D. (1989) 'BTG: The Mother of Invention', *Director*, September, pp. 121–2.

Howes, K. (1993) 'The Shield and the Sword', *Satellite Communications*, vol. 17, no. 1, pp. 6A–9A.

Johnston, R. and S. Carmichael (1981) *Australian Science and Technology Indicators Feasibility Study – Private Enterprise. Final Report*, Occasional Paper 4 (Canberra: Australian Department of Science and Technology).

Kahaner, L. (1983) 'Changes Pending for the Patent System', *High Technology*, vol. 3, no. 12, pp. 48–57.

Kass, L. (1982) 'The Right to Patent', *Dialogue*, vol. 58, no. 4, pp. 42–5.

Kingston, W. (ed.) (1987) *Direct Protection of Innovation* (Dordrecht, Kluwer Academic).

Labich, K. (1988) 'The Innovators', *Fortune*, 6 June, pp. 27–32.

Levin, R., A. Klevorick, R. Nelson and S. Winter (1987) *Appropriating the Returns from Industrial Research and Development*, Brookings Papers on Economic Activity, vol. 3.

Liebesny, F. (1972) 'Patents as Sources of Information' in F. Liebesny (ed.), *Mainly on Patents* (London: Butterworth), pp. 117–19.

Littler, D. and A.W. Pearson (1979) 'The Employee Inventor and the New Patents Act', *Planned Innovation*, vol. 2, no. 10, pp. 335–8.

Macdonald, S. (1987), 'British Science Parks: Reflections on the Politics of High Technology', *R&D Management*, vol. 17, no. 1, pp. 25–37.

Macdonald, S. (1990), *Technology and the Tyranny of Export Controls. Whisper Who Dares* (London: Macmillan – now Palgrave Macmillan).

Macdonald, S. (1998) *Information for Innovation. Managing Change from an Information Perspective* (Oxford: OUP).

Machlup, F. (1958) *An Economic Review of the Patent System*, Studies of the US Patent System No. 15, US Senate Sub-committee on Patents, Trademarks and Copyrights (Washington DC: US Government Printing Office).

Mandeville, T. (1982) 'Engineers and the Patent System: Results of a Survey of Members of the Institution of Engineers', in T. Mandeville, D. Lamberton and J. Bishop (eds), *Supporting Papers for Economic Effects of the Australian Patent System* (Canberra: Australian Government Publishing Service).

Mandeville, T. and J. Bishop (1982) 'Economic Effects of the Patent System: Results of a Survey of Patent Attorneys', in T. Mandeville, D. Lamberton and J. Bishop (eds), *Supporting Papers for Economic Effects of the Australian Patent System* (Canberra: Australian Government Publishing Service).

Mansfield, E. (1986), 'Patents and Innovation: An Empirical Study', *Management Science*, vol. 32, no. 2, pp. 173–81.

Mansfield, E., M. Schwartz and S. Wagner (1981) 'Imitation Costs and Patents: An Empirical Study', *Economic Journal*, vol. 91, no. 364, pp. 907–18.

Markham, J. (1962) 'Inventive Activity: Government Controls and the Legal Environment' in National Bureau of Economic Research, *The Rate and Direction of Inventive Activity* (Princeton: Princeton University Press).

Marschan-Piekkari, R., D. Assimakopoulos and S. Macdonald (forthcoming), 'Esprit: Europe's response to US and Japanese domination in IT', in Coopey R. (ed.), *Collaboration and Information Technology* (Oxford: OUP).

Merges, R. (1988) 'Commercial Success and Patent Standards: Economic Perspectives on Innovation', *California Law Review*, vol. 76, pp. 805–76.

Miller, W. (1988) 'Productivity and Competition: A Look at the Pharmaceutical Industry', *Columbia Journal of World Business*, Fall, pp. 85–8.

Moss, C. and A. Evans (1987) 'Protecting Ideas and New Products', *Industrial Management and Data Systems*, September–October, pp. 21–4.

Mossinghoff, G. and T. Bombelles (1996), 'The Importance of Intellectual Property to American Research-Intensive Pharmaceutical Industry', *Columbia Journal of World Business*, vol. 31, no. 1, pp. 38–48.

Nature (1929) 'The Grant of Invalid Patents', 9 November, p. 713.

Orkin, N. (1984) 'Rewarding Employee Invention: Time for Change', *Harvard Business Review*, vol. 62, no. 1, pp. 56–7.

Perry, N. (1986) 'The Surprising New Power of Patents', *Fortune*, 23 June, pp. 73–83.

Pilling, D. (2001), 'Patent Case Holds Key for Drug Groups', *Financial Times*, 18 April, p. 12.

Polanyi, M. (1943) 'Patent Reform', *Review of Economic Studies*, vol. 11, no. 1, pp. 61–76.

Porter, V. (1989) 'The Copyright Designs and Patents Act 1988: The Triumph of Expediency Over Principle', *Journal of Law and Society*, vol. 16, no. 3, pp. 340–51.

Rivette, K. and D. Kline (2000) 'Discovering the New Value in Intellectual Property', *Harvard Business Review*, January–February 2000, pp. 54–66.

Rosenberg, N. (1974) 'Science, Invention and Economic Growth', *Economic Journal*, vol. 84, no. 333, pp. 90–108.

Rothwell, R. (1992) 'Successful Industrial Innovation: Critical Factors for the 1990s', *R&D Management*, vol. 22, no. 3, pp. 221–39.

Rothwell, R. (1994) 'Towards the Fifth Generation Innovation Process', *International Marketing Review*, vol. 11, no. 1, pp. 7–31.

Schmookler, J. (1957) 'Inventors Past and Present', *Review of Economics and Statistics*, vol. 39, pp. 321–33.

Schott, K. (1981) *Industrial Innovation in the United Kingdom, Canada and the United States* (London: British North American Committee).

Schumpeter, J. (1939) *Business Cycles* (New York: McGraw-Hill).

Sciberras, E. (1986) 'Indicators of Technical Intensity and International Competitiveness: A Case for Supplementing Quantitative Data with Qualitative Studies in Research', *R&D Management*, vol. 16, no. 1, pp. 3–13.

Shapiro, A. (1990) 'Responding to the Changing Patent System', *Research Technology Management*, vol. 33, no. 5, pp. 38–43.

Shulman, S. (1995) 'Patent Medicine', *Technology Review*, vol. 98, no. 8, pp. 28–36.

Silverman, A. (1990) 'Intellectual Property Law and the Venture Capital Process', *High Technology Law Journal*, vol. 5, no. 1, pp. 157–92.

Simon, E. (1996), 'Innovation and Intellectual Property Protection: The Software Industry Perspective', *Columbia Journal of World Business*, Spring, pp. 30–7.

Takalo, T. and V. Kanniainen (1997) 'Do Patents Slow Down Technological Progress?', paper presented to the conference New Developments in Intellectual Property: Economics and Law, Oxford, March.

Tapon, F. (1989) 'A Transaction Cost Analysis of Innovations in the Organization of Pharmaceutical R&D', *Journal of Economic Behaviour and Organization*, vol. 12, pp. 197–213.

Taylor, C. and Z. Silberston (1973) *The Economic Impact of the Patent System* (Cambridge: Cambridge University Press).

Teece, D. (1988) 'Capturing Value from Technological Innovation: Integration, Strategic Partnering, and Licensing Decisions', *Interfaces*, vol. 18, no. 3, pp. 46–61.

Thurow, L. (1997), 'Needed: A New System of Intellectual Property Rights', *Harvard Business Review*, September–October, pp. 95–103.

Wyatt, G. (1977–8) *The Determinants of Inventive Activity Reconsidered*, Working Paper 2, Department of Economics, Heriot-Watt University.

3
Pro-competitive Measures under TRIPS to Promote Technology Diffusion in Developing Countries[1]

Carlos M. Correa

Introduction

Economists and policy makers face a difficult dilemma in the area of innovation: how to reconcile the aims of intellectual property, which provides innovators with incentives by restricting use of the innovation and thereby guaranteeing extraordinary gains, with a society's interest in allowing maximum use of innovative products, by keeping their price low and ensuring diffusion, imitation and improvement (OECD, 1992, p. 50).

A fair balance between the private and the social benefits of innovation requires the development of a policy framework which ensures not only that new technologies are created, but also that competitors are able to work and improve on them. As taught by the economic theory on technical change, innovation and diffusion are 'two faces of the same coin': innovation leads to diffusion, which in turn influences the level of innovative activity (OECD, 1992, p. 51).

Moreover, from a social and ethical perspective, it is essential that policy mechanisms ensure that innovation results reach those who need them. One obvious example is the case of pharmaceuticals, diagnostic kits and other health-related products.

If the policy framework leads, by exclusion of competition and lack of controls on abuses, to excessively monopolistic market structures, innovators can maintain high price/cost margins, retard further innovation and deny access to innovative products, especially to the poorer segments of the population. In contrast, a certain degree of competitive threat induces firms to continue to innovate and keep prices low. Innovation policy needs to provide incentives for both the *creation* and the *diffusion* of new technology. The monopolistic elements should diminish, in particular, where diffusion opens up important technological opportunities and where it is important to satisfy essential societal needs.

Intellectual property is a significant component of innovation policy, but its impact varies according to the sectors at stake[2] and the level of development of the country where such policy is implemented. The granting of exclusive rights increases appropriability by preventing unauthorised use. If the power conferred on the rights holder is too strong diffusion may be limited, further innovation jeopardised and many would-be adopters may be deprived of access to needed products. A sound intellectual property policy should, hence, strike a balance between the right to exclude and the right to use innovations.

The achievement of such balance is one of the stated objectives of the Agreement on Trade-Related Aspects of Intellectual Property Rights (TRIPS) (Article 7). Though the adoption of TRIPS allowed developed countries to impose on developing countries and economies in transition the core of their own intellectual property rights (IPRs) systems, it aims at balancing the rights of producers and users of technology and leaves room for establishing pro-competitive measures that may facilitate access to and further innovation on protected goods and technologies. Of particular importance are, in this regard, the provisions relating to parallel imports, exceptions to exclusive rights and compulsory licences which are examined below.

IPRs in developing countries

Developing countries account for only 4 per cent of world research and development (R&D) expenditures (UNDP, 1999, p. 67). As a result, such countries are strongly dependent on the transfer of technology from developed countries.[3] It is evident, therefore, that the effects of strengthened IPRs in those countries will be qualitatively different from those in the technologically advanced countries. While in the latter stronger rights may lead to increased profits and more innovation, in the former the main effects will be felt in terms of the prices to be paid for protected goods and technologies.

This does not mean that patents may not stimulate R&D in developing countries, particularly in those which are more advanced in the industrialisation process. It rather indicates that the development of new inventions (particularly in sectors of high R&D costs and economies of scale, such as pharmaceuticals) will be simply out of reach for most developing countries. The patent system is unlikely to work as a significant incentive to local innovations, except in those countries where a substantial scientific and technological infrastructure exists. Stronger IPRs may, at the same time, retard diffusion of new products (because of high prices) and have an ambivalent effect on the access by local firms to foreign technologies.

Arguments on the relevance of adequate intellectual property protection to foster transfer of technology are particularly strong where high, easy to imitate, technology is at stake, such as in the case of biotechnology and computer software. It is also possible to argue that in cases where 'tacit' (non-codified) knowledge is essential to put a technology into operation, the transfer is more likely to take place if it is bundled with the authorisation to use patents and other IPRs. If protection of such rights and of trade secrets in the potential borrowing country are weak, the originating firms are unlikely to enter into transfer of technology contracts.

While the lack or insufficient protection of IPRs may pose a barrier to obtain the required technologies, at the same time, changes in intellectual property legislation may affect the bargaining position of potential contracting parties and can make access to technology more problematic (Skolnikoff, 1993). A strengthened and expanded intellectual property regime is likely to lead to an increase in royalty levels and to the imposition of restrictive business practices that restrain competition.

Stimulating competition, technology transfer and innovation

As mentioned, World Trade Organization (WTO) member countries can adopt different measures in order to promote competition in a form that is consistent with their obligations under TRIPS. Some of these measures are briefly examined below.

Among the measures that developing countries may adopt are those solely or mainly aimed at encouraging price competition and access to protected products. This is notably the case for parallel imports, some exceptions to patent rights (such as the 'Bolar' exception), the granting of certain types of compulsory licence (for example in cases of emergency, anti-competitive practices),[4] and the conditional protection, under the concept of unfair competition, of data submitted for the registration of pharmaceuticals.

Other measures may be particularly relevant to encourage technology transfer. For instance, compulsory licences for government use can be utilised – as the USA has done in many cases – in order to get access to critical technologies. Compulsory licences granted because of the lack of local manufacturing of a patented product have generally been seen as an important channel for the transfer of technology, despite the fact that very few licences of this type have been actually granted in the developing world and that the patent owner cannot be generally obliged to transfer the know-how necessary for the effective use of the patented invention.[5]

Finally, some measures may be principally provided for in order to stimulate innovation. This is the case, for instance, for the experimentation exception discussed below, which is of particular importance to those sectors where incremental innovation is significant.

Parallel imports

Article 6 of TRIPS recognises the possibility of legally admitting parallel imports,[6] based on the principle of 'exhaustion of rights'. The principle was extensively developed in the framework of the European integration in order to avoid the fragmentation of markets and the exercise of discriminatory pricing by intellectual property (IP) title holders within the Community.

The doctrine of exhaustion – which justifies parallel imports – has been applied with respect to industrial property titles (for example patents and trademarks) as well as in relation to copyright (see Graz, 1988). This is also the approach followed by TRIPS. It is based on the concept that the IP title holder of goods has no right to control the use or resale of those goods once they have been lawfully put on to the market by the title holder or his licensee.

In many countries – particularly those under a common-law system – the doctrine is based on the existence of an implied licence under which the buyer (and those claiming rights through him) of a patented product is free to deal with the product as if it were not patented. The sale of a patented product, unless notified to the contrary, gives to the purchaser a licence under the patent to exercise for this product all the normal rights of an owner, including the right to resell (Cornish, 1989, p. 200; Omaji, 1997, pp. 565–6).

In other countries, such as in continental Europe, the doctrine of exhaustion of IPRs is not subject to the discretion of the title holder, but is automatic. The inventor is considered to have been rewarded through the first sale or distribution of the product. The equivalent to this doctrine in the United States is known as the 'first sale doctrine' (Yusuf and Moncayo von Hase, 1992, pp. 117–19).

The doctrine of exhaustion of IPRs was originally limited to the domestic market. In the European Communities (EC), however, it was extended by decisions of the European Court of Justice (ECJ) to the entire common market, in order to avoid the market fragmentation that the application of import bans in each jurisdiction may create. The EC exhaustion doctrine has been applied with respect to different types of IPRs, including copyrights. In the patent field, the validity of the doctrine has been upheld even in cases where the exporting EC country did not provide for patent protection (see, in particular, the decision of the European Court of Justice in *Merck v. Stephar*, case 187/80, and the more recent decisions by the ECJ, 5 December 1996, joined cases C 267/95 and C 268/95 *Merck v. Primecrown* and *Beecham Group v. Europharm*).

While the EC adopted a principle of regional exhaustion of rights, other countries moved on to implement the same principle on an international basis. This means that whichever country may be the exporting country, the IPR title holder is not granted the right to prevent the parallel importation of a product that was put on the market in the said country with his consent or otherwise in a lawful manner.

The application of the exhaustion of rights doctrine on a domestic scale only has a protectionist effect since a ban on parallel imports avoids competition from abroad. Given that the title holder has been rewarded through the first sale of the product in the country of origin, the ban on parallel imports is not necessary to secure compliance with IPRs (Yusuf and Moncayo von Hase, 1992, p. 128).[7]

Parallel imports are not a means of ignoring the patentee's right to remuneration (which is received with the first sale of the product), but a means of ensuring that patents work 'to the mutual advantage of producers and users of technological knowledge' (Article 7 TRIPS) in a global economy.

The recognition in TRIPS of the principle of international exhaustion of rights may be seen as a logical result of the process of economic globalisation. With progress in transportation and communications, and with the steady reduction of tariff and non-tariff barriers on a worldwide scale, the boundaries of 'national' markets are diluting. From an economic point of view, such a principle may contribute to the competitiveness of local companies, which may be jeopardised if they are bound to buy exclusively from a local distributor which charges higher prices than elsewhere. Likewise, consumer interests are better served if the right to purchase legitimate products from the lowest price source – national or foreign – is recognised. Parallel imports reduce prices and encourage foreign title holders to establish themselves locally in order to monitor the market and adjust business strategies to changing conditions (Reichman, 1993, p. 7).

The doctrine of exhaustion of IPRs on an international scale has been applied in two important cases by Japanese courts. The High Court of Tokyo held in *Jap Auto Products Kabushiki Kaisha & Anor v. BBS Kraftfahrzeug Technik A.G* (1994) that the parallel imports of auto parts purchased in Germany did not violate patents granted to BBS in Japan. And in the *Aluminium Wheels* case, the Japanese Supreme Court affirmed, in July 1997, that Article 4 bis of the Paris Convention ('Independence of patents for the same invention in different countries') did not apply in Japan and that the issue of parallel imports was a matter of national policy of each country.

In the United States, according to case law, parallel importation is generally allowed in the absence of enforceable contractual restrictions (Barrett, 2000, p. 984). A decision by the US Supreme Court of 9 March 1998, affirmed the exhaustion of rights principle with regard to the importation of copyrighted items sold in the 'gray market' (*Quality King Distributors Inc. v. L'Anza Research International Inc.*).[8] The international exhaustion of IPRs has been admitted in other countries at least in respect of trademarks and copyrights. This has been the case, for instance, in Australia (Omaji, 1997) and New Zealand (in respect of copyrights).

The USA questioned s. 15(c) of the South African Medicines and Related Substances Control Amendment Act 1997 which stipulates that 'the Minister may prescribe conditions for the supply of more affordable medicines in certain circumstances so as to protect the health of the public' and, in particular, the conditions on which any medicine put on the market by the patent holder or with his consent may be imported by a third party in South Africa.

Despite the legality of South African law under TRIPS, the US government and the international pharmaceutical industry put enormous pressure on the South African government to eliminate such measures[9] (see Chapters 5 and 11 by James Love and William Pretorius in this volume). Supported by a number of active NGOs (particularly those concerned with the dramatic rise of HIV-related infection in South Africa), the South African government resisted such pressures and eventually obtained the withdrawal of South Africa – in December 1999 – from the 'Special 301' list.[10]

The application of the principle of exhaustion of rights in the health sector may be of particular importance. By allowing the importation of a (patented) medicine from a country where it is sold more cheaply than in the importing country, access to the product may benefit a larger number of patients, while ensuring that the patent owner receives the remuneration for the patented invention in the country where the product was sold. The acceptance of parallel imports may be regarded as one of the measures consistent with TRIPS that member countries are explicitly authorised to take to protect public health (see Article 8.1).

Exceptions to patent rights

Exceptions to exclusive patent rights may include use of an invention for experimental purposes, for research and education and use prior to the granting of a patent. Other exceptions may be based on other public-interest reasons, such as public health or the protection of the environment.

Article 30 of TRIPS defines in very general wording the exceptions that members may allow. Under this provision, there is considerable freedom for national laws to define the kind and extent of the possible exceptions to the exclusive rights of patent owners. Based on comparative law, different types of exception may be provided for within the scope of Article 30, such as:

- acts done privately and on a non-commercial scale, or for a non-commercial purpose;
- use of the invention for research;
- use of the invention for teaching purposes;
- experimentation on the invention to test or improve on it;
- preparation of medicines under individual prescriptions;
- experiments made for the purposes of seeking regulatory approval for marketing of a product after the expiration of a patent; and
- use of the invention by a third party that had used it *bona fide* before the date of application of the patent.

Some of these exceptions are particularly important from the perspective of technological policies, such as the 'experimental' exception, and to promote competition and access to medicines on competitive terms, such as the so-called 'Bolar' exception. These exceptions are considered below.

Experimental use

Exceptions relating to research and experimentation on the invention may be an important tool to create a favourable context for innovation.

The adoption of an experimental exception may permit innovation based on 'inventing around' or improvement on the protected invention, as well as evaluation of an invention in order to request a licence, or for other legitimate purposes, such as to test whether the invention works, its sufficiency and novelty.

In some countries, such as the United States (Wegner, 1994, p. 267),[11] experimentation and research without the authorisation of the patent owner is admitted for scientific purposes only. In European and other countries, experimentation on an invention is allowed for commercial purposes as well. The Community Patent Convention,[12] for instance, provides that there is no infringement in case of 'acts done for experimental purposes relating to the subset-matter of the patented invention' (Article 27(b)). Case law relating to pharmaceutical or agrochemical products in European countries has permitted research done to find out more information about a product, provided that it is not made just to convince licensing authorities or customers about the virtues of an alternative product, and to obtain further information about the uses of a product and its possible side-effects and other consequences of its use (Cornish, 1998, p. 736).

With the exception of a few countries, most developing countries have apparently not explicitly used the room left by TRIPS to provide for an experimentation exception, including for commercial purposes.

'Bolar' exception[13]

Another important exception, first introduced by the United States, deals with the use of an invention relating to a pharmaceutical product to conduct tests and obtain the approval from the health authority, before the expiration of the patent, for commercialisation of a generic version, just after the expiration of the patent. The USA, Canada, Australia and Israel, among other countries, have admitted this exception by law or through case law.[14] In exchange for this permission, the term of a patent may be extended for an additional period in some of those countries.

The US Drug Price Competition and Patent Term Restoration Act (1984) permits testing to establish the bio-equivalence of generic products before the expiration of the relevant patent. The purpose of this exception is to help generic drug producers to place their products on the market as soon as a patent expires, and thereby allow consumers to obtain medicines at much lower prices immediately thereafter. In exchange for this exception to exclusive patent rights, the patent term of the original drug could be extended by up to five years.

Canada also adopted a 'Bolar'-type provision in 1991 explicitly allowing a third party to produce and stockpile the product for release immediately after the expiration of the patent. However, the regulatory review of a product is linked to the patent status: the generic producer must give notice to the patent holder about the intended use of the invention, and the patentee is given an automatic injunction. According to the Patented Medicines (Notice of Compliance) Regulations, the approval of a generic version may be delayed for 24 months when there is a patent dispute.

'Bolar'-like exceptions have also been established in Australia, Argentina, Israel and Thailand. Particularly if not linked to an extension of the patent term (as provided for in Argentina and Canada), such an exception is supportive of the development of a generics pharmaceutical industry, and allows consumers to get access to medicines at a lower price as soon as the patent expires.

The consistency of the 'Bolar' exception with TRIPS was analysed, as discussed below, in a case decided in the framework of the WTO. In November 1998 the European Communities and their member states requested the WTO Dispute Settlement Body to establish a panel to examine the application of the Bolar provisions in the Canadian Patent Act in relation to Canada's obligations under TRIPS. In March 2000, the Panel concluded that Canada was not in violation of TRIPS in its practice of allowing the development and submission of information required to obtain marketing approval for pharmaceutical products carried out without the consent of the patent holder. However, Canada was found to be acting inconsistently with TRIPS in its practice of allowing the manufacture and stockpiling of pharmaceutical products during the 6 months immediately prior to the expiry of the 20-year patent term (WTO WT/DS114/R).

In summary, the admission of an exception for initiating approval procedures for generic pharmaceuticals (and, in some cases, agrochemicals) before the expiration of a patent has gained growing support in developed countries but it is still relatively unusual in developing countries. To be consistent with TRIPS requirements, this exception does not need to be linked to the extension of the life of the respective patents.

Compulsory licensing

A compulsory licence is an authorisation given by the government for the use by a third party, without the consent of the right-owner of a patent or other intellectual property right. Article 31 of TRIPS expressly allows the granting of compulsory licences under certain conditions.

No specification is made in TRIPS, however, on the grounds under which such licences can be granted. A particular, but not exhaustive, reference is made to the cases of national emergency or extreme urgency, dependency of patents, licences for governmental non-commercial use, and licences to remedy anti-competitive practices. National laws can, however, provide for the granting of such licences whenever the title holder refuses to grant a voluntary licence on reasonable commercial terms (see WTO, 1995) and for other reasons, such as public health or public interests at large. The text of TRIPS is also open with respect to the rights that can be exercised by the licensee, including production or importation. The only case in which TRIPS does restrict the freedom to determine the grounds for compulsory licences relates to 'semiconductor technology', which can only be subject to compulsory licences for public non-commercial use and to remedy anti-competitive practices.

It should be noted that in some cases, for instance, emergency and public non-commercial use, there is no need previously to request a voluntary licence, as required by Article 31(b) of TRIPS. Moreover, in the case of public non-commercial use, the patent holder shall be informed after the use of the invention has taken place, 'as soon as reasonably practicable' (Article 31(b)). Licences to remedy anti-competitive practices are subject to a special treatment with regard to the remuneration to be paid to the patent holder.[15]

TRIPS also allows for compulsory licences in cases of lack of or insufficient working. Article 27.1 of the Agreement stipulates that 'patent rights shall be enjoyable without discrimination...whether the products are imported or locally produced'. The interpretation of this clause is debatable. Though Article 27.1 has been understood as prohibiting any obligation to execute a patented invention locally, this interpretation is not unanimous. The Preamble, as well as Articles 7 and 8, make it clear that one of the objectives of TRIPS is to promote technology transfer, which may be ensured in some circumstances by means of compulsory licences for non-working. The interpretation of this Article[16] is likely to be finally settled under WTO procedures if a dispute thereon arises between WTO Members.[17]

Most countries in the world, including developed countries, provided for different modalities of compulsory licences before the adoption of TRIPS (Correa and Bergel, 1996). Such provisions have been retained or expanded thereafter. The United States has had an extensive practice in this field. With regard to the granting of compulsory licences to deal with anti-competitive practices in the United States, Scherer has noted that:

> compulsory patent licensing has been used as a remedy in more than 100 antitrust case settlements, including cases involving Meprobamate, the antibiotics tetracycline and griseofulvin, synthetic steroids, and most recently, several basic biotechnology patents owned by Ciby-Geigy and Sandoz, which merged to form Novartis. My own statistical analysis of the most important compulsory licensing decrees found that the settlements had no discernible negative effect on the subject companies' subsequent research and development expenditures, although they probably did lead to greater secrecy in lieu of patenting (Scherer, 1999, p. 12).

The US Government has also made an extensive use of compulsory licences for governmental use, in a manner that has raised the complaints of the European Union.[18]

Despite the legitimacy of compulsory licences, some countries that have provided for them in their legislation have faced the threat of unilateral retaliations, or the suspension of aid, by some developed countries.[19] Of particular interest was the dispute between the USA and South Africa in relation to South African legislation aimed at allowing parallel imports and compulsory licences for medicines.

Protection of data submitted for registration

A component of any public health policy that needs to be carefully considered relates to some of the conditions for the registration of pharmaceutical products. Certainly, such products need to comply with adequate standards of efficacy and toxicity in order to be safe for consumers. As a condition of registration of new products, national authorities normally require the submission of data relating to efficacy and toxicity. The legal protection of such data, particularly in respect of the use thereof to treat subsequent applications for similar medicines, has raised different approaches and considerable controversy.

The issue of data protection is addressed by Article 39.3 of TRIPS. It leaves considerable room to member countries to implement the obligation to protect such data against unfair competition practices. TRIPS provides that 'undisclosed information' is regulated under the discipline of unfair competition, as contained in Article 10 bis of the Paris Convention. With this approach TRIPS clearly avoids the treatment of undisclosed information as 'property' and does not require the grant of 'exclusive' rights to the data possessor.

The subject matter of the protection under Article 39.3 is test data, that is the results of trials carried out by the originator company in order to prove efficacy and safety of the product. This information is obtained by applying standard protocols on a certain chemical substance, and does not constitute a creative contribution. This is acknowledged by TRIPS, which makes this kind of protection conditional upon the fact that there should have been a considerable effort to develop this information: the underlying concept is not the protection of creation but the protection of *investment*. Furthermore, TRIPS requires this protection only in respect of *new chemical entities*. There is no need to provide it for a new dosage form or for the new use of a known product.

The protection to be granted is against 'unfair commercial use' of the relevant protected information. This means that a third party could be prevented from using the results of the test undertaken by another company as background for an independent submission for marketing approval if the respective data were acquired through dishonest commercial practices. Such a party could, obviously, independently develop the relevant data and information, or obtain them from other sources. However, the duplication of tests to reach results that are already known will certainly be highly questionable from a social cost–benefit point of view. Article 39.3 would also permit a national competent authority to rely on data in its possession to assess a second and further application relating to the same drug, since this would not imply an 'unfair commercial use'.

In some jurisdictions, such as the USA and the EU, additional ('TRIPS-plus') protection for data submitted for registration is granted. In the USA, the originator of the information is given a 5-year exclusivity period for the use of this information.[20] In the EU, this period is 10 years. During the data exclusivity period, a subsequent applicant cannot rely on the information from the first registration, so it will not be able to register the same product unless it develops its own clinical test data.

However, this is not the concept of TRIPS, which does not require the granting of exclusive rights. Under the standard adopted under TRIPS in order to approve subsequent applications, national authorities may rely, for instance, on the registration made in third countries which apply high sanitary standards,[21] or on data which is already available to them,[22] provided that the equivalence (or 'similarity') of the products is demonstrated.

In sum, under TRIPS, countries have options to decide how they wish to regulate the protection of undisclosed information submitted for the registration of pharmaceutical products. They can opt for TRIPS-plus protection by granting data exclusivity, or for strictly following TRIPS standards. In making this choice, policy makers will have to weigh the protection of the interests of originator companies against the importance of creating an environment that fosters competition and increases access to drugs.

The room for maneouvre under TRIPS

The 'method of implementing' TRIPS provisions can be freely determined within the 'own legal system and practice' (Article 1.1) of each country. There are considerable differences between national IPR systems, particularly between those based on Anglo-American law, and those that follow the approach of Continental European law. These differences are noticeable, for instance, in the field of copyright and neighbouring rights, trademarks and trade secrets protection.

TRIPS only contains minimum standards. Though it will contribute to a certain degree of harmonisation of IPRs protection, it does not constitute a uniform law on the matter. An important issue is the extent to which member states have freedom to determine aspects of IPRs protection which are not specifically dealt with by TRIPS, as well as the scope for different interpretations of existing provisions.

The room for manoeuvre left by TRIPS can be used by WTO member countries to design their IPRs systems in the framework of TRIPS with a view to satisfying, within the limits permitted by the Agreement, their own objectives (South Centre, 1995). For instance, its implementation may deliberately seek to encourage competition, technology transfer, the diffusion of existing technologies and innovation (including via legitimate reverse engineering).

The GATT/WTO system has attempted to ensure, as far as possible, a predictable application of its rules by limiting the scope for discretionary interpretation, and the effectiveness of the dispute-settlement mechanism (Schott, 1994, p. 125; Hoekman and Kostecki, 1997, pp. 44–50).

Issues relating to the interpretation of TRIPS within the WTO have been raised in four cases handled under the Dispute Settlement Understanding (DSU). Several complaints have been filed under TRIPS, involving alleged infractions by developing and developed countries. In 1999 there had already been sixteen WTO dispute settlement filings based on TRIPS. This amounted to 10 per cent of all filings under the DSU, a significantly high percentage. Eleven of the sixteen filings were brought by the United States (Geuze and Wager, 1999).

The USA and later on the EU complained against India in relation to the application of the 'mail box' provided for by Article 70.8 of TRIPS. As mentioned, the EU initiated a case against Canada on the consistency of the 'Bolar' exception.[23] The USA brought another case against Canada, relating to the extension to 20 years of the term of protection for patents granted, before the entry into force of TRIPS, for a shorter period.[24] Finally, upon a complaint by the European Union, a panel found that s. 110.5(b) of US copyright law, relating to the enjoyment of certain works by customers in business premises, was inconsistent with Article 13 of TRIPS.[25]

While the relationship between TRIPS and the GATT still needs to be worked out, a panel has held that TRIPS has a 'relatively self-contained, *sui generis* status within the WTO', though it is 'an integral part of the WTO system, which itself builds upon the experience of over nearly half a century under the GATT 1947'.[26] According to GATT/WTO jurisprudence the interpretation of the WTO Agreements, including TRIPS, is to be made on the basis of principles of international customary law, as codified in Articles 31 and 32 of the Vienna Convention on the Law of Treaties (1969). WTO Panels and the Appellate Body are expressly prohibited from adding rights and obligations when adjudicating on disputes (Article 3.2 of the DSU). However, 'the line between interpretation and providing clearer parameters of the rights and obligations of Members under these agreements is often very fine' (Marceau and Pedersen, 1999, p. 33).

Only the member states are empowered to interpret the WTO Agreements, under a rule of qualified majority. As noted by Jackson:

> in many places in the Uruguay Round and WTO treaty there are gaps, and considerable ambiguities. These are beginning to emerge in the discussions and dispute settlement proceedings of the new WTO. They seem to be particularly significant in the context of the new issue text, namely GATS for services and TRIPS for intellectual property. The dispute settlement system cannot and should not carry much of the weight of formulating new rules either by way of filling gaps in the existing agreements, or by setting forth norms which carry the organization into totally new territory such as competition policy or labor standards. (Jackson, 2000, pp. 184 and 187)

Conclusions

The analysis made indicates that the new international rules for IPRs are bringing greater uniformity but not necessarily full harmonisation of national legislation and practices on the matter. TRIPS does not impose uniform law. It leaves certain flexibility for WTO member countries to adopt different legislative policies in some respects. Such flexibility may be used, in particular, in order to adopt pro-competitive measures, such as those described above, that may facilitate the diffusion of innovations and the access to goods and technologies.

The interpretation of TRIPS accepted by panels and the Appellate Body constitute a key element to determine the scope that member countries actually have to adopt different solutions, suitable to their own needs and levels of development. Of particular importance is the extent to which such bodies will accept different, but permissible, interpretations of TRIPS. In fact, TRIPS contains a number of gaps and ambiguities and leaves many issues open to interpretation by the member states. It is outside the competence of the panels and Appellate Body to fill in gaps and provide their own interpretation on such issues.

Notes

1. This paper is partially based on a study ('The TRIPS Agreement: How Much Room for Maneuver is Left?', 2000) prepared by the author for UNDP.
2. In many industries the loss of appropriability does not act as a disincentive for expenditures for innovative activities. In many cases (such as semiconductors) the crucial factor is the *lead time* in introducing new products on to the market.
3. Transfer of technology may take place through informal modes, such as movement of personnel, acquisition of equipment and dissemination of publications, or through formal modes, including non-equity arrangements (for example licence agreements, turn key plants), joint ventures and foreign direct investment. The use of these different modalities varies considerably depending on sectors involved, the maturity of technology, and the stage of development of the recipient country (Correa, 2000, p. 264).
4. It should be noted that nothing in TRIPS prevents a member country from granting a compulsory licence for the importation of a protected product.
5. See, however, the practice followed in some cases in the USA in Correa (1999).
6. 'Parallel imports' take place when a product is imported into a country by a third party without the authorisation of the IP title holder or his licensees in those cases where the product has been lawfully put on the market anywhere else in the world. The importation by the third party parallels the importation by the IP title holder or his licensee. Parallel importation does not refer to the importation of counterfeit products.
7. It may be argued, therefore, that the prohibition of parallel imports may amount to a trade restriction, contrary to Article XI.1 of GATT (1947), which does not allow the imposition of restrictions 'other than duties, taxes or other charges'.
8. The US Congress passed a law in 2000 authorising the parallel importation of medicines into the United States in cases where the product is reimported to

the USA (Agriculture, Rural Development, Food and Drug Administration, and Related Agencies Appropriations Act, 2001).

9. See Bond (1999).

10. On 10 March 2000 President Clinton issued an Executive Order instructing a flexible policy on HIV/AIDS and TRIPS for Sub-Saharan Africa.

11. A draft bill in the United States (The Patent Competitiveness and Technological Innovation Act, HR 5598, 1990) expressly stressed the link between the experimentation exception and competitiveness and innovation.

12. The Community Patent Convention was signed in 1975, but did not come into force because it did not obtain the required number of ratifications. The European Commission has continued to pursue the objective of a single patent application leading to a patent valid throughout the European Community. Its latest proposals for the creation of a community patent are to be found in draft Regulation of the EC (COM (2000) 412 Final).

13. This exception is named 'Bolar' after a case judged by US courts in *Roche Products Inc. v. Bolar Pharmaceutical Co.* (733 F 2d 858, Fed. Cir., cert. denied 469 US 856, 1984), in which the issue of the exception was dealt with. The court denied Bolar the right to begin the Food and Drug Administration approval process before the expiration of the patent.

14. In the European countries, an 'early working' exception has been gradually admitted by case law on the basis of the already mentioned right by a third party to conduct experimentation without the authorisation of the patent owner (Cook, 1997; NERA, 1998).

15. In the USA many compulsory licences have been granted in order to remedy anti-competitive practices. In some cases, these licences have been granted 'royalty free'. See Fugate (1991).

16. Article 27.1 has been generally interpreted as excluding obligations requiring the industrial exploitation of the invention. However, Article 5A of the Paris Convention (which is applicable under TRIPS) allows for compulsory licences in cases of non-working. In addition, Article 27.1 of TRIPS leaves it unclear whether the products that can be 'imported or locally produced' are only third parties' infringing products or also those of the patent owner.

17. The USA requested a panel against Brazil under the WTO Dispute Settlement Understanding in relation to the Brazilian provision (Article 68 of the Industrial Property Code) on compulsory licences for cases of non-working. The case was settled before being heard.

18. See European Commission (1997).

19. See the US Trade Representative Press Release, 30 April 1999, listing the countries that may be subject to trade sanctions under s. 301 of the US Trade Act.

20. If the product is not new, but data are submitted on new clinical investigations, a 3-year exclusivity period is granted.

21. This is the approach followed by Argentine law (No. 24.766).

22. The Federal Court of Appeal of Canada held that the national authority is able, under Canadian law and NAFTA rules, to rely on confidential information available to it (*Bayer Inc, the Attorney General and the Minister of Health and Apotex Inc. and Novopharm Ltd*, 19 May 1999).

23. See WT/DS50/R, WT/DS50/AB/R and WT/DS79/R.

24. See WT/DS170/R.

25. See WT/DS160/R.
26. See the Panel Report on USA–India–Patent Protection for Agricultural and Chemical Products, WT/DS50/R, adopted on 16 January 1998, para. 7.19.

References

Barrett, Margaret (2000) 'The United States Doctrine of Exhaustion: Parallel Imports of Patented Goods', *Northern Kentucky Law Review*, vol. 27, no. 5.

Bond, Patrick (1999) 'Globalization, Pharmaceutical Pricing and South African Health Policy: Managing Confrontation with U.S. Firms and Politicians', *International Journal of Health Services*, vol. 29, no. 4.

Cook, Trevor (1997) 'Pharmaceutical Patents and the Generic Sector in Europe', *Patent World*, issue 97, February 1997, pp. 36–40.

Cornish, W. (1989) *Intellectual Property: Patents, Copyright, Trade Marks and Allied Rights* (London: Sweet & Maxwell).

Cornish, W. (1998) 'Experimental Use of Patented Inventions in European Community States', *International Review of Industrial Property and Copyright Law C*, vol. 29, no. 7.

Correa, Carlos (1999) *Intellectual Property Rights and the Use of Compulsory Licenses: Options for Developing Countries* (Geneva: South Centre).

Correa, Carlos (2000) 'Emerging Trends: New Patterns of Technology Transfer', in S. Patel, P. Roffe and A. Yusuf (eds), *International Technology Transfer. The Origins and Aftermath of the United Nations Negotiations on a Draft Code of Conduct* (The Hague: Kluwer Law International).

Correa, Carlos and Salvador Bergel (1996) *Patentes y Competencia* (Santa Fe: Rubinzal-Culzoni).

European Commission (1997) *Report on United States Barriers to Trade and Investment* (Brussels).

Fugate, W. (1991) *Foreign Commerce and Antitrust Laws*, 4th edn (Boston, Little, Brown & Co).

Geuze, M. and H. Wager (1999) ' WTO dispute settlement practice relating to the TRIPS Agreement', *Journal of International Economic Law*, vol. 2, no. 2, pp. 347–84.

Graz, Dominique (1988) *Propriété Intellectuelle et libre circulation des marchandises*, (Geneva: Librairie Droz).

Hoekman, Bernard and Michel Kostecki (1997) *The Political Economy of the World Trading System. From GATT to WTO* (Oxford: Oxford University Press).

Jackson, John (2000) *The Jurisprudence of GATT & the WTO* (Cambridge: Cambridge University Press).

Marceau, Gabrielle and Peter Pedersen (1999) 'Is the WTO Open and Transparent? A Discussion of the Relationship of the WTO with Non-governmental Organisations and Civil Society's Claims for more Transparency and Public Participation', *Journal of World Trade*, vol. 33, no. 1.

NERA (National Economic Research Associates) (1998) *Policy Relating to Generic Medicines in the OECD. Final Report for the European Commission* (London: December).

OECD (1992) *Technology and the Economy. The Key Relationships* (Paris).

Omaji, Paul (1997) 'Infringement by Unauthorised Importation under Australian Intellectual Property Laws', *European Intellectual Property Review*, vol. 10.

Reichman, J. (1993) *Implications of the Draft TRIPS Agreement for Developing Countries as Competitors in an Integrated World Market* (Geneva: UNCTAD).

Scherer, F. (1999) 'The Patent System and Innovation in Pharmaceuticals', paper presented to 'Colloque de Toulouse: Brevets pharmaceutiques, innovations et santé publique', Toulouse, January 28–30.

Schott, Jeffrey J. (1994), *The Uruguay Round. An Assessment* (Washington, DC: Institute for International Economics).

Skolnikoff, E. (1993) 'New International Trends Affecting Science and Technology', *Science and Public Policy*, vol. 20, no. 2.

South Centre (1995) *The Uruguay Round. Intellectual Property Rights Regime. Implications for Developing Countries* (Cartagena).

UNDP (1999) *Human Development Report* (New York).

Wegner, Harold (1994) *Patent Law in Biotechnology, Chemicals & Pharmaceuticals* (New York: Stockton Press).

WTO (1995) *Environment and TRIPS*, WT/CTE/W/8 (Geneva).

Yusuf, Abdulqawi and Andrés Moncayo von Hase (1992), 'Intellectual Property Protection and International Trade-Exhaustion of Rights Revisited'. *World Competition*, vol. 16, no. 1, Geneva.

Part II

Development and Access to Technology: Genetics, Health, Agriculture, Education and Information Technology

4
Intellectual Property and the Human Genome

John Sulston

Introduction

In an extraordinary revelation just under fifty years ago, the structure of a component of our bodies, called DNA, was discovered. The special thing about this component, which is an immensely long thin molecule, is that it turned out to carry the genome – the code of instructions to make us. The same applies to any other living being, since each has its own genome encoded in DNA.

The structure of DNA is a pair of strands wound around each other. Each strand has a uniform backbone with units called bases projecting from it at regular intervals. There are four different bases, called adenine, cytosine, guanine and thymine, usually abbreviated to A, C, G and T. It is their sequence, read along one of the strands, that forms the code, just like the sequence of letters in a written language forms a code. The sequence of bases on the second strand is defined by that on the first, because the bases always form pairs like rungs of a ladder across the molecule – A with T and C with G.

It was remarkable that the secret of life turned out to be so straightforward: many had thought that it would have to be represented by complex molecules in some more distributed fashion, rather than by this simple linear code. From that moment on, it became an implicit goal of biology to read out and understand the code, starting with the simplest organisms, but some day reaching our own, human, DNA.

First people had to learn about the basics, about the way in which the information was read from the DNA, in units of instruction called genes, and how in most cases the information in a gene was translated into the structure of another type of molecule called protein. Proteins form most of the functional parts of our bodies: hair is made largely of the protein keratin, for example, whilst muscles are made from a complex assembly of different proteins.

The original concept of a gene was a hypothetical and indivisible entity that would account for the regularity of inherited characteristics as first observed by Mendel 150 years ago. Through a series of experiments, DNA was eventually recognised as the likely repository of these units of inheritance. When the structure of DNA was discovered all became clear: the genes were simply segments of the code.

In the 1970s, Fred Sanger devised an efficient method to read out the sequence, and, with modification and automation, his technique has survived to the present day. By 1990, technology was advanced enough to plan an assault on the human sequence, and over the last three years the bulk of it has been read out.

It is important to note that this is only the beginning. The code is potentially of huge value because we know that it contains all the instructions to make a human being. But we are only just starting to understand it, so most of the value lies in the future. For this scientific reason alone it is essential that the code itself remains in the public domain, but there are also, of course, strong ethical reasons for keeping this information in common ownership.

Obtaining the sequence

The origins of genomics go back to the 1980s when it became apparent to some of us that it would be worthwhile to tackle the genomes of higher organisms as a whole rather than looking at them gene by gene as had been done up to that point. Previously the route to finding a gene in an animal was through looking for individuals that had a defect in the function of interest. One then used the methods of genetics to track down the gene, and the new methods of molecular biology to isolate it and find out exactly what it did. Armed with this information one was better equipped to move on to other genes that had related functions and so build up a picture of a whole mechanism.

Two difficulties with this approach were, first, that it was slow and, second, that not all genes had detectable mutations that one could work with. So the notion of isolating all the genes at once was very appealing, if it could be done.

My own experience was with a little nematode worm that lives in the soil and breeds fast, so that the genetics part could be done quickly. The slow part was tracking down the genes. We solved that by making a map of the whole genome. We broke the DNA into fragments at random and treated them in a way that allowed them to be replicated in bacteria. We found a way of rapidly characterising each fragment so that we could tell when one overlapped another, meaning that they came from neighbouring places on the genome. Much like assembling a jigsaw puzzle we were able to build a representation of the genome, matching fragment to fragment all the way. The beauty of it was that each fragment was sitting safely inside a clump of bacteria in our freezer so that we could go back and retrieve any one we wanted. We had turned the original DNA, which was far too big to be handled on its own, into a set of manageable and mapped pieces.

This turned out to be a great boon for the biologists. They were able to line up their genetic experiments with the physical map and track down the genes much more quickly. Similar work started in other organisms, including the fruit fly and the human. Genomics – the study of genomes – had begun in earnest.

By 1990 it was time to go to the next step. The automation of Sanger's sequencing method had progressed immensely and we could seriously think about tackling the nematode. At that time it was still a huge task. Its genome was 100 million bases and the largest thing sequenced so far was only a quarter of a million. Nevertheless, people were already contemplating the human genome at 3000 million bases, and the Human Genome Project (HGP) had been officially begun for the purpose.

At first many people were unhappy about the costs. Mapping had been relatively cheap but sequencing was going to cost far more. Various short cuts were proposed, involving isolating genes and sequencing them alone, because we knew already that these large genomes had substantial areas that contributed little biological information. However, two crucial arguments prevailed: one was that it would be impossible to find all the genes in this way, the other was that the areas between them, while not densely packed with information, certainly contained important control sequences that would be lost by short cutting.

So we embarked on genome sequencing, first on the nematode and then a little later in the human. As soon as the projects were seriously under way the doubts began to fade away because it was clear to biologists that having direct access to the code gave them powerful new ways into their research problems. The nematode was completed in 1998 by two labs (the Sanger Centre and Bob Waterston's Genome Sequencing Center at Washington University, St Louis, Missouri), and was the first animal to be sequenced.

Competition for the human genome

Life was a bit more complicated in the case of the human genome because so many people wanted to be part of it. And already in the early 1990s there was a feeling that this information would be worth money some day. In 1996 we convened the first meeting to discuss the international relationships needed to get the job done. I was greatly in favour of a broad partnership because I felt strongly that our genome is our common heritage and that sharing the work and the expense would reinforce and pragmatise this feeling.

That first meeting was held in Bermuda and there we formulated and agreed the Bermuda principles – that publicly funded labs carrying out large-scale human sequencing would release all data immediately as it was produced and that they would not claim any patent rights over it. Release was a practical proposition because the Internet was becoming fast and efficient and there were three databases (in the USA, Europe and Japan) that provided permanent public archives of sequence.

The actual production of sequence was scaling up and it began to look as though our International Human Genome Sequencing Consortium would reach the goal of a finished human sequence well before the original target date of 2005. The Sanger Centre alone was committed and funded to produce a sixth by 2002. Other groups were anxious to join, if not beat us.

Then in 1998 a rival appeared. One of our number, Craig Venter, broke away and obtained private funding to start a company called Celera. The aim was to sequence the genome by a method that would cover most of it rapidly at an accuracy that was limited but sufficient to claim patent rights to some newly discovered genes and to sell access to other scientists for their own gene hunting. Celera stated at the time that the data would eventually be released free of charge and suggested that the HGP should phase out human sequencing. Some of us had doubts at the time, well founded as events turned out, both about the methodology proposed and more seriously about the wisdom of leaving so important a piece of information to private monopoly. There was nothing to guarantee that those holding stock in Celera would not abrogate the data release policy, and that's exactly how it turned out.

Led initially by the Wellcome Trust, the public funding agencies rallied and, after some agonised debate, we all agreed to a scheme put forward by Francis Collins (head of the National Institutes of Health genome effort and of the HGP) by which we too would rapidly produce an incomplete product to head off the patent and privatisation threat, but would then go on to finish it properly by 2003. In 1999 there was a huge scaling up in sequence production as both public and private sides installed hundreds of new sequencing machines. During the following year-and-a-half there was tremendous and increasing press interest in the perceived race. The HGP continued to release its sequence as it was produced. Celera released nothing but was able to pick up and incorporate the public sequence like anyone else. The company issued a series of highly optimistic statements that for some reason were generally accepted at face value by the press even though there was no supporting evidence.

In June 2000 there was a simultaneous announcement by both parties, engineered by the White House, that the 'draft' sequence had been done. This was somewhat artificial, not only because the sequence was incomplete but also in that the publicly originated sequence was public whilst Celera's was not, but it satisfied media demands for a conclusion.

Subsequently, in February 2001, there were simultaneous publications of the draft sequences. There was a scandal because Celera had persuaded *Science Magazine*, in which they published, to accept a very limited release of their sequence, going against a long-established practice that publication in a major journal would automatically require full release. Academics were entitled to a limited download under stringent conditions that would inhibit them from normal scientific exchanges with their colleagues; anyone with commercial interests had to sign a full material transfer agreement whose terms, we were advised by company lawyers, would be unacceptable for many corporations. This had never happened before and was a heavy blow against the freedom and integrity of academic publishing. Also, it was apparent that at this point the integrity of the Celera sequence was heavily dependent on that from the public consortium. Later the company issued denials of dependence claiming that they had subsequently put their sequence together independently, but by then it was not available for examination so nobody could tell.

Meanwhile Celera began to sequence the mouse genome, while the public labs primarily focused on their agreed goal of a finished human sequence. It should be noted that the latter was not an arbitrary decision. All biologists agree that the finished sequence is of much greater value than a draft and that it is essential for the public consortium to produce it.

Opensource

In 2000, seeing the disadvantages of the one-way transfer of our information to Celera with nothing coming back to the public domain in return, we began to wonder whether we could at least enforce redistribution. Our model was the 'opensource' software model which ensures that, for example, GNU and Linux software remain in shared ownership for development as well as application by everyone. We went into the possibilities in some detail and discussed them with the heads of the public databases, but in the end we all came to the conclusion that more would be lost than gained by our pursuing this line. Our role was to provide the data publicly for anyone at all to use. Not only was the released sequence immediately useful for research but also it became prior art and the process of sequencing became more obvious: both of these attributes would undermine attempts at patenting sequence in the future. Had we claimed ownership, which is what any kind of restriction would amount to, we would be abrogating the very thing that we stood for. All we could do was to let everyone know what we were doing and why. This is as true today as it was then.

Interpretation

Possession of the genomic sequence is just the beginning. As it is revealed, it is simply a string of letters. We are still at quite an early stage of understanding it. The most important analytical task is to find the genes. We think that there are 30 000 to 40 000 of them in the human genome – only about twice as many as in the worm or the fruit fly. At first sight it seems rather surprising that there aren't more, especially as about half the genes in worms and flies have counterparts in the human. This immediately illustrates the remarkable unity of life, the result of the evolutionary process that has given rise to all life on earth from a single common ancestor. Evolution tends to re-use genes rather than throwing them away and inventing new ones. Furthermore, as we trace the course of evolution leading to more and more complex creatures, we see that an increasing proportion of genes is used in a regulatory fashion. So the explanation for our modest gene count is that we have a basic set of genes similar to that of the worm or fly plus a number of our own but, most importantly, we have a larger executive class of genes that organises the basic building blocks into more elaborate forms – just as the same bricks can be used to make a cottage or a mansion.

The reason that the mouse is now important has to do with the power of comparative genomics. It's very difficult to spot genes in the human sequence because they come in pieces dispersed throughout much of the sequence that is more or less unused. Comparative genomics means lining up one genome with another to see where they are similar and where they are different. Both mouse and human are mammals and they have very similar genes. In fact the difference between them probably has more to do with the way genes are turned on and off than with the nature of the gene products. Since the two species diverged some tens of millions of years ago the DNA sequences have drifted apart by mutation where the sequence is non-functional. But natural selection has ensured that in functional regions the drift is limited because animals having mutations in these places will become disadvantaged or die. So looking for the places where the sequences are similar is a powerful way of spotting important bits – that is genes.

Variation

A frequently asked question is whose genome has been sequenced. The answer is no one person's; this first reference sequence is a composite from several anonymous donors. Different copies of the human genome are 99.9 per cent identical in most places, so the assembly from different sources was not a problem. Now that we have the reference sequence there is great interest in cataloguing the variations because these are what make each of us genetically distinct. The most common sort of variation is the single nucleotide polymorphism (SNP) – that is a place where one base is swapped for another. In 1999 a public–private partnership was set up that involved ten companies, the Wellcome Trust and several public sequencing centres. Interestingly, the companies decided that it was worthwhile forming a club to place the sequence in the public domain rather than competing privately and duplicating it. The consortium has already placed some 1.5 million SNPs in the public domain, and the correlation of these variations with people's health and susceptibility to disease will be tremendously valuable for medicine.

This activity, of course, raises questions of privacy and ultimately of human rights. Of course the data is kept confidential, but there is no such thing as a secure database. It is important, therefore, that in the long run we do not depend on keeping patients' records secret but ensure in law that nobody can be disadvantaged by their genotype. An added reason for doing so is that we all share 50 per cent of our particular variations with our nearest relatives – parents, siblings, or offspring – so information about one member of a family immediately provides probabilities about the others. Privacy is not enough: we must outlaw genetic discrimination of any kind under human rights legislation, just as has already been done for the well-known genetic characteristics of gender and race.

Medical use

There is a hierarchy of difficulty in applications, which I shall now briefly review from the easiest to the most difficult. It is crucial that the easy ones are not used to justify excessively broad intellectual property claims that will prevent the longer-term goals being achieved.

Knowledge of variants in a gene that correlate with a particular medical condition allows accurate diagnosis of patients for that condition. This is more difficult when, as is the case for many common conditions such as heart disease and diabetes, multiple genes are responsible but will still give valuable information. Diagnosis without cure may lead to advice on lifestyle (for example diet) but is not otherwise of much value to the patient. Prenatal diagnosis and termination for fatal conditions is, however, of great value in cultures where the practice is permitted and acceptable to the parents. For example, organised screening for beta thalassaemia is dramatically reducing its global incidence and this may be the best way of dealing with this disease. However, it is desirable also to proceed to improved therapies wherever possible.

Pharmacogenetics – the choice or modification of drugs to suit the patient's genotype – is expected to be of some value in the near term. At the genomic end of things it amounts to diagnosis. The extent of its use will depend on the cost of genotyping. The varying susceptibility of individuals to particular diseases (for example HIV) will provide the information needed to develop new therapies involving novel drug targets. We should also note in passing that the sequencing of pathogen genomes (for example those of the bacteria that cause tuberculosis and cholera) is providing new approaches to combating the infectious diseases, which are the major health problem in developing countries.

Much effort is going into the analysis of tumours for the genetic changes that cause them to grow and become cancerous, taking advantage of the availability of the whole genome for this purpose. It is hoped that detailed analysis of tumour genomes will reveal new targets for drugs more specifically toxic to tumours and, therefore, with fewer side-effects for the patient as well as higher cure rates. Because cancer treatment is a matter of killing rogue cells rather than improving debilitated ones, there is cause for optimism that this will lead to many new treatments in the next decade or two.

True gene therapy is the hardest, requiring delivery of a gene to the place where it is needed and having it produce its product correctly and stably. But there are some encouraging early results and in time there will be many successes.

In the long term the most important consequence of this work will be a complete parts list for the human body – the set of molecules that compose it and a full understanding of how they actually do the work. This anticipates many decades of biological research, but will bit-by-bit lead to an entirely new attitude to medicine. The workshop manual for the human body will have become a reality.

Dangers of monopoly

Keeping genomic data public requires continuing effort. Apart from the human genome itself there are many other important genomes that will help us to understand our own. For example, the mouse genome is important both in its own right and for interpreting the human genome. A public–private Mouse Sequencing Consortium was set up last year and has been freely releasing data, just as we did with the human sequence. Meanwhile Celera took advantage, as it was entitled to do, of the publicly released human sequence and switched at an early stage to sequencing the mouse. Because much of the public sequencing capacity remained tied up with finishing the human, the company was able to move ahead and now has a draft product that many scientists want to buy into. So the mouse is being used as bait to attract buyers into the database as a whole. A private SNP collection is being deployed in the same way.

In a contest between freely released and proprietary sequencing efforts there will inevitably always be a bit more data in a proprietary database (since it contains data from both) until each genome in turn is finished. Properly managed, this will allow a private company to remain a step ahead and continues to offer a possible route towards monopoly.

However, most researchers want the public sequencing effort to continue because, as in the case of the human, they recognise the need for finished sequence in the mouse. So for the moment calls from the company for the US government to cease funding public mouse sequencing have gone unheeded.

But what exactly is wrong with leaving it to a company? First, it is accepted by all that the sequence will never be properly finished that way. Second, to the extent that the data is fundamental and important it should be available to all on equal terms, not to the wealthy few. The widespread testing for beta thalassaemia, cheap because it uses low-cost local labour, would be impossible if royalties were charged for the tests as Myriad does for breast cancer. Third, the inhibition of redistribution is destructive of research effort. When signing up to a proprietary database, researchers must agree only to download what they need for their own use and not to redistribute the data. This is, of course, essential to protect the company's business, but it means that the normal exchanges between researchers are inhibited. In the case of large-scale sequence it's really essential to carry the data along with the interpretative work that's done on it because otherwise you never know exactly where you are. If redistribution of the primary data is not allowed, then all exchanges have to take place through the company's database and are restricted to subscribers. This places the company in an immensely strong position of control over this fundamental data. Not many biologists really think that this is a good way to run their research, which is why there is general support for continued public sequencing. At the same time, their perception of competition in their fields is leading many to subscribe. We should be wary of thus inadvertently supporting a slide towards monopoly. This view is reinforced by recent announcements of a drug target-discovery programme by Celera, which potentially puts it in conflict with its database customers.

Discovery and application

Because of all the media attention, it sometimes must seem that scientists in the HGP are promoting it as an end in itself. It should rather be thought of as a milestone in molecular biology as well as a beginning for the biological and medical advances just discussed. Molecular biology is the science of life at the atomic level, the one we need to go to both to understand what is really going on and to manipulate if we choose to do so. Molecular biology as a whole is a revolution in thought just as profound as that of cosmology that revealed to us our true place in the universe. To understand our own bodies in minute detail, to understand how the instructions to make them are coded and applied, is an extraordinary philosophical advance as well as a practical one. Clouds of ignorance and superstition are swept away and the amazing beauty of the mechanisms is revealed.

Not everyone feels happy about this. And it is true that viewed in one way the progress of discovery, removing us from the centre of the universe, relating us to animals and indeed all other forms of life, and now revealing us in molecular detail, can be seen as a comedown. To me it is quite the reverse. I marvel at the power of the human mind to reach out both into the vast tracts of the universe and equally to the very small within our own selves. Understanding is beautiful in itself and it adds to the beauty and wonder of the whole rather than diminishing it.

But there's more. With understanding comes the power to control and to alter – and it is here that we should pause and consider, for with power comes the responsibility to apply discoveries wisely. Furthermore, at the point of application the responsibility goes beyond the discoverer or ought to do so. There is a need for democratic involvement by everyone. The discoverer – the scientist in this case – has a special role to play in communicating what has been done and in predicting the likely outcomes of actions. But if these actions are such as to affect others or to involve ethical considerations, then the scientist should have no more of a vote in deciding what should be done than anyone else. That is what we mean by democracy. Confusing discovery and application has led to a widespread distrust of science because of the real and perceived lack of democratic control over application.

The problem has been greatly exacerbated, perhaps even largely caused, by the profit motive. So much of current research is paid for on the basis that profitable discoveries will be made that it tends to be taken as a given that exploitation will follow as quickly as possible on discovery. Of course, if there are good things to be done with the work we should get on with them, but not in secret and not without heed to the consequences.

Free release and intellectual property

Why should the data be kept free? First, this is our common heritage and nobody has a right to control access to it. We all carry our personal copies of the human genome around with us and every part of it is unique. If someone claims to own a gene, then they're claiming to own one of my genes as well. And they can't offer to share the genes between us because we both need all our genes.

Second, there are important practical considerations of utility. It seems to me that intellectual property on a gene should be confined strictly to an application that is being actively pursued – to an inventive step. Someone else may want to work on an alternative application and so need to have access to the gene as well. It's not possible to go away and reinvent a human gene. So ideally all the discovery part of genes – the sequence, the functions, everything – needs to be kept pre-competitive and free of property rights. This fits with the main point of the patent system, which is to stimulate innovation through competition and avoid permanent monopoly. You can't invent around a discovery of nature; you can only invent around other inventions. The most valuable applications for a gene come much later than the first easy ones, so this is not just a matter of principle but has extremely important consequences.

At the moment, this view is only partially accepted by the patent offices. Certainly the notion of patenting a pure sequence with some general and nominal utility such as its potential for finding genes seems to have been abandoned. I think that a major factor in ensuring that this came about was the release of so much sequence by the public consortium, which served as prior art and made plain sequence both non-novel and obvious.

But patents are being issued, and many more have been applied for, that claim rights to all uses of a gene on the basis of a limited understanding of its function. This view is defended by claims that the large sums of money required for drug development will only be forthcoming if genes can be ring-fenced against rival developers and that process patents are not defensible. Of course, it's much easier for a developer to defend product patents but the disadvantages to the rest of us of allowing monopolisation of genes in this way far outweigh the benefits. So there is a need to press for further evolution of patent practice so that there is proper competition among developers for real applications and the true inventors are rewarded rather than those who buy genetic lottery tickets.

Patents did not assist at all in the sharing of human sequence data. The field was fast-moving and, at least in the US, delays in release of data after filing meant that patent information was out of date when it was finally made public. The great majority of patents are still pending anyway.

The negative consequences of a patenting ethos, on the other hand, are striking. The secretive atmosphere in laboratories where a lot of patenting is done means that pre-patenting communication is inhibited. Most observers feel that scientific meetings have suffered from this as well. A recent survey of US academic laboratories has revealed a high proportion of researchers who feel inhibited by patent claims (Schissel *et al.*, 1999; Merz, 2000).

Conclusion

At the time, I was astounded by the difficulties we had in ensuring open access to the human genome, information of fundamental importance to medicine which the great majority of people believe should be beyond private ownership. These difficulties become more comprehensible when seen in the context of the current exaggerated belief in private ownership, many instances of which are described in this book. The documentation of them is all the more important for that, because the ambition for wealth that gave rise to them continues unabated both in terms of gene patenting and in attempts at control through proprietary databases.

Despite these concerns, much has been achieved. The draft human genome sequence is on the Internet, free and available for all to explore and use as they wish, regardless of where they are or of their ability to pay. Many discoveries have already arisen from the human sequence and more are coming all the time, but that isn't the most important aspect of it. The key thing is that it has become part of the foundation of biology and will soon no longer be visible as a separate entity. It has become a crucial element in a free and open system of biological information. Maintaining that openness is the best way of advancing knowledge of living things and of delivering healthcare universally and equitably.

Acknowledgement

My admiration and thanks to all my colleagues in the International Human Genome Sequencing Consortium for their collective achievement. I would like to thank the Wellcome Trust and the Medical Research Council for their generous support, and the staff of Oxfam for educating me in the wider issues of world healthcare.

References

Merz, Jon (2000) Statement to the Subcommittee on Courts and Intellectual Property of the Committee on the Judiciary, US House of Representatives Oversight Hearing on Gene Patents and Other Genomic Inventions, www.house.gov/judiciary/merz0713.htm.

Schissel, Anna, Jon Merz and M. Mildred Cho (1999) 'Survey Confirms Fears About Licensing of Genetic Tests', *Nature*, vol. 402, p. 118.

5
Access to Medicine and Compliance with the WTO TRIPS Accord: Models for State Practice in Developing Countries

James Love

Introduction[1]

This chapter addresses the issue of government authorisation to use a patent without the permission of the patent owner. In particular, models for compulsory licensing and government use of patents are examined, as a tool to increase access to medicines in developing countries.[2] The recommendations in this chapter are informed by the following facts.

Contrary to much of the debate over the World Trade Organization (WTO) rules for intellectual property, the Agreement on Trade-Related Aspects of Intellectual Property Rights (TRIPS) is actually fairly permissive on the issue of government decisions to authorise third parties to use patents without the permission of the patent owners. For example, for public non-commercial use, a country may use or authorise a third party to use a patent without negotiation or without a licence (Article 31(b)), the only obligation being the payment of 'adequate' compensation (Article 31(h)). This approach too can be used for emergencies, including public health emergencies (Article 31(b)). When an authorisation is granted to remedy anti-competitive practices, such as high prices from the exercise of monopoly power, the products can even be exported (Article 31(k)). TRIPS also allows a country to make virtually all of its own decisions on these issues, including those regarding compensation or appeals, through administrative processes (Article 31(c), (i), (j) and (k)). Moreover, TRIPS specifically does not require governments to grant injunctive relief to patent holders (Article 44.2) in cases where government authorisations of patent use satisfy the Article 31 framework. Taken together, these provisions in the TRIPS permit countries to create very simple and easy to administer systems for permitting production or import of generic products from the competitive sector. However, what TRIPS permits and what countries actually do are two different things, and in the end, it is national law and practice that will be decisive, both in providing access to inventions, including medicines, and in establishing the state practice framework in which TRIPS rules will be interpreted. Also, there remains an important issue with respect to the degree to which countries can tailor their laws to specific concerns regarding access to medicines, because of the Article 27.1 restrictions on discrimination of patent rights by field of technology.

Many governments have good national laws for public use of patents, which is a similar but more direct and less restrictive method of authorising non-voluntary use of a patent than a compulsory licence. For example, under 28 United States Code s. 1498, the US government can use patents or authorise third parties to use patents for virtually any public use, without negotiation. Patent owners have no rights for injunctive relief, and may only seek compensation, not as a tort, but as an eminent domain taking.[3] This is not unique, however, and the Australian, Irish, Italian, German, New Zealand and UK public use provisions also provide very similar powers, as do several other countries, including the Philippines, Malaysia and Singapore, among others. See below for examples of specific national laws on this. The TRIPS rules are designed to accommodate these practices.

Compulsory licences have been used extensively in North America, Japan and Europe for a variety of purposes, including many that have been issued for computers, software, biotechnology and other modern technologies. In 2000 the US issued several compulsory licences for tow-truck technologies. Canada has the most extensive experience with the use of compulsory licences for pharmaceutical drugs. Until pressured by the US, as a condition of joining NAFTA (North American Free Trade Agreement), to abandon a compulsory licensing approach that was nearly automatic, Canada routinely granted compulsory licences on pharmaceuticals, with compensation based upon royalties, typically set at 4 per cent of the competitor's sales price.

Despite a public health crisis of enormous proportions for HIV/AIDS, apparently no African country has issued a compulsory licence for any medicine. Given the permissive global trade framework for compulsory licensing, one has to wonder why this is so.

Virtually all national patent law systems are modelled after European and US patent legal traditions, often based upon colonial statutes, or the modern-day equivalent: laws informed by WIPO technical assistance.

The United States spends $1 billion annually on its patent and trademark office. Europe and Japan also spend large sums to examine patents. Despite these investments in rich countries, the quality of US patent examinations is poor. According to a study by Lemley and Allison of patents litigated to judgment, 54 per cent were found to be valid and 46 per cent were invalid.[4] Critics of US patent examinations believe a much larger number of issued patents are not valid under any reasonable tests of utility and invention, and would be busted if the patent owners sought enforcement. Patent examinations in developing countries, if they exist at all, are understaffed, undertrained and have less access to research materials on prior art.[5]

The costs of litigation are not trivial. In (27 December) 1998, the *New York Times* reported the median cost of US patent litigation was $1.2 million, per side, and the costs of litigation in complex cases is much higher. In *Polaroid v. Kodak*, each side reportedly spent over $100 million. Consider this quote from a judge in the AZT patent dispute:[6]

> In the twenty-five months transpiring between the filing of the initial complaint in this consolidated patent infringement action on May 14, 1991, and the commencement of the trial on June 28, 1993, approximately five hundred and forty-one pleadings have been filed and dozens of hearings on motions and discovery matters have been conducted by the court. The court has entered eighty-eight written orders and numerous bench rulings. Thus, the court is intimately familiar with the facts of this case and the legal contentions of the parties. To state that the case has been hotly contested would be an understatement. The parties have amassed learned, experienced and sizable trial teams who have represented their clients zealously and competently. The administrative complexity [of] conducting a trial of this magnitude has been enormous for the court and the parties. The sixty-year-old courtroom in New Bern, North Carolina, has been converted into a contemporary high tech facility utilizing real time court reporting and six computer-integrated video display monitors. It is highly conceivable that the cost of this trial for the parties exceeds $100 000 per day, in addition to the time and expense associated with this court and the jury. As the case enters its fourth week of trial, the parties estimate, somewhat conservatively the court suspects, that the trial will last an additional six to eight weeks.

See also this quote by Professor Michael Meurer:[7]

> First of all, frequency of litigation and the cost of litigation for biotech patents is very high. Drug and health patents are litigated more than any other kind of technology. There is one empirical study that showed that six lawsuits are spawned by every 100 corporate biotech patents.[8] There is also research that shows that most of the start-up companies are spending a comparable amount on legal costs to what they are spending on research.[9] So this is a very big concern for start-up companies.

Few if any developing countries have a significant capacity to examine patent applications, or to litigate patent claims. Some developing countries have patent registration systems that don't require patent examination at all. In the US, Japan or European markets there are substantial financial incentives for generic drug companies to bust bad patents. These incentives do not exist in small national markets. It is predictable that a considerable number of patents in developing countries will be bad patents, because the countries or competitors will not have the capacity or economic incentives to evaluate and litigate overreaching patent claims.

For a variety of reasons, poor countries are extremely reluctant to sue or be sued. Litigation is expensive, and can overwhelm already limited programme budgets. In some countries, a cultural reluctance to engage in litigation restrains public officials from pursuing courses of action likely to involve protracted litigation.

Developing countries have not enacted good TRIPS-compliant state practice models for authorising the use of patents on medicines. Prior to TRIPS, many countries simply excluded patents on pharmaceuticals from the patent system. Under TRIPS, countries must issue patents on medicines. Unless they can invent a model for state practice that will actually work in developing countries, countries will not be able to obtain less expensive medicines from the competitive sector.

Summary of good state practice

This chapter outlines a model for government authorisations of uses of patents without the permission of the patent owner. In particular, this is designed to address cases where the country or generic entrants do not maintain the capacity to invest significant resources in litigation. While I am interested in the development of a state practice model for a developing country, I have also drawn on examples from patent laws in developed countries. People looking at these issues can obtain translations of foreign intellectual property (IP) laws from the World Intellectual Property Organization (WIPO) in both paper and electronic formats. The Consumer Project on Technology has excerpted sections of several patent laws, including compulsory licensing, government use and patent exception provisions (see http://www.cptech.org/ip/health/cl/examples2.html).

The recommended features for a good state practice model are as follows:

1. The system must not be overly legalistic or expensive to administer, or easily manipulated by litigation. Some large pharmaceutical companies are masters of IP litigation and routinely misuse regulatory and IP laws, exploit loopholes and harass competitors in the courts. Any system which permits the big Pharma companies to do this will not work very well in practice. For this reason, we recommend models that rely upon administrative processes.
2. The government use provisions should be strong. The rules in TRIPS give governments very broad powers to authorise use of patents for public non-commercial use and this is one area where there are many good state practice models to consider. No developing country should have statutory public use provisions that are weaker than the US, German, Irish or UK provisions.
3. The system of setting compensation should be relatively predictable and easy to administer. It should have royalty guidelines to reduce uncertainty and to speed decisions, and an administrative process that places burdens on patent owners to disclose essential economic data if they seek to appeal administrative decisions. It is important to have greater transparency in this area. This process should also be fast, with initial decisions setting initial compensation, and revisions, such as from administrative appeals, providing forward-looking adjustments. When there are complex IP rights for a product, as is sometimes the case for medical technologies, one approach is to permit a decision setting a royalty for all claims to be paid into an escrow fund and to have the various patent owners settle claims between each other, possibly through arbitration, with the arbitration costs borne by the competing patent owners.
4. Production for export should be permitted. Under TRIPS, the most straightforward way would be to permit exports if
   (a) the administrative process found that a lack of competition within the therapeutic class of drugs has given the producer market

power, creating a barrier to access. This would be consistent with Article 31(k) of TRIPS. This can be done by a health agency, even by administrative action.

(b) A different approach would be to authorise production for export when the legitimate interests of the patent owner are protected in the export market, such as when the export market provides reasonable compensation to the patent owner, as an Article 30 exception to patent rights. A number of NGOs are also urging countries to adopt an Article 30 patent exception for products that are produced for humanitarian purposes.

The Article 31(k) and Article 30 approaches are both stronger if accompanied by an administrative finding, such as a finding that:

(a) increasing returns to scale in the production of a product are important;

(b) the product is used to treat infectious diseases;

(c) the export of the product will benefit the public health; and/or

(d) the export of the product will address humanitarian objectives.

5. There should be a provision for authorisation of the use of patents to address public health emergencies. Under Article 31(b), this triggers the same fast-track liberal procedures as exist for public non-commercial use. Many European governments have a large public-sector role in funding healthcare, but for most developing countries there is little capacity to provide expensive drugs for HIV/AIDS or other severe illnesses. In these countries, it is possible to expand access to new expensive drugs by permitting the competitive generics sector to enter the commercial market, where there are opportunities for expanded access to medicines, at least among some income groups. By declaring a public health emergency for HIV/AIDS, tuberculosis, malaria or other illnesses, a government could give general authorisation for the competitive sector to supply particular types of drug, subject to paying a modest royalty to the patent owner, and could also eliminate the steps of negotiation normally required for commercial use, saving time and lowering barriers to entry, and probably increasing the number of generic competitors. This should be done right now for all HIV/AIDS-related medicines in Africa, Romania, Thailand and other countries where AIDS drugs are protected by patent and the high price creates access barriers.

Administrative processes

As indicated above, TRIPS permits the use of administrative practices in all Article 31 decisions, including the setting of compensation and the appeals processes. The key thing for each country is to settle basic issues. It must determine which agency, official, committee or other body will make the initial decision and which will receive and act on appeals. TRIPS requires that the processes be fair, transparent and accountable relying, for example, on written records and decisions, with opportunities to provide evidence and be heard and that there exists an independent appeals process to a higher body from the one that makes the initial decision.

Several countries give very broad powers to a wide range of government officials to make decisions regarding the initial authorisation of use, when the use involves public non-commercial use. In some cases, including the US, the statute gives the power to authorise the use of the patent to any government official, for example by issuing a contract or agreement that contains the authorisation to use patents or copyrights. The agency's administrative procedures may provide additional guidance on how these decisions are made, such as, for example, the procedures spelled out in the US federal acquisition regulations.

The procedures for authorising third parties to engage in commercial use of a patent tend to be more specific about who can make such an authorisation. In Belgium, the statute provides for a committee that includes persons representing consumer, labour and small-business interests. In Switzerland, compulsory licensing decisions are made by the Federal Council. In many countries, the licences are issued by the registrar of patents or the ministries of trade or industry. In the US, the Secretary of the Department of Health and Human Services makes the determination in cases involving the Bayh–Dole 'March-In' rights (the rights of a Federal agency to require an owner of an invention to grant a licence to an applicant), while compulsory licensing of patents for nuclear energy or clean air are handled by different bodies. In Spain, the Minister of Industry is required to consult with the Minister of Health on compulsory licensing applications that involve patents which concern the public health.

Article 31 of TRIPS requires that the administrative process provide an 'independent review by a distinct higher authority'. For example, the Minister of Health could appoint an officer to make decisions and also an independent body to review decisions, with the power to overrule, modify or remand the initial decisions. The review could be provided by another office, such as the registrar of patents or the attorney-general. The task is to create a system that will carry out the purposes of the compulsory licensing or government-use programme, and to have a process that is and is perceived to be fair and straightforward. With respect to

Article 31 TRIPS is more about having a rules-based system than it is about the specific rule or outcomes, at least as far as the WTO is concerned. That is, in a WTO dispute-resolution procedure, many different approaches and outcomes will be acceptable to the WTO if they follow in good faith the procedural safeguards.

While the purely administrative process is one option, countries could also have a mixed system where the appeals are handled by a federal court. If judicial appeals are permitted, the statute could set out the basis for an appeal, and could be very specific with regard to the standards used to overturn an administrative decision. For example, the statute could make it very difficult to overturn an administrative decision, or it could make it easier for either the patent owner or the person seeking the licence to prevail on appeal. This is one of many areas where policy makers have discretion and choices to make. A decision to permit a judicial appeal does not need to include the right of the patent owner to obtain injunctive relief. For example, in the US system for public use almost any government employee can authorise use. This is not considered an infringement of the patent and the patent owner does not get the right to obtain an injunction against either the government or third parties authorised by the government. The patent holder does, however, have a right to compensation and the decisions regarding compensation, including appeals are made by federal courts.

Government use

There is a high variance in national provisions for government or public use of patents. Some are quite permissive, while others are not. These are some examples of countries with fairly liberal public use provisions in national patent laws.

The US has very broad rights to use patents for public purposes. As noted above, the government can use patents for any government purpose, is not obligated to negotiate for licences, and such use does not authorise any injunctive relief to the patent owner. The patent owner is granted compensation, as a government taking under eminent domain laws.

Italy gives the government the right to expropriate patents for 'Military or public interest' uses.

In Australia, 'Exploitation by the Crown' of a patent, including use 'by a person authorized in writing by the Commonwealth or a State', is 'not an infringement' of a patent.

In Germany, 'a patent shall have no effect where the Federal Government orders that the invention be exploited in the interest of public welfare'.

Malaysian patent law has special provisions for 'Rights of Government', which authorise 'the Government of the Federation or of any State, a Ministry or Government department or any person authorised by such Government, Ministry or Government department' to 'make use and exercise any invention', subject to the payment of 'reasonable compensation'. As in many other countries government authorised uses of patents are not considered an infringement in Malaysia.

In Singapore, the patent law has a provision for 'Use of Patented Inventions for Services of Government', which permits 'a Government department or a person authorised by a Government department' to 'make, use, exercise and vend the patented invention for any purpose which appears to the Government department necessary or expedient' for several stated purposes, including 'public non-commercial use'.

The New Zealand patent law has a provision for 'Use of patented inventions for services of the Crown', which states, 'notwithstanding any other provision of this Act, any Government Department, and any person authorised in writing by a Government Department, may make, use, exercise, and vend any patented invention for the services of the Crown and anything done by virtue of this subsection shall not amount to an infringement of the patent'. Interestingly, the only limitation on the sale of a good to the public under this provision concerns integrated circuits.

In the Philippines, the relevant provision is 'Use of Invention by Government', which states that a

> Government agency or third person authorized by the Government may exploit the invention even without agreement of the patent owner where:
> (a) The public interest, in particular, national security, nutrition, health or the development of other sectors, as determined by the appropriate agency of the government, so requires; or (b) A judicial or administrative body has determined that the manner of exploitation, by the owner of the patent or his licensee, is anti-competitive.

Like other countries, this is a separate section in the national law from the sections on compulsory licensing.

The Irish patent law has provisions for 'Use of Inventions for the service of the State', which authorises a government Minister:

> to use the invention for any purpose which appears to such Minister to be necessary or expedient for the maintenance of supplies and

services essential to the life of the community; for securing a sufficiency of supplies and services essential to the well-being of the community; for promoting the productivity of commerce and industry, including agriculture; generally for ensuring that the whole resources of the community are available for use and are used, in a manner best calculated to serve the interests of the community; for assisting the relief of suffering and the restoration and distribution of essential supplies and services in any country or territory other than the State that is in grave distress; or for ensuring the public safety and the preservation of the State.

Switzerland's patent law provides for 'Expropriation of the Patent', and states, 'If public interest so requires, the Federal Council may wholly or partially expropriate the patent'.

The UK law provides for 'Use of patented inventions for services of the Crown', and confers on 'any government department and any person authorised in writing by a government department' powers to use a patented invention.

Setting compensation

Use of a patent under Article 31 of TRIPS requires that the patent owner is compensated. The general rule is contained in Article 31(h):

> the right holder shall be paid adequate remuneration in the circumstances of each case, taking into account the economic value of the authorisation.

In many respects, this is the most fundamental obligation in Article 31. It is clear that countries have considerable discretion in setting compensation. Article 1 of TRIPS says that countries 'shall be free to determine the appropriate method of implementing the provisions of this Agreement within their own legal system and practice'.

There are, of course, limits to what would satisfy this requirement, but there is already a rich diversity of national approaches to compensation in compulsory licensing and government use. The WTO would be hard pressed to justify intrusive reviews of this. Like most Article 31 issues, the most important issue is to provide a fair process for reaching a reasonable result. There is no question about the power of states to rein-in IP rights in order to assure affordability and access, but in the process of doing so, governments are advised to provide an administrative record that explains the basis for policy and specific outcomes. This doesn't have to be complex or involve endless proceedings. It can be simple and quick.

The easiest way to proceed is to create a set of compensation guidelines, based upon reasonable royalties in most cases, that will provide a framework for decision making, and also provide some predictability and transparency for the system. These guidelines can be administrative, or even set out in a statute. In practice, a straightforward royalty guidelines system will facilitate early action. Government officials can simply pick the royalty rate from the guidelines that provides a rough match with the specific facts and then the products can be put on the market without delay. Patent owners or generic producers could appeal initial decisions, but the appeal process should not slow down the introduction of generic competitors.

One issue that should also be addressed concerns cases of complex rights on the same product, a situation that is likely to become more commonplace. One solution is to have the government set a reasonable royalty that would compensate all of the various patent owners and have the money paid into an escrow account. The owners of the patents could work out their differences, possibly through arbitration and split the escrow funds when their international differences were resolved. Again, this would permit rapid introduction of the generic products, without waiting for the distributional issues to be resolved among competing patent owners.

Japan, Germany, the Philippines and other groups have adopted various forms of royalty guidelines, and countries can invent their own models for this as well. PhRMA, the US-based big Pharma trade group, presented data to the USTR in February 2000 that 5 per cent was the average US royalty rate for pharmaceutical drugs. Japan in the past has used rates from 2–4 per cent for some purposes, while for pharmaceuticals Germany has used 2–10 per cent. In the Canadian case, which according to the WHO is the most extensive use of compulsory licensing for pharmaceutical products, the government typically ordered royalties around 4 per cent. Whatever the rate it should be manageable. There is no reason for the WTO to demand that the poor countries of the world pay top dollar on medicines while millions are dying for lack of access to treatment. Indeed, the target royalty payment could be an approximation of the average or median royalty paid on pharmaceutical products, for which there exists reasonable competition among therapeutic substitutes, or some other methodology which does not impose high royalties from blockbuster drugs as a norm for the developing country poor.

In a recent presentation to the Indian domestic competitive industry in a meeting in Mumbai, the following royalty guidelines were recommended for developing countries:

- Innovative products: 3–5 per cent;
- Production with modest innovation: 2–3 per cent; and
- Minor patents: 1 per cent or less.

There could be different numbers, a study to choose the rates, or additional compensation, such as an extra royalty payment of 1–2 per cent over the guidelines for products that are particularly useful from a therapeutic point of view, unusually expensive to develop (based upon real evidence of costs), that reach limited audiences, or that have other special considerations. There could also be a lowering of payments when the R&D for the product was supported by public-sector organisations, including tax-based subsidies, such as the US orphan drug tax credit programme.

In the best of all possible worlds there could be much more analysis, such as the thoughtful pharmoeconomic analysis conducted by the Australian government to determine reimbursement for pharmaceutical drugs. However, this is expensive in terms of both money and time in the training of staff, and not only may it be hard to justify as part of resources, but it may also make the programme harder to understand and manage.

One important innovation in this area is to place obligations on parties who seek royalties to provide basic data both to governments and for the public. For example, no company should be permitted to make entirely unsupported claims regarding the costs of developing products in order to plead for higher royalty payments. If a firm wants to argue that it has undertaken large investments and risk, as, of course, it may have done, the firm should be required to provide evidence to back up the claim. For example, the firm should disclose the actual costs invested in the development of the product using a standardised disclosure format. Standardised data would contribute to deeper public-sector and citizen understanding of the actual investments in products and the economics of new drug development. This should be accompanied by data on the actual sales of that product since its introduction to provide more information on the returns from the company's investments. No appeal of a royalty rate should be permitted without such disclosures, and indeed, countries could and I hope would require such disclosures before granting any compensation at all. Such disclosures are addressed now in the Trans Atlantic Consumer Dialogue's recent recommendations to the US and the EU on transparency in pharmaceutical economics.[10]

Discrimination by field of technology

A troublesome area of TRIPS concerns Article 27.1, which reads in part:

> patents shall be available and patent rights enjoyable without discrimination as to the place of invention, the field of technology and whether products are imported or locally produced.

The meaning of this text isn't clear, because the phrase, 'field of technology' is not a well-established legal term. The big Pharma companies cited this Article in their complaint against the South African Medicines Act:[11]

> 2.4. it is discriminatory in respect of the enjoyment of patent rights in the pharmaceutical field which discrimination is in conflict with the provisions of Article 27 of the Trade Related Aspects of Intellectual Property Rights Agreement [hereinafter referred to as the 'TRIPS Agreement'], an international agreement binding the Republic and to which Parliament has given effect by the promulgation of the Intellectual Property Laws Amendment Act, No. 38 of 1997, and consequently such provision is in conflict with Section 44(4) of the Constitution read with Sections 231(2) and 231(3) of the Constitution.

The issue of the Article 27.1 discrimination language was raised in Canada-Patent Protection of Pharmaceutical Products, WT/DS114/R, March 17, 2000, a recent WTO dispute involving Canadian patent exceptions for research and testing on generic drugs used for drug registration (the so-called 'Bolar' exception) and a Canadian patent exception that permitted stockpiling of production in anticipation of the patent expiration. The EU submission to the WTO stated:[12]

> That Canada, by treating patent holders in the field of pharmaceutical inventions by virtue of these provisions less favourably than inventions in all other fields of technology, violated its obligations under Article 27.1 of the TRIPS Agreement requiring patents to be available and patent rights enjoyable without discrimination as to the field of technology.

The WTO considered very technical arguments over whether or not Canadian patent exceptions violated Article 27.1. Canada referred to

Article 32(b) of the Vienna Convention on the Law of Treaties, which said the interpretation of treaty terms 'should not produce manifestly absurd or unreasonable results'. As summarised by the WTO panel, Canada, amongst other things, argued:[13]

> The adoption of the meaning of Article 27.1 reflected under (a) above would clearly violate that rule of construction. It would lead to a requirement for 'across-the-board' derogations from patent rights, thus compelling exceptions where there was no practical need and reducing patent protection more than was required in all areas save those in which a balancing measure was actually required. Such an incongruous result would not be consistent with the objectives of the TRIPS Agreement.

The WTO decision in the case was more than 110 thousand words, and explores a number of key issues in interpreting TRIPS. There are extensive discussions of TRIPS Articles 7, 8, 27, 28, 30 and 31, plus substantive discussions of the pharmaceutical market. The decision includes language that declares that one of the reasons for Article 27.1 was to prevent countries from enacting compulsory licensing laws that dealt specifically with pharmaceuticals. There is also text such as this concerning access to generic drugs:[14]

> Although not manufactured in all countries of the world, generic medicines of course had a role to play in promoting public health in all countries. According to the World Health Organization, more than one third of the world's population lacked regular access to essential drugs. Every year, millions of children and adults in developing countries around the world still died from diseases that could be readily treated by drug therapies, and more economically treated with generic drugs.

In the end, the 17 March 2000 WTO panel report held that the Canadian 'Bolar' provisions were not violations of Article 27.1 of TRIPS. This decision seemed to be based largely on the fact that the legislation itself did not specifically limit itself to the pharmaceutical industry, even though it was clear that this was the primary area where the legislation was having an effect.[15]

In general, the issue of permitted discrimination by sector of the economy seems to be an important unanswered question, even after the WTO's decision and poses perhaps the most difficult issue for drafting legislation. The Canadian 'Bolar' case will likely be revisited in the future. For this reason, reports by UN agencies, including the WHO, UNAIDS, UNCTAD or UNDP would be useful and timely. The issues presented by Article 27.1 on discrimination border on the absurd, as countries will find it extremely difficult to write laws to address in specific and limited ways important social concerns. The US compulsory licensing laws for clean air and civilian nuclear energy are faced with the same issues. The current thinking is for countries to adopt laws that provide for compulsory licensing in broad areas like 'health', and make the argument that health isn't a field of technology. But at a certain level it becomes ridiculous to argue that countries cannot fashion laws that have the express mission of expanding access to medicines.

Notes

1. Thanks to Robert Weissman for comments on the first draft, to Thirukumaran Balasubramaniam for research on foreign patent laws, and to participants at several seminars, including the November 2000 UNDP meeting for HR2001 consultants, the 28 November 2000 Geneva UNCTAD Workshop on Trade in Pharmaceuticals and Human Rights, a 6 December 2000 Bangladesh seminar organised by MSF (Médecins Sans Frontières) for the People's Health Assembly, and a 12 December meeting of the India Drug Manufacturers Association in Mumbai, India.
2. This is only one of many important areas in patent law. For a discussion of this and other issues, with models for state action, see C. Correa (2000), 'Integrating Public Health Concerns into Patent Legislation in Developing Countries' *Report* (Geneva: South Centre).
3. In several US cases, compensation has been based upon 'what the owner has lost, not what the taker has gained' (Leesona, 599 F2d at 969), rejecting the argument, by patent owners, that they are entitled to lost profits based upon sales at prevailing commercial market rates.
4. Lemley and Allison (1998), *AIPLA Quarterly Journal*, vol. 26, p. 185.
5. One example of the problems from underresourced patent examination involved ddI, a drug for HIV/AIDS. Bristol-Myers Squibb was able to obtain patents for formulation claims in Thailand that were rejected by the US Patent and Trademark Office. BMS used this patent to block generic production of ddI pills in Thailand, even though BMS was not the inventor of ddI, and did not own a patent on the use of ddI for treating HIV/AIDS.
6. *Burroughs Wellcome Co. v. Barr Lab.* (1993), 828 F Supp. 1208, 1209 (EDNC 1993).
7. http://www.bu.edu/law/scitech/volume6/Panel2.htm.
8. Reference quoted as: J. Lerner (1994) 'The Importance of Trade Secrecy: Evidence from Civil Litigation', paper presented to the Conference on the Economics of Intellectual Property Rights, ICARE Institute, University of Venice, Italy, 6–8 October.

9. Footnote reads, 'See Lanjouw, J. O. and M. Schankerman (1997), *Stylized Facts of Patent Litigation: Value, Scope and Ownership* 3, National Bureau of Economic Research Working Paper No. 6297 [noting that crowded fields and new fields of technology generate more patent litigation]; Lanjouw, J.O. and J. Lerner (1997), *The Enforcement of Intellectual Property Rights: A Survey of the Empirical Literature* 13, National Bureau of Economic Research Working Paper No. 6292, 1997 [correlating the number of times that a patent is cited in future applications to the value of the patent and noting that innovative technology patents are cited with increased frequency]'.
10. Trans Atlantic Consumer Dialogue (http://www.tacd.org), Doc. Health 6–00.
11. *Pharmaceutical Manufacturers' Association of South Africa, et al., v. the President of the Republic of South Africa, the Honourable Mr N. R. Mandela N.O., et al.*, High Court of South Africa, Case number: 4183/98.
12. See Canada-Patent Protection of Pharmaceutical Products, WT/DS114/R at para 3.1.
13. See Canada-Patent Protection of Pharmaceutical Products, WT/DS114/R at Para 4.16.
14. See Canada-Patent Protection of Pharmaceutical Products, WT/DS114/R at Para 4.38.
15. On the record before the Panel, there was no occasion to consider the question raised by certain third parties – whether measures that are limited to a particular area of technology – *de jure* or *de facto* – are necessarily 'discriminatory' by virtue of that fact alone, or whether under certain circumstances they may be justified as special measures needed to restore equality of treatment to the area of technology in question. The Panel's decision regarding s. 55.2.1 did not touch upon that issue.

6
Access to Medicines: Patents, Prices and Public Policy – Consumer Perspectives
Kumariah Balasubramaniam

Introduction

Health is a consumer concern. Poverty, a major determinant of health, is the commonest cause of ill health. Medicinal drugs play a critical role in the management of ill health. According to the Director General of WHO, over a third of the world's population (over two billion people) have no regular access to essential drugs and most of them do not have access to basic healthcare. The majority of households in developing countries pay for their own healthcare services (Brundtland, 1999). Poverty is the main cause of lack of access to drugs, and poverty is on the increase according to the UNDP (1999):

- Eighty developing countries still have per capita incomes lower than they were a decade or more ago.
- In 1997 it was estimated that by the year 2000, half the people in Sub-Saharan Africa would live below the poverty line.

Slow economic growth, stagnation and even decline have been forecast for 100 developing countries and countries in transition.

Poverty is the reason why over two billion people have no regular access to even the basic list of a few essential drugs. Of the World Trade Organization (WTO) multilateral agreements TRIPS (Agreement on Trade-Related Aspects of Intellectual Property Rights), when fully implemented, will deny access to essential drugs to many more millions of people. This could lead to a situation where over 50 per cent of the world population will have no access to essential drugs. This in turn is likely to produce more poverty, since sick people find it much harder to earn or maintain an income.

Consumers International Regional Office for Asia and the Pacific (CIROAP), at the request of its members and network partners, has been studying and monitoring the impact of the Uruguay Round of Negotiations and WTO/TRIPS and GATS Agreements on developing countries and presented a number of analytical papers at international fora (Balasubramaniam, 1990; 1993; 1994; 1997; 1999a; 1999b; 2000a; 2000b).

This chapter will examine the impact of TRIPS on access to essential drugs in developing countries. Based on a critical examination of empirical data the chapter will present certain public policy recommendations.

An essential prerequisite for meaningful policy formulation will be first to understand the economic, technological and commercial development of developing countries and their demographic profile. This understanding will enable us to study how TRIPS will impact on these countries. This in turn will help us to formulate public policies to avoid its negative impact.

Developing countries

The following information from 110 low- and middle-income countries has been taken from data and analysis given in the UNDP *Human Development Report* New York, OUP (1999), and *World Development Report: Knowledge for Development*, World Bank New York, OUP (1998/99).

- Ten per cent of, or 11, countries have a population of less than 100000 each; 24 countries have less than 1 million each; 65 countries have less than 10 million each;
- Twenty countries have an annual GDP of less than US$500 million each; 28 less than $1 billion each; 57 less than $5 billion each; 75 countries have less than $10 billion each;
- Thirty-five per cent or 39 countries have a per capita GNP of less than US$400. The World Bank poverty line is per capita GNP of $365;
- The per capita external debt in some developing countries is higher than the per capita GNP;
- Some poor countries are very deeply integrated in global trade, but their exports are confined to one or two primary commodities. Manufacturing merchandise in these countries accounts for less than

10 per cent of the total exports in a market where the prices of many primary commodities are declining while the prices of manufacturing goods are rising; and

- The per capita GNP in developing countries is not a realistic measure of the purchasing power of the population. The income distribution is highly skewed. There are people living in Sub-Saharan Africa on less than three cents a day (Table 6.1). In Brazil with a per capita GNP of $4720, over 16 million people are living on a dollar a day. Appropriate public policies are the only way by which these people can have access to essential drugs.

Table 6.1   Per capita GNP in 10 low- and middle-income countries and the per capita GNP of population sub-groups in each

Population sub-groups[a]	Country: national per capita GNP[b] and per capita GNP of population sub-groups (US$)				
	Sierra-Leone [200]	*Guinea-Bissau* [240]	*Nigeria* [260]	*Bangladesh* [270]	*Kenya* [330]
Lowest 10%	10	12	34	111	40
Next 10%	12	38	70	143	73
Second 20%	20	78	116	182	111
Third 20%	98	144	187	232	177
Fourth 20%	237	247	304	297	281
Next 10%	396	396	468	383	475
Top 10%	872	1017	816	640	1574
	India [390]	*Lesotho* [670]	*China* [860]	*Guatemala* [1500]	*Brazil* [4720]
Lowest 10%	160	60	189	90	377
Next 10%	199	127	284	225	802
Second 20%	254	218	481	435	1345
Third 20%	327	375	641	788	2336
Fourth 20%	423	650	959	1395	4172
Next 10%	558	1119	1427	2460	7694
Top 10%	975	2909	2657	6990	22609

Notes:
[a] Expressed as % of total population.
[b] Figures cited in square brackets.

Source: World Development Report: Knowledge for Development, World Bank: New York, OUP, 1998/99.

Research and development (R&D)

R&D requires capital investment, adequate numbers of scientists and engineers and a proper infrastructure in order for it to produce invention and innovation. These factors are either absent in developing countries or they are present in only limited ways. As a result developing countries' share in the world R&D expenditure is negligible. Table 6.2 gives the percentage share of world R&D among OECD countries, the Soviet Union, Eastern Europe and the developing countries in 1980, before the collapse of the Soviet Union, and in 1993. In 1980 the industrialised countries accounted for 74 per cent, the Soviet Union and Eastern Europe 20 per cent and the developing countries 6 per cent. Within the next thirteen years, in 1993, the industrialised countries' share of world R&D had risen from 74 to 84 per cent. Because of financial constraints, many developing countries are reducing their R&D budgets. The developing countries' share of the world R&D has declined in 10 years to 4 per cent (Correa, 1998a). Very few countries have adequate financial, human and technological resources for R&D.

Table 6.2 Distribution of world R&D in 1980, 1990 and 1993

Region	Percentage world R&D
1980	
OECD	74.0
Soviet Union and Eastern Europe	20.0
Developing countries:	
Asia	4.1
Latin America	1.5
Africa	0.4
1990	
All developing countries	4.0
1993	
10 industrialised countries	84

Source:
(i) J. Hagerdoorn and J. Schakenraa (1994), 'The internationalization of the economy, global strategies and strategic technological alliances', *in Commission of the European Communities. The European Community and the Globalisation of Technology and the Economy, Brussels*. (Data based on figures of the National Science Foundation (1989).)
(ii) UNDP *Human Development Report* (1999) p. 68 (1993 data).
(iii) Carlos Correa (1998a) (1990 data).

Table 6.3 Number of scientists and engineers engaged in R&D in a selected number of industrialised and developing countries and economies in transition (1981–95)

Countries	Scientists and engineers in R&D per million population
A. Industrialised Countries	
Australia	2477
Canada	2322
France	2537
Germany	3016
Japan	5677
Korea (South)	2636
UK	2417
US	3732
B. Advanced developing countries and the Asian tigers	
Argentina	350
Brazil	165
China	537
India	151
Indonesia	181
Malaysia	87
Mexico	95
Philippines	90
Singapore*	2512
Thailand	173
C. Economies in transition	
Belarus	3300
Bulgaria	4240
Estonia	3296
Russian Federation	4358
Ukraine	6761
D. Less advanced developing countries (for which data is available)	
El Salvador	19
Jamaica	8
Madagascar	22
Nepal	22
Nigeria	15
Rwanda	12

Note:
* Singapore is still classified as a developing country although its per capita GNP of US$32 810 is sixth in the ranking order and higher than the US with a per capita GNP of US$29 080.

Source: World Development Report: Knowledge for Development (1998/99) World Bank.

Table 6.4 Percentage share of exports of medium and high technology goods to OECD countries

Source of exports of medium and high technology goods to OECD countries	Percentage share of total exports
The top seven industrialized countries (G7)	50.6
The newly industrialised countries in Latin America and the Asian tigers	11.0

Source: L. Alcorta and W. Peres (1995) *Innovative Systems and Technological Specialization in Latin America and the Caribbean*, United Nations University/INTECH, Maastricht.

Human resources in developing countries are very limited. Table 6.3 gives the number of scientists and engineers engaged in R&D in a selected number of industrialised and developing countries and economies in transition in the period 1981–95. Industrialised countries have 2000–3000 scientists and engineers per million of their population. The advanced developing countries, including the Asian tigers, except Singapore, have only a few hundred per million. Less advanced developing countries have about 10–20 per million of their population. In this context it is relevant to note that 30 000 African Ph.D.s live abroad while the continent is left with only 1 scientist and engineer per 10 000 people (UNDP, 1999).

Low levels of R&D in even the newly industrialising developing countries are reflected in their share of exports of medium and high technology goods. Table 6.4 gives the percentage share of exports of medium and high technology goods to OECD countries from the top seven industrialised countries and all the newly industrialised countries (NICs) of Latin America and the Asian tigers.

The data in Tables 6.2, 6.3 and 6.4 clearly demonstrate that in the foreseeable future only a few developing countries can make use of technology, even if it is transferred as a public good. The capacity of these developing countries to absorb and make use of technology is very limited. The argument that strong patent protection alone will promote the transfer of technology and result in innovation in these recipient countries is unlikely to be true. These countries will have to continue to depend on, amongst other things, imported drugs. An examination of the worldwide pharmaceutical industry will show that pharmaceutical innovation is at present controlled by multinational drug companies in 10 industrialised

Table 6.5   A typology of the world's pharmaceutical production

Stage of development	Number of countries		
	Industrial	**Developing**	**Total**
A. Sophisticated pharmaceutical industry with a significant research base	10	Nil	10
B. Innovative capabilities	12	5*	17
C. (i) Those producing both therapeutic ingredients and finished products	6	8	14
(ii) Those producing finished products only	2	87	89
D. No pharmaceutical industry	1	59	60
Total	31	159	190

Note:
* These countries are Argentina, China, India, Korea and Mexico.

Source: Robert Ballance, Janos Progany and Helmet Forstener (1992) *The World's Pharmaceutical Industries: An International Perspective on Innovation, Competition and Policy*, UNIDO.

countries (see Table 6.5). These companies want to strengthen their dominant position in world markets by means of the global intellectual standards contained in TRIPS.

Technological development, pharmaceutical production, consumption and trade

Technology

The United Nations Industrial Development Organization (UNIDO) has classified countries in the following categories depending on the stage of development of the pharmaceutical sector (Table 6.5).

The following observations can be made about the categories specified in Table 6.5.

A. There are only ten industrialised countries with a sophisticated pharmaceutical industry and significant research base. These are the countries that can develop new chemical entities or new drugs. Multinational drug companies (MNCs) in these countries own most of the key pharmaceutical technologies. Under TRIPS they gain further benefits such as a minimum patent term of 20 years and patents in all fields of technology, standards which are obligatory on all WTO members.

B. Countries with innovative capabilities: These countries can produce new drugs by a process of reverse engineering. When a new chemical entity (NCE) is introduced, research scientists in these countries develop a new process different from the process invented by the innovator and protected by patent. With the new process, the same NCE is manufactured. This reverse engineering is possible only in developing countries with patent legislation that protects processes but not products. Before TRIPS a vast majority of developing countries protected processes but not products. This enabled countries such as Argentina, China, India, Korea and Mexico (see Table 6.5) to develop a strong national pharmaceutical industry and compete with the drug multinationals in the North.

C. (i) Eight developing countries have the technology to manufacture raw materials from chemical intermediates available in the world market.

(ii) Eighty-seven developing countries have the technology to formulate dosage forms from raw materials or bulk drugs available in the world market.

D. Fifty-nine developing countries do not have any pharmaceutical industry.

Countries in stages C(i) and C(ii) have access only to chemical intermediates and raw materials to manufacture multisource generic drugs in the world market but not patent-protected drugs.

As stated earlier, the five developing countries in stage B and Brazil can manufacture patent-protected drugs by a process of reverse engineering. However, with the enforcement of TRIPS these countries will not be able to carry out reverse engineering. Without the capacity to reverse engineer it is open to question whether the national pharmaceutical industry in these countries will survive.

A 'national health disaster' has been anticipated by the Indian Drug Manufacturers' Association (IDMA) as a result of the implementation of TRIPS. In India only 30 per cent of the population can afford modern medicines despite the fact that drug prices in India are amongst the lowest in the world (National Working Group on Patent Laws, 1993). A study by an IMF economist showed price increases for patented drugs ranging from 5–67 per cent. Annual welfare losses for India ranged from US$162 million to US$1261 million, with an annual profit transfer to foreign firms of between US$10 million and US$839 million (Subramaniam, 1995).

Pharmaceutical production, exports and consumption

Table 6.6 shows the global pattern of pharmaceutical production and exports in 1975 and 1990. Research-based multinational drug firms in the ten industrialised countries control about 70 per cent of the export market. Drug firms in five advanced developing countries and eleven industrialised countries account for 27 per cent of world exports. The balance of 5 five per cent is exported by developing countries. From this table it would appear that the share of developing countries exports will not be more than 20 per cent of the world exports.

Table 6.7 gives the estimated market share and consumption of pharmaceuticals in different geographical areas and economic groups. The OECD countries with 16 per cent of the world's population account for about 80 per cent of the world market with an average per capita consumption of US$357. Africa and Asia with 67 per cent of the world's population account for only 8 per cent of the world market with an average per capita consumption of just over US$8.

The argument used by the international drug industry to justify their high prices is that they need profits for putting money back into R&D. MNCs control about 80 per cent of the world's pharmaceutical market and the industrialised countries account for about 80 per cent of the consumption. The profits of MNCs from industrialised countries will not be affected by weaker patent protection in developing countries, enabling the latter to manufacture and market essential drugs at lower prices. It is also relevant to note that what MNCs lose on lower prices

Table 6.6   Global pattern of pharmaceutical production and exports, 1975–90

Stage of development and number of countries in parenthesis	Percentage world production		Share world exports	
	1975	1990	1975	1990
A. Sophisticated industry and significant R&D (10)	60	69	78	68
B. Innovative pharma industry (16)	28	22	19	27
C. (i) and (ii) Countries producing therapeutic ingredients and those producing finished drugs only (91)	12	09	04	05

Source: Ballance *et al*. (see Table 6.5).

Table 6.7 The global pharmaceutical market: estimates of market share and consumption in different geographical areas and economic groups

Asia/Group	Population		Pharmaceuticals		
	Population in million [1997]	Share of total world population (per cent)	Share of world market (per cent)	Estimates of market in US$ billion (2002)	Per capita consumption US$
Industrialised countries (North America, Europe, Japan and Australasia)	899	15.9	79.1	321.3	357
The Middle East	89	1.6	2.6	10.6	119
Latin America and the Caribbean	483	8.5	7.5	30.5	63
Economies in transition (CIS and Eastern Europe)	399	7.1	2.6	10.6	26
South-East Asia and China	1802	31.8	4.9	20.1	11
Africa	712	12.6	1.3	5.3	7.4
South Asia	1274	22.5	1.8	7.3	5.7
Total	5658			406	

Source: www.ims-global.com/insight/report/global/report.htm [market share] UNDP – *Human Development Report* (1999) (Population).

in developing countries may be compensated for by an increase in the volume of sales in these countries.

Strong patent protection will increase drug prices. Weaker patent protection will promote generic competition and lower prices. The next section provides factual evidence for this.

Patents and prices

In mid-1999, Consumers International and Health Action International (CI/HAI) conducted a survey of the retail prices of sixteen drugs in thirty-six countries. The objectives of the survey were to:

● Study the impact of pharmaceutical patents on the availability and price of essential drugs; and

- Suggest solutions to ensure regular access to essential drugs in developing countries in a globalised economy with a tighter intellectual property system.

The retail prices in US dollars of 100 units of 29 dosage forms of sixteen commonly used drugs in thirty-six countries were surveyed in July/August 1999 (Balasubramaniam and Sagoo, 2000). These included ten developed countries (OECD), twenty-five developing countries from Africa, Asia and Latin America and one from the Commonwealth of Independent States (CIS).

The most striking features in this survey were the following:

- The retail prices of proprietary drugs in some of the developing countries of Africa, Asia and Latin America were higher than the prices in the ten OECD countries. The retail prices of fifteen out of the eighteen dosage forms of eleven drugs for which comparable data are available were all higher in some of the developing countries than in the OECD countries.
- Proprietary brand forms of several of the multisource drugs surveyed were the only products available in many of the African countries even though low-priced generic equivalents were available on the world market. These countries do not offer patent protection to drugs.
- There was a very wide variation of retail prices in the countries surveyed:
  (i) The variation in the retail prices of proprietary drugs was a much wider range (1:16–1:59) than the variation in prices of generic equivalents (1:7–1:18).
  (ii) The variation in the retail prices of multisource drugs in developing countries (1:2–1:59) was a much wider range than the variations in OECD countries (1:2–1:12).

A foundational claim of economics is that free markets promote competition. It should therefore follow that in a free market competition will result in a lowering and, more importantly, a levelling of prices. This appears to be so in OECD countries and to a certain extent in the generic drugs market in the developing countries, but not in the proprietary drugs market in developing countries.

The smaller variation in retail drug prices in the OECD may be due, amongst other things, to the following:

- Co-marketing arrangement by manufacturers;
- Parallel importing;

- Reference pricing; and
- Drug pricing policies.

The wide variation in prices of proprietary drugs in the developing countries suggests that the guiding principle which the international drug industry seems to adopt in fixing prices is to set the limits according to what the market can bear. Profit maximisation seems to be the only objective. This has been described as the 'Law of the Jungle', where might is right (Balasubramaniam *et al.*, 1998; *SCRIP Magazine*, 1999).

There is evidence that price competition is possible in pharmaceutical markets. Data from India proves this. When competitors introduce their products, the originators will lower their prices and compete with the national firms. They will not withdraw from the market. It is also important to introduce generic competition as early as possible in order to prevent the originators from having time to secure brand loyalty for their products. Strong brandname loyalty leads to a continuation of monopoly profits in the post-patent period.

There is a time lag between the introduction of a drug in the world market and the introduction of a product by a competitor into the home market. It takes further time to capture adequate market share so as to increase production, lower costs and compete with the originator. The Indian data on retail prices of three drugs recently introduced and four others which were introduced much earlier illustrates this phenomenon and underscores the need for national policies on intellectual property protection with provisions to enable national firms to initiate production of new drugs as early as possible. Indian firms were able to do this by a process of reverse engineering. This was possible because the Indian national legislation on patents did not provide patent protection for products.

Under TRIPS all members of the WTO will have to provide patent protection for products and processes for 20 years. The only way national firms can initiate production before the expiry of the patent is by compulsory licensing which is still allowed under TRIPS (see Chapter 5 by James Love in this volume). Nevertheless, only a few advanced developing countries can use compulsory licensing to manufacture new drugs. The vast majority of developing countries do not have any facilities for the production of pharmaceuticals. They can have access to lower-priced drugs produced in the more advanced developing countries or by generic manufacturers in some developed countries through parallel importing. This is also allowed under TRIPS. The analysis of empirical data supports the position that compulsory licensing and parallel imports are two regulatory tools that should be included in the national legislation of all developing countries.

TRIPS and developing countries

The Third World Network has recently published three documents (Correa, 1998a,b, 2000) on TRIPS and developing countries. They refer to several publications which clearly show the adverse impact of strong IPR protection on the pharmaceutical supply system in developing countries. Although the implications of TRIPS for development, especially foreign direct investment (FDI), innovation and technology transfer, are difficult to foresee, nothing suggests that, in the absence of other factors, IPRs will automatically and positively influence FDI, innovation, access to foreign technology or other development-related activities. The determinants of FDI include availability of scientists and engineers engaged in R&D, macroeconomic policies, and infrastructure including power, communication, and so on.

TRIPS sets forth minimum standards of IPR to be applied by all members of the WTO. However, it does not create a uniform law and gives member states, particularly in the field of patents, certain degrees of freedom to legislate at national levels. How this freedom can be exercised depends on the strength and weaknesses of science and technology in the individual country. From the data provided it would appear that very few countries have adequate resources to make use of the opportunities provided by TRIPS, opportunities which in any case depend on the enactment of the right national legislation. One way forward is to develop model IPR legislation for developing countries which takes into account the health needs of their consumers.

Access to essential drugs and public policy

Policy makers need to consider two different populations in developing countries when they examine the issue of access to drugs:

(i) Those who do not have regular access to essential drugs now. These are the over two billion people who do not have access to even a few essential drugs, according to the Director-General of the WHO, because they do not have the purchasing power. The only source of supply for them is the international community and donor funding support to national governments to provide essential drugs. Lower drug prices in the international market will greatly benefit this population.

(ii) Those who have access now but will be denied access when TRIPS is implemented. This has been referred to as a potential 'National Health Disaster' by the Indian Drug Manufacturers' Association (National Working Group on Patent Laws, 1993).

This second group consists of lower income earners as shown in Table 6.1, with a per capita GNP of a few hundred dollars. This population may amount to about one or two billion. It is relevant to remember that the majority of households in developing countries pay for their healthcare out of personal savings or through borrowing.

To provide access to those who have no access to drugs, one essential policy goal is the setting up of a public health financing system based either on general taxation (the Beveridge plan) or compulsory social insurance (the Bismark plan). Both are based on an income-related contribution to taxation or social insurance. All the advanced industrialised countries in the world, except the US, have one or other system of healthcare financing. It needs to be reiterated that two billion people can never afford to pay for essential drugs, however low the prices. The vast majority of them have incomes of much less than a dollar a day and some of them only a few cents a day.

Public policy on healthcare financing is only one option and part of the solution to improve access to drugs. For the public policy on healthcare financing to be successfully implemented it should be complemented by a national policy on patents, supported by international agreements on IPRs. The next section examines this.

Access to drugs and TRIPS: policy options at national and international levels

Policy options at national levels and international trade agreements need to be examined in the context of the following:

1. The WTO multilateral agreements were negotiated on the basis of 'Level Playing Fields'. It was argued that these agreements would give equal opportunities to all WTO member states to benefit from liberalised trade and the strongly protected IPRs that result from research and development.
2. Empirical data clearly reveal the gross asymmetry between the North and the South, between industrialised and developing countries. Box 6.1 gives data on IPRs in developed and developing countries. The playing field is anything but level. The strongest consideration should be given to renegotiating TRIPS.

Box 6.1   Intellectual Property Rights, Developed and Developing Countries

- The number of patent applications worldwide in 1977 was less than 3000.
- In 1997 more than 54 000 applications were made.
- At present the industrialised countries own 97 per cent of all patents worldwide.
- In 1995 one single country, the US, received over 50 per cent of the global royalties and licensing fees paid to owners of patents.
- Ten industrialised countries controlled 95 per cent of the US patents of the past two decades.
- These ten industrialised countries captured more than 90 per cent of cross-border royalties and licensing fees.
- Seventy per cent of global royalties and licensing fee payments were between parent and affiliate in multinational corporations.
- The use of intellectual property is alien to developing countries.
- More than 80 per cent of patents that have been granted in developing countries belong to residents of industrialised countries.

Source: UNDP, *Human Development Report* (1999) p. 68.

The questions to be answered are:

- What should be the future for the WTO/TRIPS Agreement?
- Should the scope or length of IP standards in TRIPS be reduced?
- Should there be much longer transition periods for developing countries?
- Should the WTO's role in IP be restricted to trade-related issues?
- Should IP be decoupled from the WTO altogether?

Answers to these questions will help policy makers to identify national policy options based on multilateral trade agreements, taking into account the gross asymmetry between developing and developed countries. The following suggestions should be considered in any future re-negotiation of TRIPS:

- TRIPS should place public health interests above those of commercial interests.
- The scope and length of intellectual property standards in TRIPS should be flexible to allow developing countries to formulate, enact and implement national legislation on IPRs as a policy instrument for the technological, economic and commercial development of their respective countries.

- The transition period should be extended to allow developing countries to achieve competitiveness in the world market. Industrialised countries had the benefit of being able to choose the times at which they provided patent protection for pharmaceuticals. Some countries in Western Europe as well as Japan refused to grant product patents for pharmaceuticals until they had reached international competitiveness. These countries provide the most convincing argument that a *national* patent policy is essential for the technological development of a national pharmaceutical industry. France, Germany, Italy, Japan, Sweden and Switzerland, home of some of the most innovative pharmaceutical companies, persistently resisted providing pharmaceutical product patents until their industries had reached a certain degree of development. France introduced product patents in 1960, Germany 1968, Japan 1976, Switzerland 1977, and Italy and Sweden in 1978 (SELA, 1998).

During its first 100 years, the US was still a relatively young and developing country and refused to respect international intellectual property rights on the ground that it was freely entitled to foreign works to further its social and economic development (US Congress, 1986). The UK, at the time the world leader in technology, attacked the US (but did not use the word 'pirate') for not providing strong patent protection. These attacks and complaints had very little or no effect since American firms wanted the freedom to imitate British innovations and put them on the market (*Washington Post*, 1989).

The industrialised countries, having fully used the provisions in the Paris Convention to enable their pharmaceutical manufacturers to strengthen their innovative capacity, now deny the same privileges to developing countries. This is not morally defensible in a civilised society.

References

Balasubramaniam, K. (1990) 'Third World Sovereignty in Danger', a paper presented at the Third World Patent Convention, organised by the National Working Group on Patent Laws, New Delhi, 15–16 March, New Delhi, India.

Balasubramaniam, K. (1993) 'GATT and the Third World', a paper presented at the International Convention on People's Approach to GATT Negotiations organised by the National Working Group on Patent Laws, New Delhi, 18–20 February, New Delhi, India.

Balasubramaniam, K. (1994) 'Pharmaceutical Patents and the Consumer', a paper presented at the 'PCC94 Congress – Innovative Pharmaceutical Re-Engineering and Cost Control', 14–15 July, Singapore.

Balasubramaniam, K. (1997) 'Heads: TNCs Win – Tails – The South Loses' or the GATT/WTO/TRIPS Agreement, K. Consumers International, Regional Office for Asia and the Pacific, Penang, Malaysia.

Balasubramaniam, K. (1999a) 'Consumers and the WTO/TRIPS Agreement', paper presented at the International Convention on Impact of WTO/TRIPS on Access to Drugs', organised by the Ministry of Health Pakistan in collaboration with the World Health Organization Regional Office for Eastern Mediterranean, 26–30 July, Karachi, Pakistan.

Balasubramaniam, K. (1999b) 'The Impact of WTO/TRIPS Agreement on the Access of Essential Drugs for People Living with HIV/AIDS', paper presented at the 5th International Conference on AIDS in Asia-Pacific, 23–7 October, Kuala Lumpur, Malaysia.

Balasubramaniam, K. (2000a) 'Implications of the TRIPS Agreement for Pharmaceuticals: Consumer Perspectives', a paper presented at the ASEAN Workshop on the 'TRIPS Agreement and its impact on Pharmaceuticals', organised by the Ministry of Health Indonesia, 2–4 May, Jakarta, Indonesia.

Balasubramaniam, K. (2000b) 'Globalization and Liberalization of Healthcare Services, WTO and the General Agreement on Trade in Services', a paper presented at a seminar 'Health and Healthcare in a Changing Environment: The Malaysian Experience', organized by Citizens Health Initiative and Universiti Sains Malaysia, 22–4 April, Kuala Lumpur, Malaysia.

Balasubramaniam, K., O. Lanza and S.R. Kaur (1998) 'Retail Drug Prices: The Law of the Jungle', *HAI News*, No. 100, April.

Balasubramaniam, K. and K. Sagoo (2000) 'Patents and Prices', *HAI News*, No. 112, April/May.

Brundtland, G.H. (1999) paper presented at the *ad hoc* working group on the Revised Drug Strategy held in Geneva on 13 October in *Globalization and Access to Drugs Health Economics and Drugs*, DAP series No. 7 (Geneva: WHO, 1999), pp. 63–8.

Correa, C.M. (1998a) *'Implementing the TRIPS Agreement'* (Penang, Malaysia: M. Carlos Third World Network, April).

Correa, C.M. (1998b) *Options for Implementing the TRIPS Agreement in Developing Countries* (Penang, Malaysia: Third World Network, April).

Correa, C.M. (2000) *Intellectual Property Rights, the WTO and Developing Countries*, TRIPS Agreement and Policy Options (Penang, Malaysia: Carlos, Third World Network) National Working Group on Patent Laws (1993) *'Patents regime in TRIPS: Critical Analysis'*, New Delhi.

SCRIP Magazine (1999) 'Quotable Quotes', January.

SELA (Sistema Econimico Latinoamericano) (1988) 'Capitulos De Sela', October/December, Caracas; quoted in *'Patenting and the Third World: A Historical Appraisal'* by Henk Hobbelink, Co-ordinator GRAIN (Genetic Resources Action International) Appartado 233398, E08080, Barcelona, Spain.

Subramaniam, A. (1995) 'Trade Related Industrial Property Rights and Asian Developing Countries: An Analytical View', paper submitted to the Conference on Emerging Global Trading Environment and Developing Asia, International Monetary Fund, Manila.

UNDP (1999) *Human Development Report* 1999, p. 32

US Congress (1986) Office of Technology Assessment, *'Intellectual Property Rights in an Age of Electronics and Information'*, Washington DC, p. 228.

Washington Post (1989) 6 December, quoted in SELA (1988) in Hobbelink, Patenting and the Third World.

7
Agricultural Research: Intellectual Property and the CGIAR System

Michael Blakeney

The Consultative Group on International Agricultural Research (CGIAR)

The CGIAR, founded in 1971, is an informal association of public and private donors that supports an international network of sixteen international agricultural research centres (IARCs), each with its own governing body. The major sponsors are the Food and Agriculture Organization (FAO), the World Bank, the Rockefeller and Ford Foundations, the United Nations Development Programme, the United Nations Environment Programme and the aid programmes of the EU and a number of individual countries. With a budget of some US$340 million per annum, the CGIAR oversees the largest agricultural research effort in the developing world.

This agricultural research commenced with the work of Norman Borlaug, an American plant breeder, who won the Nobel Prize in 1970 for his work in developing high-yielding wheat varieties for Mexico. Borlaug was the founding father of the Centro Internacional de Mejoramiento de Maiz y Trigo (CIMMYT), which became the first of the CGIAR centres.

Following the establishment of CIMMYT, fifteen other international agricultural research centres have been established, each focusing on crops and materials of interest to developing countries.[1] In addition to conducting research, the CGIAR supports a collection of germplasm, which currently comprises over 600000 accessions of more than 3000 crop, forage and pasture species which are held at the research centres. These germplasm collections are held under the auspices of the FAO 'in trust for the benefit of the international community, in particular the developing countries' and include up to 40 per cent of all unique samples of major food crops held by gene banks worldwide. The FAO

Commission on Genetic Resources for Food and Agriculture determines the policy under which the network of *ex situ* collections operates.

In addition to the so-called 'designated germplasm', which is held under the trust relationship with the FAO, the various CGIAR centres have developed 'elite germplasm' and biological tools, such as isogenic lines, mutants and mapping populations, from the materials which have been deposited with them.

The significance of the CGIAR

The CGIAR was established as a catalyst for what became known as the Green Revolution, namely the achievement of high crop yields in developing countries through plant breeding. Crop improvement in developing countries continues as one of the principal objectives of the CGIAR. Its work focuses on increasing food security for the world's poorest people. Because of this focus, the CGIAR centres undertake the sort of agricultural research which is not likely to be undertaken by private corporations. Thus the various CGIAR centres are concerned with research into the sustainable management of natural resources, including tillage and water management, the development of integrated pest-management systems, agro-forestry and small aquaculture systems, as well as the improvement of crop species in impoverished and marginal environments. Examples of the latter include the development of drought-tolerant maize, millets and sorghum, disease-resistant lentils, beans, bananas, cassava and rice.

The importance of agricultural research which conduces to poverty alleviation is self-evident but an important feature of the modern environment within which the CGIAR operates is that the resources available for agricultural research are steeply declining.[2] Similarly, donor funds available for agricultural research in the South have also been declining. For the most part, the research undertaken by the CGIAR centres is not of much interest to the countries of the North, where both the agricultural systems and significant food crops are different. Consequently, significant private corporate donation for the sort of research undertaken by the CGIAR is unlikely.

A major exception to this general picture is the research undertaken by CIMMYT into wheat, which is of great interest to the major Northern food producers. Also, as is discussed below, with the development of recombinant DNA technologies, the genetic qualities of some of the poor farmer crops might be of interest to the North. Thus, for example, bacterial blight resistance in rice can be introduced into tomatoes.

The development of gene technologies as a vehicle for modern agricultural research and the proprietisation of those technologies is an explanation of the growth of private agricultural research in the OECD at an annual rate of 5.1 per cent, compared with the 1.7 per cent growth rate for public agricultural research (Alston *et al.*, 1998).

The considerable investment in life sciences patenting is an explanation for the multibillion dollar acquisitions and mergers, which have characterised this industry in the North.[3] A commercial consequence of the intrusion of intellectual property (IP) into agricultural research has been the concentration of key IP rights in the hands of a small and declining number of private life-sciences companies. A result of this market concentration is to lock up key intellectual property rights in the hands of a few powerful entities and to raise the barriers to market entry of others wishing to participate in these activities. Thus by the end of 1998, the top five vegetable seed companies controlled 75 per cent of the global vegetable seed market (Havenga, 1998).

This market concentration in private hands has also raised questions about the future role of public-sector plant breeding. To what extent will private-sector plant breeding, render public plant breeding superfluous? Will the owners of IP rights in key technologies make them available to public plant breeding programmes on affordable terms? What restrictions will be attached to the supply of these technologies? To what extent will public plant-breeding institutions seek intellectual property rights in their own technologies or germplasm, as a bargaining counter, with a view to the cross-licensing of intellectual property rights? To what extent will public plant-breeding institutions seek IP rights as a source of revenue? To what extent will public plant-breeding institutions enter into joint research activities with private institutions?

CGIAR and intellectual property

In recent years difficult questions have been raised concerning the legal status of the CGIAR germplasm collections. A number of the gene banks which make up the CGIAR were established in the 1960s and 70s as facilitators of the agricultural research which precipitated the 'Green Revolution'. At that time the questions of ownership and IP rights in the collections were not addressed, being very much subordinated to the mission of the CGIAR to increase crop yields to feed a burgeoning world population.

IP rights have had a profound impact upon the CGIAR in three contexts. First, the burgeoning significance of plant variety protection, through the activities of the International Union for the Protection of

New Varieties of Plants (UPOV) and the inclusion within Article 27.3(b) of the Agreement on Trade-Related Aspects of Intellectual Property Rights (TRIPS) that countries are obliged to protect plant varieties, through patent laws or *sui generis* legislation or both. The advent of plant variety protection has rendered the germplasm collections of the CGIAR a tempting source for privatisation.

There have been a number of high-profile instances of attempts by third parties to obtain proprietary rights in material obtained or derived from CGIAR germplasm. For example, ownership concerns were raised in 1998 as a consequence of Plant Breeders' Rights applications made in Australia by agricultural research institutes there in relation to a peavine and a lentil which had been bred from genetic stock obtained from ICARDA and from ICRISAT (Edwards and Anderson, 1998). Research by the high-profile NGO, Rural Advancement Foundation International (RAFI), suggested that there were numerous other instances of 'biopiracy' by other Australian agricultural research institutes. Reacting to the biopiracy controversy, CGIAR called for a moratorium on the granting of intellectual property rights over plant germplasm held in its centres. CGIAR chairman, Dr Ismail Serageldin, explained the call for a moratorium as 'the strongest signal the CGIAR can send governments to ensure that these issues be resolved and the materials in the CGIAR remain in the public domain' (CGIAR, 1998).

Secondly, the application of modern biotechnological techniques to agricultural research has enhanced the value of the germplasm collections of the CGIAR as sources of interesting genetic material. An illustration of this development is the way in which a researcher from the University of California at Davis, working at the International Rice Research Institute (IRRI) as a post-doctoral fellow, was able to secure patent rights for her university in the genetic material responsible for bacterial blight immunity in rice and other crops. The immunity had been developed by IRRI researchers in a breeding programme over a 15-year-period, utilising a strain of rice collected in Mali.

Thirdly, the way in which modern agricultural research is conducted has obliged CGIAR researchers to seek access to enabling proprietary technologies, such as patented genes, promoters, enhancers, selectable markers and terminators. Often these rights are held by multiple owners and are subject to various conditions which might constrain the researcher's freedom to operate. The constraints which the private owners of these technologies may seek to impose on CGIAR centres and their researchers will be antipathetic to the public goods culture of the CGIAR. For example, the obligation of recipients of proprietary technologies to make a prior disclosure to the technology providers of the results of any research utilising these technologies obliges CGIAR centres to introduce a climate of confidentiality in which the disclosure of research information is policed.

An illustration of the sorts of tensions which can arise in public–private research collaboration are those which were generated by the offer of Monsanto, made at the Global Forum on Agricultural Research meeting in Dresden in May 2000, to make its research on the structure of the rice genome available to researchers. The first problem was the perceived taint of the association of the public agricultural research community with a company which had attracted bad publicity, particularly in the South, from its work with the so-called 'terminator technology' (technology which permits the function of a gene to be switched off). Secondly, Monsanto required recipients of this information not to make research data resulting from its use available to Monsanto's commercial rivals. This would involve a significant departure from the CGIAR philosophy of open access to the fruits of its publicly funded research. Thirdly, since the structural information provided by Monsanto would be unpatentable without the functional genomics which would be established by IRRI and its research collaborators in the national agricultural research organisations (NAROs), the CGIAR would be inadvertently drawn into a commercial collaboration with the private sector.

Negotiating the access of CGIAR centres to these proprietary rights will impose significant transaction costs, as well as imposing substantial management burdens (Blakeney, 1999a). For example, the International Service for the Acquisition of Agri-biotech Applications (ISAAA), in an analysis of the proprietary technologies underlying IRRI's proposal to investigate the development of protein and carotene enhanced rice, reported the existence of 70 separate IP rights that had to be navigated before this research could be undertaken. RAFI's deconstruction of the ISAAA report[4] is illustrative of the legal complexities for the CGIAR centres in working with proprietary rights.

These three impacts have raised the importance for the CGIAR centres of the ownership of their germplasm collections and the management of intellectual property generated by them and of the proprietary technologies which are utilised in their research.

Structure of the CGIAR and the ownership and management of IP

As an informal association of international agricultural research centres, the CGIAR has no legal personality and, consequently, can currently play no formal role in the ownership and control of the germplasm collections of the individual centres. With the various intellectual property problems, described above, which have begun to afflict the system as a whole, consideration is being given to the centralisation of the ownership and control of IP rights in the CGIAR system. In 1998, the International Service for National Agriculture Research (ISNAR), a CGIAR centre which was established as a policy and training facility for the CGIAR, commissioned a report on the use of proprietary technologies by CGIAR centres (Cohen *et al.*, 1998). Following the observations made by this report, each of the CGIAR centres commissioned audits of their IP management policies. A Central Advisory Service (CAS) was established to provide IP services for the centres. The CAS was located at ISNAR.

Another factor which has obliged the CGIAR to address the ownership and management of the system's IP is the tightening of donor funds. In the face of the many competing claims upon donor aid, international agricultural research can no longer command priority in funding. Part of the problem is the fact that donors are unhappy with the unauthorised privatisation of germplasm and research tools, which are created with the public monies provided to the CGIAR centres. This, in turn, has generated suggestions that centres regard the IP which they generate as an exploitable asset. At the CGIAR's 1999 International Centres Week meeting the suggestion was floated that the IP assets of centres be regarded at least as 'bargaining chips' for dealings with the corporate owners of proprietary technologies. Previous discussions, for example on the obvious advantages of system-wide negotiations in acquiring access to software, had recommended the advantages of more centralised ownership and management of the centres' IP.

In July 2000, the chair of CGIAR's Committee of Board Chairs (CBC) and the Centre Directors' Committee (CDC) commissioned a report on options for such centralisation. The resultant report proposed models where the CGIAR was incorporated as the holding company of the centres and the assignee of their IP and where the centres' IP was vested in a trust or foundation. Obviously the issue of CGIAR IP was subordinate to more general proposals for the governance of the system. In any event, the individual centre directors-general, when called upon to comment on the options paper, considered the centralised models to be premature. At a centre directors' retreat held at ISNAR, 2–4 September 2000, it was proposed that the centres would form a 'Federation of Centres' with an independent legal personality and an independent board of 9–11 'eminent' persons. Under the model, the Federation would take over the FAO–CGIAR Trust Agreement and would manage the system's intellectual property policy. It is as yet unclear how the new legal entity will manage the IP, which is owned by the various centres. It is also unclear how this management will interrelate with the IP assistance currently provided by the CAS and ISNAR. The International Plant Genetic Resources Institute (IPGRI) has also begun to assume IP policy functions within the CGIAR by taking upon itself the promulgation of a new IP policy for the organisation.

RAFI's comment on the 'Federation' model was that 'although it has useful and interesting features, it is what you get when you ask the people most at risk from change to recommend change' (RAFI, 2000). RAFI was particularly critical of the lack of representation in the CGIAR of Southern nations at the senior executive levels of the organisation and it saw no proposals to remedy this deficiency. RAFI proposed that:

> In order to give the System a real political base for governance and policy, over a ten year period the IARCs should evolve into 7–8 'regional' entities governed by boards made up by half of research partners within the region and half of people from other parts of the world. Rather than functioning as 'centres', they should be science animateurs or research provocateurs helping regional collaborators to identify needs and solutions and assisting in directing funding toward whatever institutes – inside or outside the region – can most appropriately do the task on a contract basis. (RAFI, 2000)

A threshold difficulty with this sort of stratagem is the difficulty of persuading some or all of the sixteen research centres to relinquish their autonomy to permit the creation of the federation.

The CGIAR centres and ownership and control of IP

The question of the ownership of the CGIAR germplasm collections by individual centres arises in two main contexts. First, the status of a centre's germplasm collection upon the dissolution or relocation of a centre. Secondly, the question of the authority of the centres to permit third parties to exploit their genetic resources. The starting place for these inquiries commences with an analysis of the legal status of these institutes themselves. The legal status of these collections has always been problematic. In 1986 the FAO had conducted a review of the legal status of all national and international institutions operating genebanks (FAO, 1986). In relation to the CGIAR centres, the FAO report concluded that, as control over their operation was shared between national and international representatives, they were not international in the strict sense because they were not created by any international instrument or organisation. On the other hand the report concluded that because they were neither in the private sector nor under the control of any state or national authority, the CGIAR centres were *sui generis*. Consequently, the report reached no firm conclusion on the ownership of the genetic resources controlled by the centres.

A similar study by the Technical Advisory Committee of the CGIAR suggested that genebanks established as a result of international collaboration should be considered to be held on trust for CGIAR purposes (TAC, 1988). This study highlighted the importance of the agreements of genebanks with their host countries and recommended that where necessary these agreements be amended to provide that in the event of closure of a research institute the germplasm be transferred to an alternative institution to be held on trust, as recommended. This trustee concept was adopted as CGIAR policy in 1989. Its 1989 policy statement on plant genetic resources, under the heading 'ownership', states that 'it is the CGIAR policy that collections assembled as a result of international collaboration should not become the property of any single nation, but should be held in trust for the use of present and future generations of research workers in all countries throughout the world'.

In 1994 twelve of the CGIAR centres entered into Agreements with the FAO which placed their collections into an International Network under the auspices of the FAO. Through these agreements, the centres accepted that their designated germplasm was held 'in trust for the international community' and that they would not 'claim ownership, or seek intellectual property rights over the designated germplasm and related information'.

The trusteeship principle adopted by CGIAR in 1989 admits of a number of problems. A threshold, but not insuperable, problem was the fact that the concept of the trust, although well-defined in legal systems deriving their law from the equity courts of English origin, was largely unknown in the civil law system. This may be remedied in large part by the negotiation in 1984 of the Hague Convention on the Law Applicable to Trusts and on Their Recognition.[5] This Convention provides for the recognition of trust principles such as the sanctity of trust property and the binding obligations of trustees. Thus, for example, genebanks established as trusts for CGIAR purposes could not be used for purposes inconsistent with CGIAR principles. This Convention has not yet secured wide support. To date the only non-common law countries which have ratified it are Italy, Luxembourg and the Netherlands.

However, it has also been signed by the United Kingdom and the USA, which should attract greater support for the instrument.

A more difficult problem is the fact that a number of the CGIAR agricultural research institutes, such as CIAT, CIMMYT, IITA, IRRI and WARDA, predate the establishment of CGIAR. This presents a problem in ascertaining the legal status of their gene collections established prior to their membership of CGIAR. In 1994, each CGIAR centre placed its genebank under the superintendency of FAO, through the administration of the Commission on Plant Genetic Resources.[6] An additional question raised by this 1994 action is the status of dispositions of genetic material prior to 1994. An illustration of this problem is the transmission by ICARDA of the Syrian legumes to the Australian Centre for Legumes in Mediterranean Agriculture, which became the subject of an Australian Plant Breeder's Rights Application. The director-general of ICARDA was reported to have defended its actions by explaining that the legumes were sent to Australia prior to the implementation of the 1994 Agreement (Edwards and Anderson, 1998).

Another problem with the CGIAR policy on plant genetic resources is that it does not specifically define the obligations of trustees of CGIAR genebanks. The CGIAR policy contains the general statement that genebanks should be held in trust 'for the use of present and future generations of research workers in all countries throughout the world'. CGIAR policy is silent on the use which these workers would make of this resource. A reasonable interpretation would be that these workers would be allowed to use CGIAR germplasm for purposes within CGIAR's general objects, for example, to make the agriculture of developing countries more productive and to protect the environment and to preserve biodiversity. As trustee, could a CGIAR centre permit a third party to secure intellectual property rights over germplasm held by the centre?

Under the trust concept a trustee is under a duty both to keep control of and to preserve trust property. Should a third party be permitted to obtain intellectual property rights, for its own benefit, over germplasm held by a centre, a breach of trust could be argued. On the other hand, if those intellectual property rights were held for the benefit of the centre and for the benefit of CGIAR objectives, this may well be consistent with the trustee's obligations to secure the preservation of germplasm. However, it is difficult to conceive of a situation where a third party will assume the very considerable trouble and expense of intellectual property protection in order to preserve plant genetic resources for CGIAR purposes. This is conceivable where, for example, a patentee might waive its rights in developing countries. But to accomplish this the rights owner would have to have secured those rights in the country in which they are to be waived, which is not likely to occur.

Aside from general principles of trusts law, the disposition of a centre's germplasm will ultimately be governed by the laws of the host country and by the headquarters agreement between the centre and the host country. For example, where a centre is established as a domestic corporation, the disposition of its germplasm will depend upon what is provided for on the headquarters agreement for dealings in both tangible and intangible property and where the agreement is silent on these matters, what the domestic corporate and property laws provide on these subjects.

Almost entirely ignored in discussions about the ownership and control of the germplasm collections of the CGIAR are the rights, if any, of the farmers and local communities who may have contributed germplasm, as well as the source countries in which the germplasm might have been collected. The question of benefit-sharing arising from access to genetic resources is addressed in a number of the key provisions of the Convention on Biological Diversity (CBD), as well as being embraced within the notion of 'Farmers' Rights' (Blakeney, 1999b). The protection of traditional scientific and cultural knowledge is currently being addressed by the World Intellectual Property Organization (WIPO) (Blakeney, 2000).

In the event that the CGIAR is reorganised into a federation of thematic or regional centres, this may involve the closure or merger of existing centres. The disposition of the germplasm and other IP of those centres will be governed by their headquarters agreements and relevant local legislation. For example, were IRRI's research facilities and germplasm collection to relocate from the Philippines, this relocation would be constrained both by Philippines corporate law and Executive Order 247, which regulates the access to biological and genetic resources in the Philippines.

Among the issues which have not yet been canvassed is whether a budget will be provided to the CGIAR's Federation's IP managers to protect its IP rights and to enforce the restrictions against commercialisation, which are contained in the material transfer agreements (MTAs) under which germplasm is made available to researchers.

Modern biotechnology and the CGIAR

Underlying the perception of a crisis in the governance and management of the CGIAR is the impact of modern biotechnology upon agricultural research. Genetic engineering has permitted the expeditious introduction of a wide range of desirable traits into plants. These include:

- pest-control traits such as insect, virus and nematode resistance as well as herbicide tolerance;
- post-harvest traits such as delayed ripening of spoilage prone fruits;
- agronomic traits such as nitrogen fixation and utilisation, restricted branching, environmental stress tolerance;
- male and/or seed sterility for hybrid systems; and
- output traits such as plant colour and vitamin enrichment. (Lindner, 1999)

The production of transgenic plants has become possible through the development of a number of enabling and transformation technologies. These technologies, together with the introduction of beneficial plant traits, have become the subject of intellectual property protection, as a consequence of the favourable decisions of courts in the USA and Europe. An indication of the impact of these decisions is the increase in patent applications for DNA sequences, which increased from 4000 in 1991 to some 500000 in 1996 (Enriquez, 1998). As is mentioned above, the expense of the IP process is a major reason why agricultural research is shifting away from the public to the private sector. The difficulties which the CGIAR as a publicly funded, public goods entity is having in coming to terms with the presence and the influence of the private sector is a first area of difficulty.

At a more profound level are the widely articulated concerns that genetic engineering is a questionable technology for agricultural research. RAFI has repeatedly questioned the ethics and the morality of obtaining IP rights in relation to plant varieties and genetic materials. There is also a burgeoning scholarship on whether the application of genetic engineering techniques to agriculture has been proven to be safe. Indeed, there is an influential scholarship which even questions whether the Green Revolution was as successful as claimed. For example, it is claimed that the increase in diseases afflicting the new super crops is attributable to increases in the biomass associated with the crops, the necessity for increased fertiliser use with the new varieties and the vulnerability to stress of the uniform crop strains. A corollary to this scholarship is the suggestion that the claimed advantages of genetic engineering might be better secured by non-genetic techniques, such as natural resource management. It is beyond the competence of this author to assess the science of these claims. However, from an IP perspective, if the international community takes the position that food security is too important a matter for private IP rights, then it is open to the community either to permit the exclusion of this subject from patentability and plant variety rights protection, or to qualify any IP rights which may be granted to provide a research exception to the enforcement of patent rights.

The future – IP, human rights and biological diversity

The promulgation of TRIPS as a membership obligation for countries wishing to participate in the WTO has firmly established IP as a world trade issue (Blakeney, 1995). Thus countries wishing to enjoy the benefits of WTO membership are obliged to comply with the IP norms which are mandated by TRIPS. As is mentioned above, this has had a direct impact upon global agricultural research, particularly the requirement in Article 27.3(b) that WTO members provide patent and/or *sui generis* protection for plant varieties. TRIPS provides the legal infrastructure for the global propertisation of research tools and research products. Part of the explanation for the existence of TRIPS is the lack of success which WIPO had had in attempts to harmonise the interests of industrialised and developing countries in the existing international IP regime which dated back to the Paris Convention of 1883. The failure to achieve any success in the Paris Revision negotiations, over a 15-year period, had induced the USA, in particular, to look to the GATT as an alternative forum within which to consider IP. The success of the TRIPS negotiators, during the Uruguay Round, in securing a consensus on IP norms was largely achieved because of the absence of developing countries in the negotiating process (Drahos, 1995). The developing countries had largely boycotted the negotiation of TRIPS on the basis that WIPO was the proper forum for IP discussions.

The South is now trying to come to terms with the fact that TRIPS is an established part of the international IP landscape. The expansion of the membership of the WTO to include most developing countries and their active involvement in the TRIPS review process is likely to result in the same sort of irreconcilability and lack of consensus which bedevilled the Paris Convention negotiations within WIPO. One important difference, however, is that TRIPS is part of a disparate package of agreements and it is feasible that concessions on IP might be extracted as part of a broader package. Thus it may be possible to bargain for amendments to TRIPS which could, for example, exclude food crops from patentability or provide exemptions from IP protection for public agricultural research.

The perceived transcendental impact of the new IP regime upon all aspects of human enterprise has caused questions to be raised about the human rights implications of IP. In its Report, *Human Rights and Human Development*, the UNDP suggested that TRIPS might be inconsistent with the International Covenant on Economic, Social, and Cultural Rights and the International Covenant on Civil and Political Rights (UNDP, 2000).

On 17 August 2000 the UN Sub-Commission for the Protection and Promotion of Human Rights,

> Noting... that actual or potential conflicts exist between the implementation of the TRIPS Agreement and the realization of economic, social and cultural rights in relation to, *inter alia*, impediments to the transfer of technology to developing countries, the consequences for the enjoyment of the right to food of plant variety rights and the patenting of genetically modified organisms, 'bio-piracy' and the reduction of communities' (especially indigenous communities') control over their own genetic and natural resources and cultural values, and restrictions on access to patented pharmaceuticals and the implications for the enjoyment of the right to health,

adopted a resolution calling into question the impact of TRIPS on the human rights of peoples and communities, including farmers and indigenous peoples worldwide (UN Commission on Human Rights, 2000). The resolution noted 'the apparent conflicts' between the IP rights embodied in TRIPS and international human rights law, particularly that 'the implementation of the TRIPS Agreement does not adequately reflect the fundamental nature and indivisibility of all human rights, including the right of everyone to enjoy the benefits of scientific progress and its applications, the right to health, the right to food, and the right to self-determination' (UN Commission, 2000). The resolution reminded 'all Governments of the primacy of human rights obligations over economic policies and agreements' (UN Commission, 2000).

The resolution did not specifically address the issue of IP and food crops and agricultural research beyond urging the Conference of Parties (COP) to the Convention on Biological Diversity to consider human rights principles and instruments in undertaking its assessment of the relationship between biodiversity concerns and intellectual property rights, in general, and between the CBD and TRIPS in particular (UN Commission, 2000).

At the TRIPS Council meeting held on 21 March 2000, the Chair set out a list of issues to structure discussions on the review of Article 27.3(b) of TRIPS. The list included:

- Ethical issues relating to patentability of life forms;
- The relationship to the conservation and sustainable use of genetic material; and
- The relationship with the concepts of traditional knowledge and farmers' rights.

In response to this list, Brazil issued a paper suggesting that 'moral and ethical consequences of inventions are better dealt with directly – that is, by inhibiting the development of the technologies themselves instead of creating obstacles to their patentability'.[7] Thus, it was recommended that

> whenever a Member considers that some specific technologies related to patents on technology are contrary to ethical, cultural or religious standards, Article 27.3(b) should consider the possibility of providing flexibility for Members to limit or to deny intellectual property rights over such technologies, in order to prevent that their development is encouraged.[8]

WIPO had already commenced an examination of the impact of human rights upon IP in the context of the IP rights of indigenous peoples in their traditional knowledge (Drahos, 1999). Since 1996, a number of meetings and fact-finding missions had been organised by WIPO to investigate the issue of IP protection and traditional knowledge (Blakeney, 1999b). In a Note to WIPO, dated 14 September 2000, the Permanent Mission of the Dominican Republic to the United Nations in Geneva submitted two documents on behalf of the Group of Countries of Latin America and the Caribbean (GRULAC) as part of the debate in the WIPO General Assembly on 'Matters Concerning Intellectual Property and Genetic Resources, Traditional Knowledge and Folklore' (WIPO Doc. WO/GA/26/9). The central thrust of these documents was a request for the creation of a Standing Committee on access to the genetic resources and traditional knowledge of local and indigenous communities. 'The work of that Standing Committee would have to be directed towards defining internationally recognised practical methods of securing adequate protection for the intellectual property rights in traditional knowledge' (WIPO Doc. WO/GA/26/9: Annex 1, 10).

In order to clarify the future application of intellectual property to the use and exploitation of genetic resources and biodiversity and also traditional knowledge, it was suggested that the Committee could clarify:

(a) the notions of public domain and private domain;
(b) the appropriateness and feasibility of recognising rights in traditional works and knowledge currently in the public domain, and investigating machinery to limit and control certain kinds of unauthorised exploitation;
(c) recognition of collective rights;
(d) model provisions and model contracts with which to control the use and exploitation of genetic and biological resources, and machinery for the equitable distribution of profits in the event of a patentable product or process being developed from a given resource embodying the principles of prior informed consent and equitable distribution of profits in connection with the use, development and commercial exploitation of the material transferred and the inventions and technology resulting from it;
(e) the protection of undisclosed traditional knowledge.

Finally, it was suggested that in concert with the secretariat of UPOV, the Committee could embark on the exploration of possible options for defining *sui generis* systems for the protection of genetic resources and biodiversity.

At the WIPO General Assembly the member states agreed the establishment of an Intergovernmental Committee on Intellectual Property and Genetic Resources, Traditional Knowledge and Folklore. Three interrelated themes were identified to inform the deliberations of the Committee; intellectual property issues that arise in the context of:

(i) access to genetic resources and benefit-sharing;
(ii) protection of traditional knowledge, whether or not associated with those resources; and
(iii) the protection of expressions of folklore (WIPO, 2000).

It was proposed that the Committee would hold its first session in the spring of 2001 and that the next draft programme and budget would provide for the Committee to meet twice a year in the 2002–2003 biennium. The Committee would report any recommendations for action that it might formulate to the WIPO General Assembly. It is not unfeasible to suggest that this intergovernmental committee also considers the issue of the impact of IP upon public agricultural research.

Notes

1. These centres are: the Centro Internacional de Agricultura Tropical (CIAT), Center for International Forestry Research (CIFOR), Centro Internacional de la Papa (CIP), International Center for Agricultural Research in the Dry Areas (ICARDA), International Center for Living Aquatic Resources Management (ICLARM), International Center for Research in Agroforestry (ICRAF), International Crop Research Institute for the Semi-Arid Tropics (ICRISAT), International Livestock Research Institute (ILRI), International Institute of Tropical Agriculture (IITA), International Plant Genetic Resources Institute (IPGRI) International Rice Research Institute (IRRI) and the West Africa Rice Development Association (WARDA).
2. In a recent article in *Foreign Affairs* Paarlberg noted that foreign aid for agriculture in the South fell by 57 per cent between the publication of the Brundtland Commission report in 1988 and The World Food Summit of 1996 and that World Bank loans for agriculture and rural development fell by 47 per cent over the same period, Paarlberg (2000) 'The Global Food Fight', *Foreign Affairs*, vol. 79, no. 35.
3. Since a single patent application, carried to completion in key markets costs an estimated US$200 000. Defending a patent application costs at least this amount again.
4. RAFI argues that there are only eleven IP rights which are relevant for this project, RAFI (2000) *Golden Rice and Trojan Trade Reps*, Occasional Paper Series, vol. 6, no. 2, October, www.rafi.org.
5. See International Legal Materials (1984) vol. 23, p. 1388.
6. In 1995 the Commission was renamed as the Commission on Genetic Resources for Food and Agriculture (CGRFA).
7. WTO (2000) Council for Trade-Related Aspects of Intellectual Property Rights, *Review of Article 27.3(b)*, Communication from Brazil, Doc.IP/C/W/228, 24 November.
8. WTO, *Review of Article 27.3(b)*, para. 16.

References

Alston, J.M. Pardey, P.G. and Roseboom, J. (1998) 'Financing Agricultural Research: International Investment Patterns and Policy Perspectives', *World Development*, vol. 26, p. 1057.

Blakeney, M. (1995) 'Intellectual Property in World Trade', *International Trade Law and Regulation*, vol. 1, p. 76.

Blakeney, M. (1999a) 'Agricultural Research and the Management of IPRs', in J. Cohen (ed.), *Managing Agricultural Biotechnology. Addressing Research Program Needs and Policy Implications* (Wallingford: CABI Publishing), pp. 228–39.

Blakeney, M. (1999b) 'The International Framework of Access to Plant Genetic Resources', in M. Blakeney (ed.), *Intellectual Property Aspects of Ethnobiology* (London: Sweet & Maxwell, 1999), pp. 1–22.

Blakeney, M. (2000) 'The Protection of Traditional Knowledge under Intellectual Property Law', *European Intellectual Property Review*, vol. 6, p. 251.

CGIAR (1998) Press Release 'CGIAR Urges Halt to Granting of Intellectual Property Rights for Designated Plant Germplasm', February 11, http://www.cgiar.org:80/germrel.htm.

Cohen, J., C. Falconi, J. Komen and M. Blakeney (1998) *The Use of Proprietary Biotechnology Research Inputs at Selected CGIAR Centers* (The Hague: ISNAR, March).

Drahos, P. (1995) 'Global Property Rights in Information: The Story of TRIPS at the GATT', *Prometheus*, vol. 13, p. 6; M. Blakeney, *Trade Related Aspects of Intellectual Property Rights. A Concise Guide to the TRIPS Agreement* (London: Sweet & Maxwell), ch. 1.

Drahos, P. (1999) 'The Universality of Intellectual Property Rights: Origins and Development', in *Intellectual Property and Human Rights* (Geneva: World Intellectual Property Organization), pp. 13–41.

Edwards and Anderson (1998) 'Seeds of Wrath', *New Scientist*, vol. 14, no. 2121, February, pp. 14–15; 'Editorial. Lest We Starve', *New Scientist* p. 3.

Enriquez (1998) 'Genomics and the World's Economy', *Science*, vol. 281, p. 925.

FAO (1986) Commission on Plant Genetic Resources, Legal Status of Base and Active Collections of Plant Genetic Resources, Doc. CPGR/87/5, December.

Hayenga, M. (1998) 'Structural Change in the Biotech Seed and Chemical Industrial Complex' vol. 1(2) *AgBioForum*, p. 43.

Lindner, (1999) 'Prospects for Public Plant Breeding in a Small Country' paper at ICABR Conference, The Shape of the Coming Agricultural Biotechnology Transformation: Strategic Investment and Policy Approaches from an Economic Perspective, University of Rome 'Tor Vergata', 17–19 June.

RAFI (2000) *In Search of Firmer Ground*, October, www.rafi.org.

TAC (1998) CGIAR Policy on Plant Genetic Resources, TAC Doc. AGR/TAC:IAR/88/4 February.

UN Commission on Human Rights (2000) Sub-Commission on the Promotion and Protection of Human Rights, Fifty-second session, Agenda item 4, The Realization of Economic, Social and Cultural Rights, Intellectual Property Rights and Human Rights, Doc. E/CN.4/Sub.2/2000/7, Art. 2, Art. 3, Art. 13, 17 August.

UNDP (2000) *Human Development Report 2000, Human Rights and Human Development* (New York: UNDP), pp. 83–8.

WIPO (2000) 'Matters Concerning Intellectual Property Genetic Resources Traditional Knowledge and Folklore', WIPO Doc. WO/GA/26/6, 25 August.

8
Don't Ignore Copyright, the 'Sleeping Giant' on the TRIPS and International Educational Agenda

Alan Story

> Who pays Cervantes his royalties for intellectual property? Who pays Shakespeare? Who pays the ones who invented the alphabet, those who invented numerals, arithmetic, mathematics? ... What man's intelligence has created should be the patrimony of all mankind.[1]

Introduction

Since TRIPS (Agreement on Trade-Related Aspects of Intellectual Property Rights) and the WTO (World Trade Organization) became such frequently disparaged global acronyms in the late-1990s, most of the growing opposition to both this trade agreement and to the organisation administering it has focused on issues related to patents, and especially their negative effects on countries of the South.[2] 'Stop biopiracy', 'no patents on life', or 'people's health before pharmaceutical patents' have been typical mobilising slogans of citizen and producer groups, NGOs, anti-globalisation activists, and others advancing a global justice agenda from Seattle to Cape Town to Manila and hundreds of other communities in between. The contents of this book reflect this concentration on a range of literally 'life and death' patent questions: farmers' rights and seeds, biopiracy and pharmaceuticals, as well as the contested role of patents in the transfer of technology and the stimulation of innovation. This focus is not surprising; all are, undoubtedly, significant global justice and intellectual property issues. Yet, attempting to answer the question, 'What Future for the WTO TRIPS Agreement?', by solely addressing patent-related questions overlooks, I would argue, a significant aspect of TRIPS and the 'new world order' that the WTO is trying to establish in this era, the much-touted era of the 'information economy.'

This chapter and the following chapter by Gary Lea, which introduce several key international copyright, globalisation, information technology and educational issues for countries of the South, try – however partially – to fill this sizable and potentially misleading gap in our collective understanding of the increasing global reach of intellectual property and of the ideology which infuses it.

Although patents and copyright contain numerous differences as distinct categories within intellectual property law doctrine, their recent transformation from an 'international to an internationalised' legal phenomenon[3] also exhibits a number of similarities. Under the TRIPS/ WTO regime, all WTO members (actual and aspiring) are required to embrace a particular world view which considers that all expressions, ideas and inventions – that is, the works or creations (more accurately, the re-creations and reformulations) of the human intellect – *must be* first, and usually exclusively: (a) private property; (b) the private property of their 'owners' (who are often not the actual creators of the work); thence (c) commodities; thence (d) items of international trade and commerce; and finally (e) protected as enforceable and legally binding trade rights *for the benefit* of intellectual rights holders, chiefly large corporations of the developed world, and *to the detriment* of both legitimate users and so-called 'pirates' of these expressions and inventions in the same and other countries. Patent and copyright issues raise related questions. Take the case of HIV/AIDS, its treatment and its prevention. The well-known South African pharmaceuticals case, launched in 1998 by more than forty large drug companies but then collapsing in April 2001 after a wave of worldwide protest and revulsion, once again refocused our attention on the patent implications of TRIPS and the possibilities of compulsory licensing. What is rather less well-known is that South African healthcare lecturers who want to distribute non-governmental printed materials (on a non-profit basis) to their students about HIV and sex education must often pay copyright royalty charges to large multinational publishing companies for this 'privilege'.[4] If it is wrong to charge the same rates for anti-HIV drugs in Durban or Harare or Manila as in New York or London, how can it be right to charge burdensome 'first world' copyright royalty charges to students or teachers in South Africa who want to read and teach about this condition and how to limit its further spread? (We can add that there is also a basic similarity in the stated rationales for both policies. Without the broadest and fullest patent protection as an incentive, it is argued that no drugs would be invented nor, without copyright, would any books be written.[5]) Other copyright-related problems, such as the costs of expensive copyright-protected computer software, the lack of protection of folk-lore, the barriers in gaining access to texts and other teaching materials (via the Internet or in traditional hard copy format) reveal how the privatisation and commodification values of TRIPS have been accorded a trumping role over competing values.

Copyright as a property right

What are these competing values? They start from a recognition that the protection of intellectual property and copyright, our main concern here, should be narrowly tailored; the main danger, experience has repeatedly shown, lies in its over-protection, exclusivity, and the erection of more and more lucrative user-pay turnstiles. The degree and scope of copyright protection permitted should only be that which is necessary for the *instrumental purpose* of satisfying other values and goals: the creation of knowledge, the spread of knowledge, public access and public use.[6] In fact, what level of copyright protection is actually necessary to achieve these societal goals is often greatly exaggerated.[7] And what is often forgotten is that copyright, as a property right, operates in many of the same ways as do the ownership and exclusive use of private real or personal property, such as land, buildings or corporate shares. Copyright expresses a power relationship *between persons* and represents not only the state's grant of sovereignty to a private party but also *power OVER other people*.[8] In other words, deciding and enforcing laws such as who can legally enter on to private land and, conversely, who is a trespasser, are legal decisions of the same order as the power to decide who can use a book or proprietary software and who cannot; at issue is who can gain admission at no cost or through a user-pay turn-stile, such as the payment of a copyright royalty fee – or is refused access altogether. Moreover, given that copyright in a work commonly exists as private property for well over hundred years after that work is created, ownership of a work can also determine, as Morris Cohen explains, 'future distributions' and 'what men [and women] shall acquire'.[9] And, we could add for our analysis here, what whole regions, such as the 'copyright-rich' countries of the North, shall acquire from other regions, including from the South. (As is explored later, the global balance-of-payments implications of copyright revenue flows are stag-gering.) Conversely, the cumulative effects of systematic exclusion from copyright-monopolised intangible property can often have greater eco-nomic and social ramifications, now and in the future, than who can or cannot have access to a piece of land or other types of tangible property.

Yet, all of this seems forgotten in the mystique surrounding intellectual property. If the UN established an agency called the World Property Organisation, the WPO, some numbers of people would surely wonder, 'is protecting global property holders really the UN's mission?' But create a UN agency organisation called the World Intellectual Property Organization, WIPO, and it takes on a certain air of legitimacy and transcendence.

Two slogans circulating on the Internet starkly set down the competing perspectives: 'Knowledge is power. And now it means money as well. Sell what you know at xxxx.co.uk' *v.* 'Knowledge – the more you share it, the more there is.' What I want to explore in this chapter is whether the growing internationalisation of copyright, as demonstrated by the terms and assumptions of TRIPS, is carrying out the *instrumental project* of improving education and educational opportunities in countries of the South. In other words, is TRIPS leading to a sharing of knowledge and the collective development of more knowledge? Or, alternatively, is TRIPS a harbinger/catalyst for the 'more power and more money' school of thought about the purposes of copyright? It is, after all, a seldom-disputed truism that the improvement of education in underdeveloped countries is one of the essential, if not the essential, requirement for their economic, social and political development. If the over-protection of copyright does not serve these goals and, in fact, hinders their realisation, then it is copyright's presumptions, rather than the educational needs and aspirations of peoples of the South, that need to be challenged and reformulated.

Two caveats

Before starting such an analysis, however, two major caveats must be set down. First, although this chapter focuses mainly on the question of access to knowledge, including technical knowledge, by countries of the South from countries of the North, this focus does not imply that the countries of the North are the principal repository of 'knowledge' in the world or that countries of the South are somehow 'backward' and lacking in inventiveness and ideas. Such an implication is a typical conceit of Western capitalist countries and closely linked to the notion that, without copyright and strict copyright laws, the expression of ideas and creativity would be severely stifled or would cease altogether. In the same vein, it also needs to be appreciated that copyright, as a legal and ideological concept, is the product of Western societal development at a particular historical moment and remains a foreign concept in many

other societies. For example, a number of societies, including indigenous societies, in countries of the South take a radically different
approach to 'what constitutes property or what may be rightfully be the
subject of private ownership';[10] such societies consider, for example,
that the 'copying' and sharing of expressions within a given community
is a signal of respect and recognition, not of piracy or rip-off or the
infringement of a private property right. TRIPS thus is not only a trade
agreement, it is also a multifaceted project to export to all corners of
the globe a particular set of values and presumptions about the need
to propertise both ideas and the expression of those ideas. To take,
for example, the values embedded in proprietary computer software,
one of the key copyright-protected works of our era, TRIPS represents an
attempt to promote the 'Microsoft-ification' of the world.

Global copyright revenues and trade flows

If few would dispute that patent issues have taken the centre stage in
popular protests and academic commentary since TRIPS became law
in January 1996, it is certainly arguable that it was: (a) the well-organised
demands of the 'copyright industries', as they call themselves; and (b) the
further expansion of copyright, its scope and its global enforcement
which were central to the vision and the victory of the pro-TRIPS countries and lobbying forces at the Uruguay Round of the GATT in the early
1990s. Indeed, these copyright victories were perhaps even more important than the prize of expanded patent protection, even if TRIPS itself
changed global patent laws more than it did copyright laws. Consider a
few statistics. The US copyright industries (including movies, TV, home
video, music, publishing and computer software) are 'America's greatest
trade prize', Jack Valenti, President of the Motion Picture Association of
America, has concluded.[11]
  As Valenti explains:

> We bring in more revenues than aircraft, more than agriculture and
> auto parts. What is more astonishing and more valuable is that the
> Copyright Industries have a *surplus balance of trade with every single
> country in the world*. No other American business enterprise can make
> that statement; particularly in view of a $400 Billion trade deficit in
> 2000.[12]

A recent Economists Incorporated study revealed not only that 'core US
copyright industries'[13] had contributed an estimated US$457.2 billion

to the US economy in 1999, but also that the value of such industries to the gross US domestic product had increased by an astounding *360 per cent* between 1977 and 1999. More importantly for a global copyright analysis, 'conservative' estimates revealed that foreign sales and exports of US copyright-protected products totalled US$79.85 billion.[14] (This last figure is greater than the total gross domestic product of many less-developed countries.) These 1999 foreign earnings represented an increase of 15.1 per cent over 1998 figures for US companies and, for the sake of comparison, were more than *five times greater* than the total exports of the US drug and pharmaceutical industries. Stressing the importance of the global 'harmonisation' of copyright laws – in harmony, it should be stressed, with the strong intellectual protection provided by the Berne Convention, the leading international copyright convention – the US Senate Judiciary Committee stated in 1995:

> Uniformity of copyright laws is enormously important to facilitate the free flow of copyrighted works between markets and to ensure the greatest possible exploitation of the commercial value of these works in world markets for the benefit of US copyright owners and their dependants.[15]

Whether the interests of US copyright industries and exporters (and those in Europe, Japan and other developed capitalist countries) are the same as the interests of educational users – the teacher, the librarian, the professor and the student from the countries of the South – is far less certain. What certainly is clear, especially in this era of the Internet (at least in the developed world), is that this flow of commodified information is intended to be primarily a one-way flow: from IP owners in the North, especially in the US, both to users in other countries of the North and to users in the South. As the same US Senate committee concluded, 'in an age where the information superhighway offers widespread distribution of copyrighted works to almost anywhere in the world at limited costs, harmonisation of copyright laws is imperative to the international protection of those works and to the assurance of their continued availability'. But the Senate committee was not talking about the 'availability' in the US (or Europe for that matter) of the breathtaking art of the Yoroba people of Nigeria or of Brazilian-produced samba music, but rather the availability in Nigeria and Brazil of Microsoft's Windows 2000 or the latest Hollywood blockbuster. Their populations of, respectively, 108 million and 167 million people, are coveted present, and especially future, copyright marketplaces for the multinationals.

Recent balance-of-payment figures provided by the International Monetary Fund show how unequal is the flow, how unequal is the exchange, between the world's countries when it comes to intellectual property. According to 1999 IMF figures for the global trade in royalties and licences (primarily for intellectual property), the United States received a total of US$36.5 billion on its intellectual property exports, while paying out US$13.3 billion to other countries, for a net surplus of more than US$23 billion.[16] No other country in the world had a net surplus of over $1 billion; the UK was second and very far behind with US$900 million. (Other rich countries, such as France, Germany, Canada and Australia all had substantial intellectual property deficits, while a number of poorer countries had no calculable international intellectual property revenues whatsoever.) Although this US$23 billion US surplus is not divided into copyright and patent-related income, the earlier-cited Economists Incorporated study highlights the predominance of copyright-related income. I think it is hard to dispute, then, that the main global function of TRIPS is the protection, expansion and longevity of these massive copyright and patent revenue streams.

A few basics of copyright law

Before proceeding further, we need to summarise the basics of both domestic and international copyright law so that the legal restrictions and possibilities at stake for countries of the South are clear. In a few paragraphs this is a tall order, but here goes: copyright generally protects, as private property, a wide range of expressions and technical manifestations of these expressions; these range from books, poems, musical works, records and CDs, photographs, films and computer software to works as mundane as a chocolate chip recipe or the artistic component in the slanting letters on a VISA card. Although there are some 'fair dealing' or 'fair use' exceptions (for example, private studying or a review in a newspaper), the owner of the copyright (sometimes the author or composer, but often not) is given *the exclusive right* to make a copy of the work (hence 'copyright'), to issue copies to the public (this is usually the most important and lucrative right for printed works), to perform or show the work in public (for example, a play or a movie), and to adapt the work, which means, among other things, to translate the work from one language into another or to turn a book into a movie. If these exclusive rights are allegedly infringed, for example, by photocopying an entire book and selling it to someone else, the owner has the legal right to launch a copyright infringement action. (Whether that owner actually possesses sufficient financial resources to commence such an action and carry it through to the trial stage is another matter; 'the right' in copyright is generally dependent on the holder's abilities to enforce it.) Finally, copyright protection arises 'automatically' upon creation; there is no registration requirement as with patents and trademarks. These are the basics of domestic copyright law.

Now I will say a few words about international copyright; in the nineteenth century, when books and other forms of expression became increasingly important items of international trade, the main problems which rights holders faced were: how can copyright works be protected outside the national borders of the rights holder and what should be the level or standard of protection? Neither was a simple matter. The Berne Convention of 1886,[17] initiated by a number of European countries and copyright holders, came up with one solution: national treatment. So while the various signatories at Berne could not agree on one global standard for protection, they did agree that a work originating in one of the Berne member countries (Y) must be given the same protection in every other Berne member country (Z) that Z grants to the works created by its own nationals. In other words, a novel written by a Canadian author and published in Canada (Y) is given the same degree of copyright protection in France as a novel written by a French author in France (Z) (known as the principle of national treatment). The other important aspect of the Berne convention that needs to be mentioned in this brief survey is that all Berne convention countries are required to enact certain minimum standards of protection for all types of literary, artistic, musical and similar media of expression in whatever form. That is, Berne signatories are prevented from excluding certain types of expression from protection or protection below minimum levels. For example, a developing country (or any other country for that matter) cannot decide that textbooks should only be protected by its own domestic copyright laws for as long as the author is alive or for, say, twenty years after publication; Article 7 of Berne prohibits the enactment of such a law. At the same time, however, signatory countries are free to create significantly higher and more extensive levels of protection, a 'freedom' which recently has taken on great significance, as is discussed in the next section, with regard to the duration of copyright protection. Duration of copyright raises the issue of how long a copyright-protected work should exist as private property before it enters the public domain and can be used by all.

Yet, until recently, international copyright law was a rather arcane and 'feeble' field of law because, among other reasons, rights holders had a very limited ability to enforce, extraterritorially, their copyright and to start legal proceedings in the event of a purported infringement occurring within the boundaries of another country. Further, many countries were outside the Berne Convention; total membership was only seventy-five countries, the United States did not join until 1989 and many members were essentially members in name only. This situation changed dramatically in the mid-1990s with the establishment of the WTO and the adoption of TRIPS. Any country wishing to join the WTO must also sign up to TRIPS and all signatories to TRIPS must agree to comply with all of the key sections of the Berne Convention, namely Articles 1–21 and the Appendix.[18] As a result, this once rather 'arcane' field of law has now become a tiger with claws; countries allegedly infringing the copyright in works owned by foreign corporations and nationals are being taken before the WTO's dispute-settlement and enforcement mechanisms (see Chapter 14 by Sol Picciotto in this volume). TRIPS also brought certain key changes to international copyright doctrine, especially with regard to computer software and databases (see Chapter 9 by Gary Lea in this volume).

A sampling of key educational copyright issues

With this brief legal background, I now want to examine four of the most important copyright-related and education-related problems that countries of the South are now facing; most of these issues and problems stem directly from the provisions of TRIPS, from increasing globalisation and/or from long unresolved conflicts in copyright doctrine, domestically and internationally, that are now coming to the fore.

(a) The owner/user imbalance

There is one statement that you will find in almost all contemporary analyses of copyright policy and legislation: the main aim of copyright is to maintain 'a proper balance between the rights of copyright owners and copyright users'. This statement tends more to obscure than clarify copyright relationships. Most attempts to readdress any imbalance in favour of users are quickly met with the cry from rights holders, 'but that would take away our property rights!'. Moreover, it is hardly debatable that the overall relationship between users and owners has become further 'out of whack' in recent years and that the provisions of TRIPS have put another weight on one side of the purported 'balance'.

With countries of the South being primarily copyright users rather than owners, the consequences for them have become magnified.

One key provision of TRIPS (and also of the Berne Convention) is, I think, sufficient to make the point. As is explained above, both agreements contain what are called 'minimum standards' provisions, but include no prohibitions against enacting 'maximum standards'.[19] On the issue of copyright term, the Berne Convention requires that most types of work be protected for a period of life of the author, plus a further fifty years. But for legislators in the United States and the European Union, this period was viewed as 'too short' and over the past eight years, they have both changed their laws to increase the term to life of the author, plus 70 years.[20] As TRIPS and Berne are both essentially rights holders' charters, users are powerless to employ any of their many clauses to challenge such an important change; it is change which means that a virtual library of books and other materials that might have come into the public domain and be available for free use and access have now been maintained as private property for a further twenty years. More recently, the United States has embarked on its 'TRIPS Plus' agenda and is requiring selected countries to adopt its life plus 70 years formulation. The main point is this: TRIPS is but the latest example of how, for rights holders in the North and for users everywhere, all trips (pardon the pun!) on the TRIPS copyright escalator go in only one direction: up.

(b) Proprietary computer software

In the schools and universities of the North, the widespread use of computers and ever-increasing access to the Internet have been important pedagogical developments of the past decade. But for most schools and universities in countries of the South, the 'Internet revolution', let alone the computer revolution, is still many years in the future. There are many reasons for this 'digital divide', including the well-documented economic disparity between countries of the North and the South, the pressures on Southern countries to repay debts, significant limitations in their telephone systems and electrical power grids, and the high costs of computer hardware. But one other significant factor is the costs and inaccessibility of computer software and the highly restrictive conditions under which schools, universities and individual users in the South (as well as the North) can obtain and use most of this software. Here global copyright issues and the provisions of TRIPS come to the fore.

Although computer software was not protected as intellectual property when it was first being developed – and incidentally these were, in fact, the most creative and collaborative days in the history of software – lobbying by large software companies led to legislative changes. Starting in the 1980s, software was protected first by domestic copyright statutes (the source code was controversially considered 'a literary work' and in the same conceptual category as a poem or novel) – and then later, in some countries such as the United States and Japan, by patent laws as well. In the case of copyright, such protection is now global and mandatory. Article 10 of TRIPS states: 'Computer programs, whether in source or object codes, shall be protected as literary works under the Berne Convention (1971).' The uninitiated, the uninformed or computer 'phobes' might assume from the language of this section that all computer software is necessarily copyright-protected, necessarily the private property of its owners. Nothing could be further from the truth. In fact, there are, to simplify greatly, two forms of software: (a) proprietary software (that is, software owned exclusively during its copyright life by a software owner and hence controlling all aspects of its pricing, use and even plug-ins); and (b) non-proprietary software (that is, software which mandates various types of sharing or cooperative usage of the source code and improvements to the software – or, in some cases, self-ownership and hence potential copyright protection by a subsequent developer, but not the 'original' developer.) The best-known examples of proprietary software are Windows and Word, the operating and word-processing packages of Microsoft; the best known non-proprietary alternatives include 'open source' software, Linux and 'freeware'.

The use of proprietary software creates a range of problems for countries and schools of the South, our focus here. The first one is cost. Unlike non-proprietary software which can often be downloaded for free from the Internet or involves, at most, a small one-time charge, full ownership of proprietary software remains with a company such as Microsoft; the user receives only a licence to use it on the terms set by Microsoft. (Given Microsoft's dominant position in the operating systems market, the possibilities for users to 'shop around' or actually bargain licensing terms are minuscule.) Increasingly, Microsoft's expensive licensing fees must be paid annually and are determined, in the case of a university, by the number of 'desks' (using computers) at that institution. Moreover, the 'per desk' licensing cost may be the same whether that institution is Harvard University, Oxford University or a poorly funded university in Asia, Africa or South America.[21] Microsoft's 'alternative' pricing strategy is based on the deep discounting of software, a strategy designed to achieve maximum market penetration and consumer dependence.

A second serious problem is that Microsoft and other proprietary-based companies retain exclusive use and control of the all-important underlying source code; it is copyright-protected and essentially considered a trade secret. However, modifying, improving, integrating and 'tweaking' source codes is a centre-piece of the software development 'trade'; these activities lead to computer innovation and make software such a wonderful communications tool. Microsoft licences forbid making such improvements; such attempts may result in a copyright infringement suit, an action which Microsoft has become rather specialised at initiating against alleged infringers. Further, how a school in Calcutta or Santiago wants to use computerisation to teach its students or administer its programmes will, we can safely predict, be rather different from how things are done in a school in Kansas City or Liverpool. Again, proprietary software hinders such individual tailoring to individual needs.[22]

Non-proprietary systems and open-source technology, by comparison, are based on fundamentally different principles, philosophically, technically and economically. To take but one example:

> the source code (of open source) must be available to anybody [and] ... if you use the source code that is protected under an open source licence, you must contribute your code to the community of users ... intellectual property is not part of the business model, so piracy is not an issue.[23]

And with the all-important cost structure of non-proprietary software also radically different, its benefits and potential for countries of the South and their schools are becoming clearer on a daily basis.

Not surprisingly, protests against Microsoft's global 'lock' on computer software are starting to mount and have not been calmed by Microsoft's claim that open-source software is 'un-American' and 'an intellectual property destroyer'.[24] In June 2001, the city government in Florence, Italy passed a motion which said that the extensive use of proprietary software was creating the 'computer science subjection of the Italian state to Microsoft'.[25] French legislators are also looking at alternatives to the 'Microsoft way' and, in South America, 'software libre' has become this movement's slogan. In the Philippines, there have also been protests after Microsoft initiated a raid on illegal software at a school and threatened others with law suits.[26]

Yet the struggle to treat software as a facilitating language or tool and a foundation of our global and national public communications infrastructure – one cannot even imagine the profits to be made if a single corporation 'owned' another communications tool, the English language – is far from an easy one. In Lebanon, for example, there was vigorous opposition in its Parliament during both 1997 and 1999 to draft government legislation on the subject of computer software. A number of MPs argued that software should not be protected by copyright and, in particular, that copyright owners such as Microsoft should be required to grant a compulsory software licence to poorer students and to educational institutions.[27] This was hardly an outrageous demand, but as a result of pressures from the US software industry, Lebanon was put on a US Trade Representative Special 301 watch list (that is, given a warning that the US could decide to impose trade sanctions) for refusing to protect software and other copyright-protected works sufficiently in the US view. In the end, the multinationals got their own way. Still, I think it is safe to predict that the battle over restrictive copyright protection of software will be a key one for countries of the South in coming years.

(c) Translations and the licensing of book rights to Third World publishers

Some inspiration for such a campaign may come from the protracted battle waged by a number of African and Asian countries in the 1960s against some specific provisions of the Berne Convention and the Eurocentric philosophy of copyright generally. More than one commentator at the time labelled the conflict a 'crisis in international copyright'.[28] These countries, many of which had just gained political independence and were now trying to put a priority on mass education, literacy and economic development, proposed a number of reforms to obviously one-sided international copyright protocols. Two of their more important education-related criticisms were the inability of Third World publishers to acquire rights to translate books and materials into their own national languages and to acquire licences and reprint rights to publish books that were originally published elsewhere, but not distributed in Asia or Africa or were priced too steeply. Gaining concessions on both demands would not only assist the severely underdeveloped publishing sector in Southern countries, but also make such materials much more accessible to students and teachers alike in these countries. After a nearly seven-year-long campaign and making a number of key concessions, these countries did succeed in having an Appendix added to the Berne Convention in 1971 that was aimed at overcoming, in a very limited way, several of the previous access and use problems in developing countries. For example, the possibility of obtaining compulsory licences for translations and rights were incorporated into Berne, although, again, in restricted circumstances.

Thirty years later, severe access problems remain. The definition of what is 'a developing country' is far too restrictive; South Africa, for example, is excluded from provisions of the Appendix which means that students in Soweto are treated, for copyright purposes, as if they were living in a leafy suburb of Boston. Multinational publishers, especially British ones, often expect African publishers to be their local agents and salespersons, not 'real publishers'. Acquiring reprint and translation rights remains an overly complicated process and, as one Kenyan publisher explained, 'in the few exceptional cases where European publishers grant rights to their African counterparts, this is usually done on harsh and unfavourable terms'.[29] Writing in 1987, Ricketson bluntly concluded that ' it is hard to point to any obvious benefits that have flowed directly to the developing countries from the adoption of the Appendix'.[30] With the non-digitalised printed word still remaining so central to education in countries of the South, re-visiting these key issues and formulating a new reform strategy has clearly become a priority in the TRIPS era.

(d) The protection of folklore

Back in 1996, a German rock group named Enigma put out a hit which was near the top of the international pop charts for more than six months. 'Return to Innocence' sold more than five million copies worldwide, put the term 'world-beat' on the musical map, and even was featured as background music for advertisements promoting the 1996 Olympic Games in Atlanta. 'Return to Innocence', however, was *not* Enigma's song and the background to this musical rip-off reveals a serious limitation of copyright for countries of the South. Briefly, here is what happened:[31] a group of more than thirty indigenous singers from Taiwan was invited by the French Ministry of Culture to perform Taiwanese tribal songs at concerts across Europe. The French Ministry recorded the concerts and issued a CD which the German music magnate, Michael Cretu (à la 'Enigma'), heard and liked very much. He decided to use significant sections of this Taiwanese song in his own musical recordings; to accomplish this, Cretu purchased the rights to this music from the French Ministry. When recorded by Enigma, this music was called 'Enigma's Return to Innocence'. As for the Taiwanese folk-singers, they received neither recognition nor financial compensation; in fact, they were not even told about any of these dealings.

Under current copyright doctrine what the French Ministry and Enigma did was perfectly legal, if morally abhorrent. According to 'classic' copyright theory (and the practice of both the Berne Convention and TRIPS), a work cannot be protected unless it is original, fixated (that is, written down) and created by an individual (or perhaps by joint authors). In the case of this Taiwanese musical work, it was not 'original' (in the Western copyright sense of being linked to the independent work of a known individual author or authors), it was not written down as it arose from an oral story-telling tradition, and was the product of a communal indigenous culture and not, as the 'romantic author' conception behind copyright theory suggests, the creation of an individual starving composer (or author) living in a garret. As Riley comments, 'indigenous works fail to fulfil individualistic notions of property rights that underlie the structure of Western law'.[32]

This Eurocentric approach leads both to problems of cultural preservation, to serious misappropriation and to copyright 'rip-offs' in a wide range of art forms, including the non-consensual copying of Aboriginal art from Australia and Maori images and tattoos from New Zealand. The educational implications are also serious. Noting that African oral literatures and traditions cannot be claimed as the 'intellectual property of anybody in particular', Kenyan publisher, Henry Chavaka, explains that 'as soon as this (area) is researched into, and the material compiled and published by the researcher (most of them from the North), it becomes his [or her] copyright, and no one can use it without his permission'.[33] The 'no one' includes local publishers and classroom teachers. Access to traditional material becomes more problematic because even if, for example, a teacher seeks to avoid using the copyright version of the traditional work by, for example, inviting a traditional musician into the class, the possibility of copyright infringement arises because of the exclusive rights that copyright law grants to copyright owners (including the right to perform the work in public), as well as the law relating to indirect copying and the legal inferences that operate when two works are objectively similar (as they are likely to be in the case of the copyright version of a traditional work).

Conclusion

Writing six years ago just as TRIPS was coming into force, Philip Altbach, who has commented extensively on copyright issues in countries of the South and who, as someone connected to a publishing company, is a strong supporter of copyright, suggested that:

> Copyright, from its beginnings in England in the sixteenth century, has been a means of protecting the 'haves' – of limiting access to books and information in order to maintain order and discipline, of

creating a monopoly over knowledge ... [Today] there is no recognition that the legacy of colonialism and the power of the multinationals has, to a significant extent, created the highly unequal world knowledge system ... There is a kind of OPEC of knowledge in which a few rich nations have a great deal of control over how and where books are published, the prices of printed materials, and the nature of international exchange of knowledge ... There has, in fact, been relatively little expansion in the number of knowledge producing countries – and the price of entry into the cartel increases as the cost and complexity of knowledge production goes up.[34]

TRIPS has further consolidated this power, he wrote, before concluding that 'what is needed now is an affirmative action programme to ensure that books and knowledge products are not kept from Third World nations because of the restrictions of the copyright system'.[35]

Other Southern voices are more insistent and direct. From South Africa:

Oh the woes of the student. Where to get information? How much must we pay for information? Do we actually study? Can we afford to study? What is this thing called Intellectual Property? Do we have to pay that much for information? Do these people not realise that they are going to die one day and that the world actually belongs to the youth? ... Give us information, enlighten us, and educate us for we are the future leaders of this world. Accept the fact that we are not fools, that we understand that one has to pay your way in life and that we do and in future will pay for our leisure however, allow us the same privileges that you had. Allow us to study and become the kind of citizen of the world that they would be proud of ... Woe is the life of the modern day student living in 'Darkest Africa' for obviously we are still being kept in the slave quarters of the world. Harsh words? My friends, try and live in a society where such Acts as the Intellectual Property Acts of the world impede your advancement in life.[36]

Or from the Philippines in response to the comment from a lobbyist for the US Business Software Alliance that 'copying licensed software is a form of stealing':

If it's a sin for the poor to steal from the rich, it must be a much bigger sin for the rich to steal from the poor. Don't rich countries pirate our best scientists, engineers, doctors, nurses, and programmers?

When global corporations come to operate in the Philippines, don't they pirate the best people from local firms? If it is bad for poor countries like us to pirate the intellectual property of rich countries, isn't it a lot worse for rich countries like the United States to pirate our intellectuals? In fact, we are benign enough to take only a copy, leaving the original behind; they are so greedy they take away the originals and leave nothing for us.[37]

Yes, copyright issues are the 'sleeping giant' on the TRIPS and international educational agenda.

Notes

1. Fidel Castro (1967) Speech at Guane Ceremony in Cuba, 30 April; available from: http://lanic.utexas.edu/la/cb/cuba/castro/1967/19670430_.
2. There is no uniformly 'good' phrase that can be used to designate these countries. I have chosen the word 'the South' while recognising its limitations.
3. R.L. Gana (1995) 'Has Creativity Died in the Third World? Some Implications of the Internationalization of Intellectual Property', *Denver Journal of International Law and Policy*, vol. XXIV, p. 109.
4. Interview with South African higher education copyright expert.
5. There is not the space here to challenge this view in detail. On the question of whether there is a correlation between pharmaceutical innovation and patents, recall the comments of Dr Jonas Salk, inventor of the Salk polio vaccine in the 1950s. When asked who owned the vaccine's patent, Salk replied 'Well, the people, I would say. There is no patent. Could you patent the sun?' See: http://members.nbci.com/poliostory/salk.html. Similarly, numerous studies, including even those conducted by publishers, reveal that most academic and instructional writing (for example on how to prevent the spread of AIDS) is not motivated by a financial incentive or by the incentive of copyright. See Association of Learned and Professional Society Publishers (1999) *What Authors Want*, June. Available from: http://www.alpsp.org.uk/pubs.htm
6. On the instrumental, as opposed to 'proprietarian', purpose of IP, see P.F. Drahos (1996) *A Philosophy of Intellectual Property* (Aldershot: Dartmouth). The 'copyright' clause in the US Constitution (s. 8. subs. 8) is one of the clearest statements of an instrumental approach, though repeated US cases have ignored the words and underlying philosophy of their own constitution.
7. This tendency is perhaps most graphically represented by extending the duration of copyright (generally life of the author plus 70 years).
8. M. Cohen (1927) 'Property and Sovereignty', *Cornell Law Review*, vol. XIII, p. 8.
9. Cohen, in *ibid.*, based this 'future distributions' insight on the ownership of land and machinery, but it works equally well in the case of intellectual property. In fact, given the economics of the licensing of IP (that is, most licensing income goes straight to a company's 'bottom line' without further investment or expenditure), ownership of IP is even more determinative of future acquisitions than ownership of machinery. For example, the lyrics to the song

'Happy Birthday to You' (written in 1893, copyrighted in 1935, expiration date of 2021) have already earned copyright royalties of £39 million and the lyrics still have another twenty years to go as an earner for Warner Communications, the current owner. See A. Salamon (1981) 'On the Other Hand, You Can Blow Out the Candles for Free', *Wall Street Journal*, 12 June p. 1, col. 4.

10. Gana, 'Has Creativity Died ... ?' pp. 115–16.
11. Motion Picture Association of America (2001) 'Valenti Warns of Potentially Devastating Economic Impact of Copyright Theft', 3 April; available from: http://mpaa.org/jack/2001/2001_04_03a.htm.
12. *Ibid.* (emphasis in original).
13. 'Core copyright industries' are defined as those industries that create copyright-protected works as their primary product.
14. The International Intellectual Property Alliance (2001) *'Copyright Industries in the US Economy – The 2000 Report'*; available from: http://www.iipa.com/copyright_us_economy.html.
15. US Senate Judiciary (1996) Senate Report No. 104-315, 104th Cong. 2nd Sess. 10 July; see: http://www.public.asu.edu/~dkarjala/legmats/s483rep104-315.html#.
16. International Monetary Fund (2001) *Balance of Payments*, vol. 55.
17. The Berne Convention has been revised a number of times since 1886; the current version is available at http://www.law.cornell.edu/treaties/berne/overview.html.
18. TRIPS, Article 9.1.
19. For copyright term, see Berne Convention, Article 7.6.
20. Some countries such as France and Germany already used a life plus 70 years calculation prior to the European Duration Directive of 1993. But others, such as the United Kingdom, were required to increase their copyright term as a result of this Directive. Here is how 'life of the author plus 70 years' calculations work: if a person has a book published in 2002 and dies in the year 2040, copyright extends until 2110, regardless of who actually holds copyright. Often copyright is/must be transferred, for example to a publisher, record company or employer, at the time of publication, in this case in 2002; copyright still would not expire until 2110.
21. Earlier in 2001, the Microsoft sales office in Vietnam, for example, quoted me a roughly similar 'per desk' licence price for software at a Vietnamese university as is charged for similar software in the United States. (Details on file with author.)
22. This very brief survey necessarily omits many other issues, including the critical one of technological transfer of software development skills and how to create 'Silicon Valleys' in the South.
23. For a much fuller explication of these issues, see the unpublished paper by Halbert, D. (2001) 'Asian Futures: Piracy, Open Source and the International Intellectual Property Law', September. (On file with author.)
24. P. Festa (2001) 'Governments Push Open-source Software', *CNET News*, 29 August, available from http://news.cnet.com/news/0-1003-200-6996393.html?tag=tp_pr.
25. *Ibid.*

26. 'Philippine Greens Protest the Visit of #1 U.S. Cyberlord Bill Gates', 20 March; available from http://www.hartford-hwp.com/archives/29/048.html.
27. The International Intellectual Property Alliance (1999) *Lebanon, Report 301/99*, see http://www.iipa.com/rbc/1999/rbc_lebanon_301_99.html.
28. The most detailed account of this largely forgotten history is C.F. Johnson (1970) 'The Origins of the Stockholm Protocol', *Bulletin of the Copyright Society of the USA*, vol. XVIII, p. 91.
29. H. Chakava (1995) 'International Copyright and Africa: The Unequal Exchange' in P. Altbach (ed.), *Copyright and Development: Inequality in the Information Age* (Chestnut Hill, Mass.: Bellagio Publishing Network Research and Information Center), p. 22 (hereafter Altbach).
30. S. Ricketson (1987) *The Berne Convention for the Protection of Literary and Artistic Works: 1886–1986* (London: Centre for Commercial Law Studies), p. 663.
31. For a much fuller account of these events and an insightful solution to the problem, see A. Riley (2000) 'Recovering Collectivety: Groups Rights to Intellectual Property in Indigenous Communities', *Cardozo Arts and Entertainment Law Journal*, vol. XVIII, p. 175.
32. *Ibid.*, pp. 177–8. For more on these issues, see R.J. Coombe (1998) *The Cultural Life of Industrial Properties* (Durham, N.C.: Duke University Press).
33. Chakava, in Altbach, p. 20.
34. Altbach. 'The Subtle Inequalities of Copyright', in Altbach (ed.), *Copyright and Development*, pp. 2–6.
35. *Ibid.*, p. 6.
36. L. Szente (2001) '*Misers or Sharers?*', WIPOUT (The intellectual property counter essay contest), September; available at: http://www.wipout.net/essays/0923szente.htm.
37. R. Verzola (1996) 'It's Only Piracy if You're Poor', *Perspectives*, 18 November, available from http://www.news.com/Perspectives/Soapbox/rv11_18_96a.html.

9

Digital Millennium or Digital Dominion? The Effect of IPRs in Software on Developing Countries

Gary Lea

Introduction

In November 1998, a meeting on 'IT in the global village' organised under the auspices of the United Nations Industrial Development Organisation endorsed what is now known as the Bangalore Declaration; this document started with the proposition that information technology (IT) presented a 'historic window of opportunity' for developing nations both to create national wealth and to break the poverty cycle. The delegates, however, were cautious optimists; they recognised a number of drawbacks and dangers inherent in the development of IT infrastructure and information services including increases in debt, social/technical dislocation, loss of cultural diversity, loss of privacy and increased national security risks (Resolutions 24–7).

The Bangalore delegates may well have been right to be cautious: as *The Economist* pointed out in 'Solving the Paradox' (21 September 2000), many economists are still unsure that the big productivity gains promised for IT and predicted by their more optimistic colleagues are actually coming into play. However, if we take as a reasonable mid-point the proposition that heavy investment in IT could result in a boost to GDP growth of between 0.5 and 1 per cent per annum, this would amount to at least as great a contribution to economic development as electrification in previous decades.

What sorts of economic advantage could accrue? Leaving aside the issues of priority sectors described in Resolutions 6–7, they are, broadly speaking, the same as for developed countries:

- process automation as a major efficiency boost to industry, agriculture and commerce;
- general information access as a way to improve health, education and other public services; and
- access to a wider range of other services such as e-shopping and entertainment.

However, one major roadblock exists in creating this 'computopia': besides IT hardware, developing countries have to acquire the relevant software; for present purposes this term covers computer programs, databases, digitised content, manuals or any combination thereof, for example multimedia training products.

In one sense, obtaining software is not difficult, even today: if one goes to the markets or bazaars of virtually any developing country, one can find unauthorised copies of many different types of software for a small fee even in the local currency. The Internet, too, has allowed both infra- and international distribution of electronic copies of software and, according to the International Intellectual Property Alliance's (IIPA) 2000 Report to the US Trade Representative, one fairly recent example of the impact of these various modes of availability is that in 1999, approximately 97 per cent of the software used in Vietnam was unauthorised: 'street' copies retailed for between 1 and 10 per cent of estimated retail price.

The real issue, of course, is what one makes of these figures: many in the developed world, and particularly those in the software industry, regard this as straightforward 'piracy', a breach of intellectual property (IP) rules and a loss of revenue. By contrast, many in the developing world regard it as a necessary, if not legitimate, type of 'technology transfer' as the recommended retail price for the product is simply too high for the local economy to bear.

When we talk of a breach of IP rules, though, what sorts of IPRs are *potentially* involved? Leaving aside trademark issues arising in relation to packaging or labelling, there are two: copyright/neighbouring rights and patents. Later, we must also add consideration of protection afforded when encryption, watermarking or other content security measures are taken but, to start, note how the IPRs 'accumulate'; taking a CD-ROM multimedia teaching package as an example, see how it acts as the physical embodiment of a number of different types of material to which many different rights may attach:

CD-ROM – Multimedia Teaching Package

(a) Copyright and neighbouring rights
The bundle of rights may include:

- copyright in literary works, e.g. program code and textual data
- copyright in artistic works, e.g. illustrations, displays and other static visual data
- copyright in musical works, e.g. song tunes
- copyright/neighbouring rights in cinematographic/audiovisual works, e.g. video clips
- neighbouring rights in sound recordings, e.g. audio clips

(b) Patent law
There may be patents over one or more inventions embedded or realised in the software (e.g. a method for ensuring effective video/audio streaming from CD-ROM)

In principle, carrying out an act which falls within the bounds of the rights listed above is infringement unless it is done with authorisation by the relevant rights holder or by law: in practice, the law of the country concerned may not extend to the material(s) in question and, even if it does, the civil or criminal sanctions for infringement may be inherently weak and/or limited through poor enforcement-mechanisms. In the case of Oman, for example, there was no copyright system at all until a Royal Decree of 1996 and, even when the Decree came into effect, there were no mechanisms for enforcement of rights in software until the Copyright Enforcement Decree 1998 was amended with effect from 1 July 1999.

One may well ask why Oman changed its law given the obvious developmental advantage of having no protection and 'freeriding'? The answer, of course, lies in the ever-tightening noose of international trade and IP agreements, a noose with trade sanctions woven through as the reinforcing thread.

A brief global history of software protection: 1964–1992

Until the 1970s, IP issues relating to software were largely of academic interest: the number of computers in use was fairly small, even in developed countries, and software was usually supplied as a bundle with hardware. The consequence was that users were tied very closely by sales and service contracts to the software providers.

However, the leading producer-consumer, the United States, saw a change in industry patterns during the 1970s: following on from a US antitrust settlement agreement by IBM to unbundle software in 1969, the development and mass-marketing of microcomputers and PCs attenuated the hitherto normal contractual links as software was increasingly developed by independent producers: accordingly, the US was faced with software industry calls to provide some form of intellectual property protection to its products, protection not dependent on contract with the customer *per se*. The question, then, was the form that protection might take.

Outside the US, there had been relatively little by way of legislation but the dominant view in proposals of the time was that the computer program element of software required a tailor-made or *sui generis* form of protection; this was because, whilst there were no problems with manuals and similar elements of software, there were doubts as to how the 'core' part of the product might fit into the existing copyright and patent framework.

Within the US during the 1970s, however, the emphasis began to be put on copyright as the main vehicle for program protection; because the US Copyright Office had been dealing administratively with programs as works since 1964, there was no real push to build on *sui generis* protection proposals. Nor was there any real inclination towards using the patents system; this was because, for reasons of administrative convenience, the US Patent Office had issued restrictive guidelines on patenting software technology in 1968 and the Supreme Court had subsequently issued a decision which appeared even more limiting (*Gottschalk v. Benson* 409 US 63 (1972)).

The US Copyright Act 1976, although supposedly neutrally drafted to maintain the status quo pending a report by the Commission on New Technological Uses (CONTU), contained several provisions which would make program protection easier, in particular the widening out of the definition of copies to cover electronic copies properly and the expansion of the definition of 'works' to cover any mode of expression. In 1978, the CONTU Report accepted, by a majority, that copyright should be extended to computer programs; this was done by the Computer Software Copyright Act 1980.

What was the significance of this for the rest of the world? At first, not a great deal: indeed, because of the poor drafting of the 1980 Act it took nearly four years for the US Federal courts to decide what had actually been intended. However, following *Apple Computer Inc v. Franklin Computer Corp* 714 F 2d 1240 (3rd Cir., 1984), it was clear that computer programs were to be treated, regardless of form or mode of expression, as literary works. Subsequently, however, the US approach to these matters was vital: the growth of the US software industry to span the globe led to increasing interest in and concern about the international trade issues arising from poor/limited protection in other countries. In short, the US began to consider the battle to protect software as a significant part of its trade war.

The first real casualty of the software war was not, in fact, a developing country and nor was the problem with a lack of protection: in 1983, Japan announced proposals for *sui generis* protection which featured a short protection period and compulsory licensing provisions. The US response to this, however, sent out a stark warning and set the tone for all future dealings in this area: its trade representative made representations to the Japanese Government in 1984 that protection should be through copyright and that the level of protection should be the same as that under US law. Failing that, an investigation would be launched under Trade Act 1974, s. 301, which, if it established inadequate protection of software IPRs, would result in withdrawal of trade concessions, higher import duties and market access restrictions. Perhaps unsurprisingly, the Japanese Government and Diet introduced what became the Author's Right Amendment Law 1985; by this time, WIPO proposals for *sui generis* protection had also been quietly dropped.

The first developing countries to face such hard-line tactics were South Korea (1985) and, subsequently, Malaysia; in both cases, the countries concerned were 'encouraged' to join at least the Universal Copyright Convention (UCC) and, preferably, the Berne Convention whilst, at the same time, introducing specific provisions for software protection. By the late 1980s, such cases were becoming commonplace as the 'special 301' procedures (see Chapter 10 by Peter Drahos in this volume) were made available under the Omnibus Trade and Competitiveness Act 1988: as Poland and Taiwan found, the monitoring system and 'fast-track' sanctions system made trade sanctions both a greater threat and a greater weapon if used.

The US, it is true, did not specifically 'pick out' developing countries at this point: in its 1992 Report, the IIPA placed both Germany and Italy on their proposed watch list with estimated piracy rates of 76 per cent and 82 per cent respectively. However, it is vital to remember that Germany and Italy always had the ability to pay for the software in question and, following the entry into force of EC harmonisation measures on program protection in that year, their piracy rates began to drop steeply. Thus, by the mid-1990s it was increasingly the case that developing countries were 'in the frame' and neither concessions nor recognition of their difficulties was forthcoming; indeed, as we will see, they were being exacerbated by ever stricter international IP protection and trade rules.

Prior 'failure to accommodate': the copyright and technology transfer initiatives

The great irony was that, in previous decades, some limited efforts had been made to try and provide support mechanisms for developing countries within the international IP and trade frameworks. Regrettably, however, both main initiatives were petering out even as the issue of software protection was moving to centre stage.

In relation to copyright, the issue of the position of developing countries had become a major issue by the 1960s. The senior copyright convention, Berne, had been revised in 1948 to increase the overall level of protection applied to works and to remove most instances of the ability of countries to make 'reservations' (that is, to register to disapply certain provisions); this had caused difficulties for many newly independent countries and some, such as Indonesia, had even withdrawn from the system altogether. Some relief had been afforded by the creation of a less-demanding sister convention, the UCC, in 1952 but those developing countries which were attached to Berne – usually a position 'inherited' after separation from a colonial power – were barred by a reservation clause in Berne from switching straight to the less onerous UCC system.

The Berne Convention was revised at Stockholm in 1967 and, as part of the package, a so-called 'Protocol' was developed which gave developing countries a number of concessions on the copyright protection they were obliged to offer:

(a) copyright term could be reduced;
(b) translation rights would end after a set time unless used;
(c) subject to certain conditions, compulsory licences could be granted to translate even within the currency of translation rights;
(d) subject to certain conditions, reproductions in the original language could be made for 'educational or cultural purposes' without authorisation;
(e) subject to certain conditions, broadcasts of works could be made without authorisation and, partially overlapping with but exceeding all the above;
(f) compulsory licences could be granted where the end use was for educational research or study.

The Protocol never came into force because of rearguard opposition from a number of developed countries in the shape of failures to ratify; this precipitated a near-breakdown of relations in the copyright system and the creation of a further revision to Berne at Paris in 1971. The replacement for the Protocol was an Appendix to the Paris Act, which provided watered-down provisions allowing translation or reproduction in the original language under very tightly controlled circumstances. Few developing countries took up the allowances under Appendix and, of those which did, few made much use because of the in-built limitations: as at 15 July 2001, only 8 of the 148 members of the Berne Union had taken advantage. Nor was there any additional help to be gained under the UCC; this was revised in tandem with Berne at Paris in 1971 and so its 'help' provisions are virtually identical: see Articles V-V$_{quater}$.

In principle, in the case of computer programs and databases, the position was complicated because of their uncertain classification status: whilst the *domestic* laws of countries began to treat programs as literary works from the start of the 1980s, it was by no means clear that this was the case for Berne or the UCC and these doubts were not to be entirely resolved until the 1990s. The reason that programs and databases were not dealt with at Paris was because, at that stage, it was by no means clear whether existing IPRs would be adapted to embrace them or whether new *sui generis* forms of protection would be created. However, as has been shown, such niceties had no bearing on whether or not the US could demand protection *as if* programs were literary works within Berne or the UCC.

On the patent side of the fence, there were also complications. In 1980, attempts were made to revise the Paris Convention, the senior industrial property convention which, *inter alia*, provided for patent 'national treatment' (i.e. allowing those from signatory state X to enjoy the same rights in respect of patent matters in signatory state Y as any national of Y) and 'priority' (that is, in effect, backdating of applications to filing dates in other Convention countries); these efforts included proposed measures allowing use of patented technologies in developing countries but political and business pressures prevented any changes from being implemented.

In one sense, this did not matter as computer programs, one of the 'core' pieces of any software product, were pushed out of the scope of the patent system during the 1970s: initially, the Rules of the Patent Cooperation Treaty 1970, which put in place a filing, search and preliminary examination system for applications designating a number of countries, stated that applications involving computer programs did not have to be searched or examined to the extent that the relevant international authority did not have the ability to do so. However, following US practice, countries and regional patent groupings progressively began to exclude programs from patentability *per se*: see Article 52, European Patent Convention 1973.

The hidden difficulty here was that any limitations or doubts on the role of patents or copyright in relation to computer programs protection (a) had absolutely no bearing on whether software technologies were positively being 'made available' and (b) did not mean that there were other forms of IP relating to software as a whole which could not be licensed (for example, copyright in training manuals, trade secrets/ know-how for use or development). The same lack of provision of other – patentable – technologies without expensive and onerous patent/ know-how licence agreements had lead to a push in the 1970s for so-called 'technology transfer' under the aegis of the United Nations Conference on Trade and Development (UNCTAD). Starting in 1976, UNCTAD set about the task of creating an international Code on Technology Transfer; this would have, amongst other things, controlled or eliminated certain practices of royalty pricing and restrictive terms which had hampered take-up of advanced technologies in developing countries. Once again, however, progress was stifled by a hardening of attitude amongst developed countries and work on the Code stopped in 1985. Thereafter, not only were old licensing practices retained but dealings of all sorts were increasingly put on a strictly commercial, rather than humanitarian, footing.

In summary, none of the initiatives in the copyright, patent or technology transfer field to assist developing countries which had started in the 1970s bore any fruit. What made matters worse was that, in the 1980s and 1990s, the increasing reliance of developed countries on revenues from intangibles such as services and IPRs for GDP growth meant that political and economic pressure was to swing the trade and IP policy towards tighter, rather than looser, control over activities in developing countries.

TRIPS

Until the 1980s, developing countries could, as we have seen, restrict IPR protection in a number of ways: having no IP legislation, withdrawing from the international agreements or failing to enforce whatever laws existed. From the 1980s onwards, there was the risk of trade sanctions by the developed countries affected; this, however, was a risk that, even in the case of the US, many were still prepared to take, particularly given that there were no positive legal requirements for them to do otherwise.

During the development of the 1986–1993 Uruguay Round of the General Agreement on Tariffs and Trade (GATT), things were to change dramatically: starting out from a modest proposal to deal with counterfeit goods, a negotiating strand developed which was to expand dramatically into the Agreement on Trade-Related Aspects of Intellectual Property Rights (TRIPS). In brief, the aim of TRIPS was to ensure two things: (a) broad and strong minimum standards of protection across a wide range of IPRs; and, perhaps even more significantly, (b) direct legal responsibility for enforcement to fall on all the signatories.

Why did the vast majority of developing countries agree to sign up to what ultimately emerged? Apart from the usual threats of trade sanctions, the US, EC member states and other developed countries held out two incentives: the immediate prospect of concessions on agricultural products and textiles; and the future prospect of greater foreign direct investment (FDI) by virtue of possession of 'suitable' IP regimes. Thus, ironically, the strict imposition of monopolies and quasi-monopolies in the shape of IPRs came to be a part of the progressive moves towards global free trade, a far cry from the grudging permission to have IPRs under Article XX, GATT.

Leaving aside the requirements relating to enforcement such as full availability of interim remedies, damages and final injunctions (Articles 41–61), TRIPS required its signatories to offer protection which covered *and* exceeded the relevant existing IP treaties for each IPR (so-called 'Convention plus') *even if* the signatory was not a signatory to the relevant treaty or treaties. The 'Convention plus' TRIPS provisions affecting software can be summarised as follows:

TRIPS

Art. 10(1): Computer programs to be treated as literary works under Berne.

Art. 10(2): Compilations of data and other material to be accorded copyright if, by reason of selection or arrangement, they are 'intellectual creations'. Copyright under this head does not extend to the data/material and does not affect any other copyright(s) therein.

Art. 11: Copyright to be extended to provide a rental (control) right in the case of, *inter alia*, computer programs.

Art. 27: Patents to be granted for inventions in all fields of technology provided they are new, show inventive step and are capable of industrial application. The number of exclusions which signatories could impose was limited and did *not* expressly include computer programs.

TRIPS imposed a rolling timetable for implementation of its measures: save for a limited number of special exemptions for the least developed countries (Article 66), signatories were obliged to adjust their laws and administrative practices by 1 January 2000. Finally, it should be noted that a number of Articles have in-built review processes; whilst there is still considerable debate on the matter, it is likely that these reviews will be rolled together to create the basis for the creation of a new TRIPS round which will tighten protection still further. Perhaps unsurprisingly, the governments of many developing countries are worried, hoping that, at least for a few decades, TRIPS would be a 'ceiling' rather than a 'floor' for their international IPR obligations.

The reality is that TRIPS has made 'freeriding' a considerably more difficult option to pick; this is particularly so in the case of software since the copyright status doubts over computer programs and databases are effectively eliminated. The impact, too, of Article 27, which appears to mandate computer program patentability by the back door (see below), is also considerable. A developing country now has a stark choice: either forgo the trade advantages under World Trade Organization (WTO) membership or work on the TRIPS package. In this context, the fact that, as at the beginning of 2002, 144 countries and territories were WTO members compared with a UN membership list of 189 speaks for itself.

The WTO is an international organisation which came into existence on 1 January 1995 as a result of the Uruguay Round; it acts as the administrator for previous (GATT) and future (WTO) trade agreements, a forum for trade negotiation and a handling body for trade disputes. A key question here – could a country join WTO and pay lip-service to TRIPS? Beyond the short term, no because: (a) there are monitoring and review systems which oblige WTO members to inform the relevant authorities of their progress in TRIPS implementation and, perhaps more significantly, (b) once transitional measures expire, it is possible *in extremis* for a member to be punished for non-compliance following complaint by another: failing settlement under the procedures of the Dispute Settlement Body (DSB), Articles 22.2 and 22.6, WTO Agreement allows a complainant country to implement trade sanctions where authorised by the DSB.

Although no disputes relating to software IPRs have gone through the WTO system yet, an example from the wider ambit of copyright is instructive in how no country can avoid imposing stronger protection: in *US/Section 110(5) of the US Copyright Act* (DS/160/R, 2000), the EC and others had complained against the US about the so-called 'homestyle' and 'business exemption' exceptions to copyright; these were supposed to allow otherwise infringing public performances of works via domestic-type audio-visual in small bars and restaurants and, latterly under more generous terms, certain other businesses. The EC's argument was that s. 110.5 as amended was too widely drafted in terms of size of outlet and the current lack of any real technological difference between 'domestic' and 'professional' audio-visual equipment; it was allowing, in effect, a massive loophole which deprived musicians of licensing royalties from public performance licensing. The DSB agreed in relation to the second (business exemption) part; relying on Article 13 of TRIPS, it held that it was not permissible to create exceptions to copyright that were so broad as to 'conflict with normal exploitation of the work and unreasonably prejudice the rightholder's legitimate expectations'.

Given all the above, it is unfortunate that, still, behind TRIPS lurks the spectre of unilateral action by developed nations: TRIPS was supposed to eliminate this possibility but it would appear that the US and many others still retain their capacity to strike out. Whilst the DSB report in *US/Sections 301–304 of the US Trade Act 1974* (DS/152/R, 1999) indicated that the US trade disputes system was in line with the Dispute Settlement Understanding upon which WTO dispute-settlement procedures are founded, nevertheless it observed that this was only because of current administrative practice and policy rather than in-built statutory limitation.

Furthermore, the US and many other developed countries still press on with bilateral trade negotiations which are, often, only loosely connected to the WTO framework: in particular, it is not uncommon for such bilateral deals to provide standards of IP protection even higher than those currently mandated by TRIPS, e.g. under the US–Vietnam Bilateral Trade Agreement 2000, Vietnam was not only obliged to provide TRIPS cover but additionally to establish IPRs in respect of satellite signals.

The WIPO Copyright Treaty

Those countries that are already signatories to Berne now have the option of joining up to the WIPO Copyright Treaty 1996 (WCT); this, together with its sister convention on performers' rights and rights in phonogram recordings (WIPO Performances and Phonograms Treaty 1996), provides 'advanced' copyright protection which, in reality, will probably represent the substantive 'floor' of copyright-protection levels under TRIPS Round 2.

What does WCT do that is different from Berne? It does three significant things: (a) increase the range of protected subject matter; (b) expand the range of modes of disseminating works which are regarded as infringing acts; and (c) introduce a requirement to provide civil and criminal remedies to prevent any interference with technical measures to restrict access to copyright content (for example, encryption, access codes) or any rights management information (RMI) related to the same.

In terms of subject matter, the changes are not radical if viewed from the perspective of TRIPS; Articles 4 and 5 are very similar to Articles 10.1 and 10.2 in the latter agreement. Moving on to the issue of dissemination, the same is also true for the rental right (Article 7) but the creation of a freestanding right of distribution (Article 6) and a uniform right to control communication to the public (Article 8) goes well beyond TRIPS, let alone Berne. The combined effect of Articles 6 to 8 is to prevent *any* physical *or* electronic dissemination (for example via the Internet) of protected works unless authorised by the rightsholder or by law. Whilst Article 10 WCT still allows for certain special case exceptions (for example permitted acts, fair uses, free uses), it will doubtless be interpreted restrictively (see, by analogy, the WTO 'home-style' decision above).

Perhaps, though, the most far-reaching effect will not be from the copyright changes but the imposition of controls relating to technical measures and RMI under Articles 11 and 12; this could prove to be 'the tail that wags the dog'. First of all, there are no express requirements, even permissions, for exceptions or limitations on these controls; certainly, the first efforts at implementing them (for example provisions in the Digital Millennium Copyright Act 1998 in the US and the 2001 Directive on Copyright in the Information Society in the EU) have far fewer exceptions/limitations than copyright. The problem is that, since the rights run parallel to copyright, where material is both copyright-protected and subject to qualifying technical measures/RMI, then permission to use could still be required in relation to the latter *even if* a permitted act or fair use applies to the former.

Secondly, and perhaps more difficult from a developing-country point of view, is that unlike the purely legal protection of copyright, proper technical measures would form a direct and immediate barrier to use of the protected subject matter (for example computer program, database, digitised content). Whilst, of course, no technical measure is likely to prove 'uncrackable' over more than the medium term, nevertheless it is yet another hurdle to the easy acquisition of software.

Finally, it is worth noting that as WCT is adopted and its provisions are reflected in national law, it will become increasingly easy to launch cross-border lawsuits relating to infringement of software IPRs elsewhere. Within the EU, the Brussels Convention and its successor instruments have already made it possible to sue in other member states: the creation of ever more uniform and widely drafted IP laws will make the issue of choice of law much easier once the basic question of jurisdiction is established. At the international level, the proposed creation of a new Hague Convention on Jurisdiction and Foreign Judgments in Civil and Commercial Matters is likely to have the same impact.

Software patenting

One phenomenon which has added to the burden of problems for developing countries is the re-emergence of software patenting. Starting with the decision of the Supreme Court in *Diamond v. Diehr* 450 US 175 (1981), the US authorities slowly lowered the barrier to patenting of software-related inventions (SRIs): by the time of *State Street v. Signature Financial* 149 F 3d 1368 (Fed. Cir., 1998) and *AT&T v. Excel* 176 F 3d 1352 (Fed. Cir., 1999), provided that the SRI in question was not a pure idea, pure discovery or pure mathematical formula, it could be patented – previously barred subject matter such as e-business method patents and applied mathematical techniques had, by then, become fair game.

Naturally, just as with the development of copyright in computer programs, the change in the US domestic line was rapidly reflected in international trade and IP policy: the ultimate wording of TRIPS, Article 27 was, one might conclude, designed to allow the pushing forward of the desirability of software patenting. The US and US corporations have certainly pushed hard for the *State Street/AT&T* approach to be reflected in patent laws elsewhere: for example, the US Government has agreed with Jordan that the latter will, in effect, apply *State Street/AT&T* criteria to SRI patentability (see, related to the US–Jordan Free Trade Agreement 2000, Article 5, Memorandum of Understanding on IP Protection) and, relying on TRIPS, Article 27, IBM has successfully limited the effect of the computer program exclusion under European Patent Convention (EPC), Article 52 (see *IBM/Computer programs II* T1173/97 [2000] EPOR 219). Following software industry representations, it is likely that the EU will remove the bars to patentability of SRIs under member state law as part of a 'harmonisation' measure; if this happens, the EPC will almost certainly have to be revised to drop the bar altogether. In short, if the EU is unable to resist US pressure on this issue, it is highly unlikely that developing countries will.

A final additional problem for developing countries in relation to the effect of software patents is that, at least in relation to the Internet and other international networks, the structure of *existing* infringement rules makes it possible for a person to infringe a US or other developed-country patent without even being in the jurisdiction: in effect, State Street and US law can have extraterritorial effect.

Where now and where next?

From a position of being able to 'freeride', at the present time, developing countries are faced with the following in relation to software:

- Strong IP protection with multiple IPRs involved;
- Strong technical measures/RMI controls coming on-stream;
- Increasing ease of cross-border lawsuits to control infringement;
- A set of international trade agreements that makes minimal (and shrinking) concession to developmental status;
- No mechanisms built into the IP treaties to ameliorate the burden; and
- No technology transfer agreements to ameliorate the burden.

Assuming the developed countries wish to help, what can they do? The next real point where these issues could be raised and dealt with would be at any hypothetical TRIPS II Conference; so, in the first instance, time must be set aside and suitable agenda entries drawn up.

The real trick will be to work out what form the necessary changes should take but, for the moment, we can identify four broad and non-exclusive groups:

- special 'developing country' IPR limitations/exceptions;
- technology transfer controls;
- 'pharma-style' pricing reforms; and
- (other) voluntary measures.

Whilst doubtless effective if well drafted, it is unlikely that IPR limitations/exceptions, even if time-limited, will be any more acceptable to developed countries today than they were in the Berne Protocol era; having pushed to raise IPR protection levels, they will not see the 'net' level slip.

Turning to technology transfer, this would probably be more acceptable and there is no reason why the draft UNCTAD Code work abandoned in

1985 could not be picked up as a basis for this: ensuring fair and reasonable licensing practice has become an important competition/antitrust issue so there is less reason to deny it in the international domain.

Perhaps the single most effective measure, whether integrated with, linked to or standing apart from TRIPS II, would be to deal with the cause of so much piracy: pricing. If software producers were prepared to offer cheaper developing-country pricing in return for proper monitoring and preventive work against re-export or re-transmission of software by the relevant national authorities, the problem would begin to disappear. With decent localisation of product, local support schemes and judicious use of technical measures/RMI controls, users in developing countries could not only be pulled away from pirate materials but positively encouraged to switch.

Under other voluntary measures, we can place the final hope that the software industry will ultimately recognise the principle that as much can be achieved by carrot as by stick: why don't the software producers team up with the hardware producers to provide low-cost second-user systems and software as part of a concerted, large-scale aid scheme?

If none of these reforms comes to pass, developing countries will continue to be disadvantaged but there is one possible scenario that should both give heart to them and, at the same time, strike fear into software producers: the eventual emergence of competing products, processes and even technical standards from developing countries that have adopted non-proprietary software, a possibility explored and supported by Alan Story in Chapter 8 of this volume. In January 2000, the Institute of Software, Chinese Academy of Sciences (ISCAS) announced the launch of Red Flag Linux, a sophisticated Chinese development of the globally popular operating system; at that time, there were reports that the PRC Government was planning to stop the official use of proprietary software such as Windows and, whilst this has not happened, Red Flag is being used as a platform to give Chinese programmers just the sort of resources necessary to develop world-leading technologies. The message, then, is clear: there is both a moral and a commercial imperative for software industry-leaders to consider how they can extend genuine and long-lasting help to developing countries; if they do not, they will suffer the consequences on both counts.

Part III

Knowledge and Access: Who Makes the Rules?

10
Negotiating Intellectual Property Rights: Between Coercion and Dialogue

Peter Drahos

Why did England in the seventeenth century begin a journey that would lead it to economic growth and empire while Spain began one that would lead to its economic contraction? One suggestion is that the long run performance of economies has much to do with efficiently defined property rights (North, 1990). Designed in the right way property rights will reduce negative externalities, allow for bargaining and avoid tragedies of the commons. Naturally, this gives rise to the question of how a society arrives at a set of efficient property rights. The economist, Douglass North (1990), suggests that it probably has something to do with democratic institutions.

The claim that democracy and efficiency are linked is a claim worth taking seriously. The next section of this chapter suggests that the link between the two has much to do with bargaining under conditions of non-domination. The chapter then proceeds to examine the conditions under which international intellectual property regimes have emerged, including the Agreement on Trade-Related Aspects of Intellectual Property Rights (TRIPS). Intellectual property regimes are an example of regulatory globalisation. If the connection between efficiency and democracy holds at the national level it may also hold at the international level. The global welfare effects of these regimes may be dependent upon democratic processes of international bargaining. The second and third sections of the chapter show that, to date, international standard-setting in intellectual property has proceeded under conditions that do not correspond to the ideal of bargaining amongst equally well-informed and resourced international actors. The fourth section discusses the current strategy of the US and EU on TRIPS. The final section of the chapter sets out a reform agenda for TRIPS based on the use of dialogic webs.

Democracy, efficiency and property rights

Efficiency in the case of intellectual property rights is generally thought to involve a balance between rules of appropriation and rules of diffusion (Easterbrook, 1981). Overly strong intellectual property protection leads to the problem of excessive monopoly costs of intellectual property rights while weak protection leads to the problem of excessive freeriding and therefore underinvestment in innovation. The difficult trick for any legislature is to find a balance between the rules of appropriation and the rules of diffusion in the case of intellectual property rights.

Are there reasons to think that in democracies this balance is likely to be struck in ways that produce efficiency? Economic theory suggests that bargaining amongst self-interested and rational actors can produce efficient outcomes by allowing resources to go to those actors who value them most (Cooter and Ulen, 1997, ch. 4). The link between bargaining and democracy probably lies in the fact that democracies are better at supplying those networks of institutions that allow for all kinds of bargaining amongst citizens to take place. These institutions include contract, property and the rule of law. Even more important though is the fact that a rights-based democratic culture allows for the formation of interest groups which bargain over resources that matter to them. This is one explanation for why democracies have proved to be better than communist societies at moving towards environmental regimes that to some extent reflect the true costs of using environmental resources. One can imagine an interest-group model of democracy in which bargaining takes place amongst equally well-resourced and -informed groups. In a democracy where producer and consumer interests in the production of information were equally well represented and where those interests had roughly equal powers of influence one might expect an efficient set of intellectual property rules to develop. Consumers would concede that some level of intellectual property was necessary in order to secure dynamic efficiency, but would not agree to rules that unduly restricted the diffusion of information or competition in markets.

There are also reasons why democracies might fail to arrive at efficient definitions of intellectual property rights. For example, Mancur Olson's (1965) theory that diffuse public interests will go unrepresented because the costs to individuals of organising large groups will be outweighed by the small gains to each individual might lead to the prediction that small numbers of intellectual property producers are more likely to organise than large numbers of consumers of intellectual property. And then, even if producer and consumer interest groups are equally well represented, inequalities of power might destroy the efficient balance of intellectual property rules that bargaining might otherwise deliver. Both healthcare consumers and pharmaceutical companies lobby in Congress, but it is only the Pharmaceutical Research and Manufacturers Association that has 297 lobbyists working for it – one for every two Congressional representatives.[1]

The same tensions that exist between producers and consumers of intellectual property at the national level also exist at the international level amongst the community of states (Subramanian, 1991). Most states are in the position of being net importers of intellectual property rights. Certainly all developing countries are in this category. For countries which are importers of intellectual property the temptation is not to recognise the intellectual property rights of foreigners, thereby allowing for the possibility that their nationals will be able to freeride on the research and development activities of foreigners. For exporters of intellectual property rights the aim is to extend the length and breadth of intellectual property rights in order to gain the maximum return from the trade in intellectual property rights and the goods and services to which they relate.

At least some of the tensions between intellectual property exporters and importers may be resolved through a process of negotiation. A state which had industries that engaged in freeriding on the R&D of another state's industries might agree not to export copied products to the latter state's markets in exchange for that state doing nothing about the freeriding. In order for cooperative solutions to emerge amongst states, conditions of democratic bargaining have to obtain. This allows genuine bargaining to take place. Domination by either producer or consumer states is less likely to produce international standards of intellectual property that promote efficiency gains.

In order for democratic bargaining to take place amongst sovereign states at least three conditions need to obtain. First, all relevant interests have to be represented in the negotiating process (*the condition of representation*). (This condition, however, entails neither the participation of all at all stages nor equality of outcome for all interests.) Secondly, all those involved in the negotiation must have full information about the consequences of various possible outcomes (*the condition of full information*). Thirdly, one party must not coerce the others (*the condition of non-domination*). The use of coercion to overcome the will of another is the very antithesis of negotiation. If robbed by a gunman, most of us would say not that we had been the victims of a negotiation, but rather the victims of a robbery. In the two sections that follow we ask to what extent international intellectual property standard-setting has met the three conditions that characterise democratic bargaining.

Empires and coercion: intellectual property's past

The international movement of intellectual property rights has been from developed to developing countries. It has largely been a spread from key Western states with strong intellectual property exporting lobbies to developing countries. There are some exceptions to this. Prior to the beginning of liberalisation in Vietnam in 1986 its intellectual property laws were modelled on those of the former Soviet Union.

In most cases the transplant of intellectual property laws to developing countries has been the outcome of processes of empire-building and colonisation. For example, in parts of pre-independent Malaysia it was English copyright law that applied (Tee, 1994). Patent law in the Philippines also reveals the forces of empire at work. While the Philippines remained a Spanish colony, it was Spanish patent law that applied. After December 1898 when the US took over the running of the Philippines, patent applications from the Philippines went to the US Patent and Trademark Office and were assessed under US law (Astudillo, 1999). The direction of Korean patent law was affected by military conflict. In 1910 the Japanese replaced Korean patent law with their own. In 1946 Korea acquired another patent law as a consequence of US military administration. In the 1980s South Korea was amongst the first to have its intellectual property laws targeted by the US under US trade laws. India had a patent law before many European countries, having acquired one in 1856 while under British colonial rule.

Colonialism had a profound impact on the expansion of copyright (Ricketson, 1987). Four major colonial powers ratified the Berne Convention for the Protection of Literary and Artistic Works (Berne Convention) in 1887, the year in which it came into force: France, Germany, Spain and the UK. Each of these colonial powers included their territories, colonies and protectorates in their accession to the Convention. The Berne system was run to suit the interests of copyright exporters. Each successive revision of the Berne brought with it a higher set of copyright standards. By the time many countries shed their colonial status, they were confronted by a Berne system that was run by an Old World club of former or diminished colonial powers to suit their economic interests. Former colonial powers continued to watch over their former colonies. When eleven Sub-Saharan states joined Berne they were 'so totally dependent economically and culturally upon France (and Belgium) and so inexperienced in copyright matters that their adherence was, in effect, politically dictated by the 'mother country' during the aftermath of reaching independence' (Lazar, 1971, p. 14).

After World War II many developing countries that had been colonies became independent states. Some of them began to review the operation of the intellectual property systems that had been left to them by their colonisers. So, for example, after India's independence two expert committees conducted a review of the Indian patent system. They concluded that the Indian patent system had failed 'to stimulate inventions among Indians and to encourage the development and exploitation of new inventions' (Vedaraman, 1972, p. 43). Interestingly, India did not choose to abandon patent law as a tool of regulatory policy, but instead to redesign it to suit her own national circumstances – a country with a low R&D base, with a large population of poor people and having some of the highest drug prices in the world. Passed in 1970, India's new patent law followed the German system of allowing the patenting of methods or processes that led to drugs, but not allowing the patenting of the drugs themselves.

India was not the only country that began to reform its patent law. During the 1970s Brazil, Argentina, Mexico and the Andean Pact countries all passed laws that saw patent rights in the pharmaceutical area weakened. Developing country generic manufacturers also became a threat to the Western pharmaceutical cartels that had dominated the international pharmaceutical industry. Mexico's entry into the manufacture of steroids in the 1960s, for example, contributed to the end of the European cartel that had dominated production until then (Gereffi, 1983). Developing countries, in adjusting their intellectual property laws to suit their national interests, were only doing what they had observed developed countries doing. So, for example, fearing the might of the German chemical industry the UK changed its patent law in 1919 to prevent the patentability of chemical compounds.

During the 1960s and 1970s developing countries began to ask questions about the international standards of intellectual property that had emerged in previous decades, particularly in relation to the two main conventions, the Paris Convention and the Berne Convention. The theme of these questions was always the same. Were the international standards tilted too far towards the appropriation of knowledge rather than its diffusion? Developing countries sought adjustments to both the international copyright regime and the international patent regime. In both cases they were unsuccessful. Their attempts to adjust copyright rules to meet their needs in mass education precipitated a crisis in international copyright in the 1960s (see Chapter 8 by Alan Story in this volume). Similarly, the attempts to revise the Paris Convention broke down. The Paris Union, once a quiet club devoted to the elevation of the international patent regime, became a battleground. Developing countries began to push a reform agenda that would enable them to gain access to the technology of multinationals on favourable terms. The fiercest debates took place over the revision of compulsory licensing of patented technology (Mills, 1985). The revision of the Paris Convention that had begun in 1980 was never completed.

The disappointments of the 1970s in intellectual property standard-setting led the US in the 1980s to adopt a strategy of forum-shifting (Braithwaite and Drahos, 2000, ch. 24). In fora such as WIPO, UNCTAD and UNESCO, the US faced the problem that developing-country blocs could defeat its proposals on intellectual property or advance their own. The US began to argue that the issue of intellectual property protection should become the subject of a multilateral trade negotiation within the General Agreement on Tariffs and Trade (GATT). The GATT was a forum in which the US was the single most influential player. Largely because of the efforts of the US and the US big-business community the Ministerial Declaration, which in 1986 launched the Uruguay Trade Round, listed the trade-related aspects of intellectual property rights as a subject for negotiation. When in 1994 Ministers met to sign the Final Act of the Round, TRIPS was there as a multilateral trade agreement binding on all members of the future World Trade Organization (WTO).

TRIPS and democratic bargaining

Someone who was interested in defending TRIPS might argue that it was an agreement that was produced as a result of bargaining amongst sovereign and equal states all having the capacity to conclude treaties and which agreed to TRIPS as part of a larger package of trade-offs in which there were gains for all. This line of defence becomes stronger if one can show that some form of democratic bargaining did take place amongst states on TRIPS. Conversely, if TRIPS does not meet the minimal conditions of democratic bargaining this raises questions about its efficiency, as well as its legitimacy.

The first condition of democratic bargaining requires that developing-country interests were represented at the TRIPS negotiations. On the face of it this condition seems to be met. Not all developing states participated in the TRIPS negotiations, but key developing-country leaders on intellectual property, most notably India and Brazil, did send negotiators. Lying behind representation in democratic bargaining is the idea that the representatives have some continuity of voice in the process. In other words, exclusion must not be practised. Here the track record of the GATT was not very good from a developing-country perspective. This was one of the reasons why the US had chosen it as a forum for intellectual property. In the Tokyo Round, the EEC, US, Japan, Switzerland, NZ, Canada, the Nordic Countries and Austria on 13 July 1978 released a 'Framework of Understanding' setting out what they believed to be the principal elements of a deal. Developing countries reacted angrily pointing out that they had been left out of a process that was laying the foundations for a final agreement. The then Director-General of the GATT, Oliver Long, in his report recognised the problem of exclusion, but defended this behaviour as a practical necessity (GATT, 1979). The deeper problem with this process was that it involved a strategy in which a non-representational inner circle of consensus was expanded to create larger circles until the goals of those in the inner circle had been met.

The TRIPS negotiations saw the use of circles of consensus reach new heights. GATT negotiations had developed a traditional pattern, known as the 'Green Room' process:

> In the 'Green Room' process, negotiators from all engaged countries face each other across the table (traditionally in the Green Room on the main floor of the WTO Building) and negotiate. Drafts are exchanged and progress is noted as differences are narrowed and brackets are removed in successive drafts. (Gorlin, 1999, p. 4)

This Green Room process had, in the case of TRIPS, been profoundly shaped by the consensus-building exercise that the private sector had undertaken outside the Green Room. The European Commission was brought round to the US view on the importance of securing a code on intellectual property. The Quad states (US, EC, Japan and Canada) were all enrolled in support of the US business agenda, as were the business communities of the other Quad states. Then there were the meetings of the Friends of Intellectual Property Group in places such as Washington where the US circulated draft texts of a possible agreement. After the negotiations on the detail of TRIPS began in 1990, and especially after the breakdown of the Uruguay Round talks in Brussels over agriculture in 1991, further groups were created within the TRIPS negotiations to move the process towards a final deal, most notably the '10+10' Group which consisted of a mix of developed and developing countries. As the TRIPS negotiations descended into higher levels of informality the '10+10' was contracted or expanded to '3+3' or '5+5' or a group of 25 depending on the issue. It was in these informal groupings that much of the real negotiating was done and where the consensus and agreement that mattered was obtained. A list of these groups in roughly their order of importance would be:

1. US and Europe
2. US, Europe, Japan
3. US, Europe, Japan, Canada (Quad)
4. Quad 'plus' (membership depended on issue, but Switzerland and Australia were regulars in this group)
5. Friends of Intellectual Property (a larger group that included the Quad, Australia, and Switzerland)
6. 10+10 (and the variants thereof such as 5+5, 3+3)
   (the US and the European Community were always part of any such group if the issue was important. Other active members were Japan, Nordics, Canada, Argentina, Australia, Brazil, Hong Kong, India, Malaysia, Switzerland and Thailand)
7. Developing country groups
   (for example, the Andean Group – Bolivia, Colombia, Peru and Venezuela; Argentina, Brazil, Chile, China, Colombia, Cuba, Egypt, Nigeria, Peru, Tanzania and Uruguay combined to submit a developing countries draft text in 1990)
8. Group 11 (the entire TRIPS negotiating group – about 40 countries were active in this group).

It was the first three circles of consensus that really mattered in the TRIPS negotiations. Through the use of these circles of consensus the TRIPS process became one of hierarchical rather than democratic management. Those in the inner circle of groups knew what TRIPS had to contain. They worked on those in the outer circle until the agreement of all groups to a text had been obtained. TRIPS was much more the product of the first three groups than it was of the last five.

The use of circles of consensus also makes it difficult to claim that the second condition of democratic bargaining, namely full information, was fulfilled. It can be seen from the list of groups that the US and Europe could move amongst all the key groups. This allowed them to soak up more information than anyone else about the overall negotiations. Whenever they needed higher levels of secrecy they could reform into a smaller negotiating globule. The claim that the TRIPS negotiations were a model of transparency is difficult to defend. In truth it was the transparency of a one-way mirror. This arrangement of groups also allowed the US and the EC the fluidity to build a consensus when and where it was required. For certain issues, such as how royalties from collective licensing were to be divided, they retreated to the bilaterals. Even though they were not able to always secure an agreement between themselves their disagreement did not derail the TRIPS process itself. Developing-country negotiators knew that the bilaterals were going on. Progressively they came to feel that they were wasting their time in the TRIPS negotiations.

It is also worth observing that all states were in ignorance about the likely effects of TRIPS in information markets. That there would be trade gains for the US was beyond doubt, but the real world costs of extending intellectual property rights and their effects on barriers to entry in markets were not at all clear. Multinationals had better information about the strategic use of intellectual property portfolios in various markets around the world than did most governments.

It is the third condition of democratic bargaining, the absence of coercion, on which TRIPS lies most exposed. The US in its Trade and Tariff Act of 1984 had begun adapting s. 301 of its 1974 Trade Act to its objectives on intellectual property, as well as linking its negotiating objectives on the protection of high technology to intellectual property trade barriers.[2] (Section 301 is a national trade enforcement tool that allows the US to withdraw the benefits of trade agreements or impose duties on goods from foreign countries.) In 1988 there were further significant changes to the US Trade Act of 1974 in the form of what came to be known as the 'Special 301' provisions. These require the USTR to identify foreign countries that deny adequate and effective protection of intellectual property rights or deny fair and equitable market access to US intellectual property holders.[3] Also significant were the changes to the system of Generalised Special Preferences (GSP) that the 1984 Act had wrought. The President, in deciding whether a developing country's products were to gain preferential treatment under the GSP system, had to give 'great weight' to its protection of foreign intellectual property rights.[4] For many developing countries gaining access to the closed and subsidised agricultural markets of developed countries was the main game. The whole point of the GSP system was to improve this access. At a meeting of the GATT Committee on Trade and Development in November 1985 some developing-country representatives had suggested that the US was using its GSP system in a way that was 'quite alien to the spirit and purpose of the generalized system of trade preferences in favour of developing countries' (Report of Committee on Trade and Development, 1984–85, p. 26).

When the US began to push for the inclusion of intellectual property in a new round of multilateral trade negotiations at the beginning of the 1980s, developing countries resisted the proposal. Their line of argument was that the GATT was primarily concerned with trade in goods and not personal rights of property in intangibles. Such rights fell within WIPO's brief. The countries that were the most active in their opposition to the US agenda were India, Brazil, Argentina, Cuba, Egypt, Nicaragua, Nigeria, Peru, Tanzania and Yugoslavia (Bradley, 1987, p. 81). After the Ministerial Declaration of 1986 these countries continued to argue for a narrow interpretation of the Ministerial mandate on the negotiation of intellectual property. Breaking the resistance of these 'hard-liners' was fundamental to achieving the outcome that the US wanted. 'Special 301' was swung into action in the beginning of 1989. When the USTR announced the targets of 'Special 301', five of the ten developing countries that were members of the hard-line group in the GATT opposing the US agenda found themselves listed for bilateral attention. Brazil and India, the two leaders, were placed in the more serious category of Priority Watch List, while Argentina, Egypt and Yugoslavia were put on the Watch List (Abbott, 1989, pp. 708–9). US bilateralism was not confined to these countries. By 1989 USTR fact sheets were reporting other successes: copyright agreements with Indonesia and Taiwan, Saudi Arabia's adoption of a patent law and Colombia including computer software in its copyright law.

TRIPS was less a negotiation and more a 'convergence of processes' in the words of someone who was a US trade negotiator at the time. Opposition to the US GATT agenda was being diluted through the bilaterals. Each bilateral the US concluded with a developing country brought that country that much closer to TRIPS, 'so that accepting TRIPS was no big deal' (interview, US trade negotiator, 1994).

The use of the 301 process by the US against India and Brazil was particularly important.[5] For decades these two countries had been a thorn in the sides of multinationals seeking to globalise intellectual property standards. India especially had technical expertise with which to counter the OECD-led analysis upon which the US was relying in order to achieve its agendas on intellectual property, investment and services. The Brazil–India axis was one that had to be broken. There was a second vital reason to discipline Brazil. It was a regional leader in South America. For the US pharmaceutical and information technology sectors there could only be one voice on intellectual property policy in the Americas. In July of 1987, the USTR had begun a 301 investigation of Brazil on the issue of patent protection for pharmaceutical products, an investigation that had led the President to authorise tariff increases on Brazilian goods in October of 1988. The tariff penalties came less than two months before the meeting of Trade Ministers at the December mid-term review in Montreal. For the first time the US had followed up its threat under 301 in relation to intellectual property and actually lowered the trade boom – it imposed tariffs on Brazilian paper products, non-benzenoid drugs and consumer electronic items.[6] In June 1990, the President of Brazil announced that he would seek the legislation that the US wanted. On 2 July 1990 the increased duties were terminated by the USTR. In the negotiating rooms in Geneva, India started to find that there was less support coming from Brazil.

The US retaliation against Brazil also sent a message about the level of the US private sector's commitment to the intellectual property cause. The Brazilian economy of the 1980s was one in which US multinationals, amongst others, had a strong presence. By imposing trade sanctions on a wide range of Brazilian goods, the risk was that the US would affect goods that were being made in Brazil by US multinationals. The internationalised nature of production set some limits on the use of 301. In the case of Brazil, however, the stakes were so high that US business was prepared to wear the possible costs of a 301 action in order to project the steely will of earlier conquistadors.

The negotiations on TRIPS are often said to have begun properly in the second half of 1989 when a number of countries made proposals, or the first part of 1990 when five draft texts of an agreement were submitted to the negotiating group.[7] A more sceptical view is that the negotiations were by then largely over. An even more sceptical view is to say that no real negotiation ever took place. Developing countries had simply run out of alternatives and options. If they did not negotiate multilaterally they would each have to face the US alone. In the GATT they were not part of the circles of consensus that set the agendas. Furthermore, if they resisted the US multilaterally they could expect to be on the receiving end of a 301 action. This was anything but a veiled threat by the US. Its 1988 Trade Act made resisting the US in a multilateral forum part of the conditions that could lead to a country being identified as a Priority Foreign Country and therefore the subject of a Special 301 investigation.[8] There could be no clearer articulation of a threat than to enact it as law. At least if developing countries negotiated multilaterally there was the possibility that they would be able to obtain some limits on the use of 301 actions. This at any rate was what they were being told by developed country negotiators and the GATT Secretariat. From 1990 onwards the main issue to be decided was how far an agreement on intellectual property would deviate from the blueprint that had been provided to negotiators in 1988 by Pfizer, IBM, Du Pont and other members of the international business community in the form of a draft proposal entitled *Basic Framework of GATT Provisions on Intellectual Property: Statement of Views of the European, Japanese and United States Business Communities* (Intellectual Property Committee (USA), Keidanren (Japan) and UNICE, Union of Industrial and Employers' Confederations of Europe (Europe)).

Post-TRIPS – coercion or dialogue?

US bilateralism on intellectual property rights did not cease after TRIPS came into operation on 1 January 1995. One of the major disappointments of TRIPS from the point of view of US business was the transitional provisions that gave developing and less developed countries extra time in which to comply with TRIPS standards. The simple truth was the companies that had backed the vast lobbying efforts which had gone into TRIPS wanted to see some immediate returns. The result was that the USTR began on a bilateral basis to suggest that developing countries should adopt the standards of TRIPS earlier rather than later.

The 301 process in fact grew bigger, better and stronger after TRIPS was concluded. The Clinton Administration, ignoring or perhaps not knowing the implications of stronger intellectual property rights for human rights such as health and education, strengthened 301 by introducing immediate action plans for foreign countries on intellectual property rights as well as out-of-cycle 301 reviews. The then USTR, Charlene Barshefsky, began to use 'Special 301' announcements to publicise the actions on intellectual property that the US would take in the WTO against countries. The symbolism of these announcements is interesting. It is almost as if the WTO dispute-resolution process has been folded into the US 301 process. Certainly US trade law does not defer to TRIPS. As 'Special 301' makes clear, a country may be still be determined to deny adequate and effective protection of intellectual property rights even if it is in compliance with TRIPS. In her *2000 Special*

301 Report Barshefsky pointed out that more than seventy countries had been reviewed under 'Special 301'. She named 59 foreign countries that failed to meet standards of intellectual property that were satisfactory to the US; 59 countries which had been graded into various categories; 59 countries whose laws and practices on intellectual property had to be watched, analysed and acted upon.

A trade enforcement tool such as 301 is costly to run. It is only really possible because corporate America picks up the tab. It provides the global surveillance network, the numbers for the estimates on piracy and much of the evaluation and analysis. The US state in return provides the bureaucracy that negotiates, threatens and if necessary carries out enforcement actions. It is a system that has complete bipartisan support in the US. US bilateralism on intellectual property rights remains relentless.

It would be relatively easy to draw a bleak conclusion about intellectual property standard-setting in the post-TRIPS era. Congress and the Executive continue to demonstrate a bipartisan unity on an agenda of ever stronger and more globalised intellectual property rights, an agenda written for them by big business. The US now has more enforcement strategies at its disposal than before TRIPS:

- It continues to monitor on an annual basis the performance of all countries under its 301 process;
- Bilaterally, it continues to negotiate intellectual property agreements with states, sometimes bundling intellectual property standards into agreements establishing free trade areas between itself and other governments (for example, the Agreement between the US and Jordan on the Establishment of a Free Trade Area concluded and signed in 2000). Regionally, it continues to link trade agreements to the provision of adequate and effective protection of intellectual property rights (for example, the Andean Trade Preference Act of 1991 which was modelled on the Caribbean Basin initiative of the 1980s);
- It uses a litigation strategy of going to the WTO dispute resolution process, if it thinks countries are in breach;
- It uses TRIPS Council processes and TRIPS reviews to put pressure on countries with respect to implementation.

One view is that the US, Europe and multinational corporations will continue to dominate the international standard-setting process in intellectual property. The WTO and WIPO will be used as alternative multilateral fora for standard-setting exercises. Where desirable and possible WIPO standards will be folded into the WTO. TRIPS standards will be a floor from which further bilateral, regional and multilateral standard-setting exercises will proceed, a floor with no ceiling above. Article 18 of the Free Trade Agreement between the US and Jordan, for example, allows for fewer exclusions from patentability than does Article 27 of TRIPS. Over time the US and European Union[9] may well develop a web of free-trade agreements that globalise a new set of minimum international standards of intellectual property protection higher than those contained in TRIPS. The economic price for this will be less competitive markets with no real corresponding gains in innovation, as well as new and more sophisticated global knowledge cartels.

TRIPS and the dialogue of reform

This chapter concludes by suggesting another possible future for intellectual property standard-setting in the post-TRIPS era. The reality of intellectual property standard-setting has been that of an insiders' game dominated by a few producers of intellectual property supported by states with the most to gain. Developing countries for most of the time have not been able to influence international standard-setting. Following TRIPS, however, another type of actor has become interested in how intellectual property standards are set. Increasingly, the members of civil society are making TRIPS the subject of transnational advocacy networks. For the time being, it is patent standard-setting and its effects on biodiversity, the prices of drugs and agriculture that most interest these networks. As their analytical understanding of intellectual property norms improves they will begin to ask questions about other areas of intellectual property such as trademarks and copyright. In his classic study of barriers to entry into a market, Bain concluded that trademarks constituted an even bigger barrier than did patents. This is something that is understood by developing countries, for in the 1970s Mexico, Brazil and India attempted to reform their trademark law as it related to pharmaceutical products (Gereffi, 1983). Amongst other things, they were interested in seeing foreign pharmaceutical marks being used in conjunction with local marks as well as having the generic name accompany the use of the mark. For a variety of reasons, most of these reforms never made it into law. During the TRIPS negotiations the EC, the US, Switzerland and Japan united on the drafting of a trademark provision that would make it difficult for developing countries to impose special requirements on the use of trademarks in areas such as the pharmaceutical sector.[10]

It is not only NGOs which have become more interested in the intel-lectual property standard-setting process. The increase in the length and breadth of intellectual property rights, a process that was occurring before TRIPS, has seen users of information, including business users, take much more interest. Second-generation computer software compa-nies such as Sun Corporation have called for much more balance in the setting of copyright standards[11] and have taken an active role in special-ist areas such as licensing issues under the Uniform Commercial Code. Educational institutions have also become more engaged as they have come to realise the cost implications of stronger copyright protection for mass education.

Nationally and internationally the process of intellectual property standard-setting is becoming caught up in webs of dialogue, webs in which an increasing number of non-state actors and non-business actors participate.[12] The discussions about the impact of intellectual property rights on biodiversity in the context of the Convention on Biological Diversity and on agriculture in the context of the negotia-tions on the International Undertaking are examples of these webs.

From the point of view of a theory that links the efficiency of interna-tional intellectual property standards to a theory of democratic bargain-ing, dialogic webs help to meet conditions 1 and 2 of democratic bargaining. Such dialogic webs help to represent interests that were pre-viously not represented, as well as providing fuller information about the effects of the standard-setting process. Even more importantly, webs of dialogue can help to displace the use of webs of coercion, which in the case of intellectual property exist and have been used. In a study of global business regulation Braithwaite and Drahos (2000) found in their interviews of more than 500 actors that almost all had a preference for playing games of global regulation through dialogic webs rather than webs of coercion. The reasons for this relate to the high costs of using coercion. The USTR cannot and does not act on every recommendation of coercion that Washington business lobbyists make. So, for example, when the USTR called for public comments on the operation of the Caribbean Basin Economic Recovery Act in the mid-1990s the Inter-national Intellectual Property Association, a key copyright lobbyist, expressed 'concern that USTR has never formally acted upon, or even acknowledged, any petition filed to remove countries from the CBERA (Caribbean Basin Economic Recovery Act) program for violations of the intellectual property rights of the US copyright industries'.[13] Why the USTR would not want to poison its dialogue with the Caribbean states on its doorstep is readily understandable. The announcement on

1 December 1999 by the USTR and the Secretary of Health and Human Services (HHS) that they would develop a 'co-operative approach on health-related intellectual property matters' and the participation of the HHS on the Special 301 Trade Policy Staff Sub-Committee is also an example of a strand in a dialogic web.[14] Even if a single strand seems weak, the construction of a web with many strands lessens the likelihood of a precipitous rush to coercion.

It follows that weaker actors should continue constructing dialogic webs around the intellectual property standard-setting process, taking into account the fact that TRIPS and the WTO form only a part of a much more complex process of system of standard-setting that has bilateral, regional and global aspects. NGOs focusing on intellectual property must not lose sight of the importance of standard-setting at the national level. One of the reasons that the social cost of the patent system remains unacceptably high is that many of those who sit on the policy committees that quietly advise the important patent offices around the world are drawn from the large industries that are the biggest users of the patent system. It would be rare for such committees to have members drawn from health, food, environmental and consumer movements even though all these areas are profoundly affected by patents. National standard-setting in intellectual property will be highly significant in determining the way in which TRIPS evolves. Once states begin to negotiate specific positive standards of the kind to be found in TRIPS they inevitably look to their national systems for precedents and models. For those better-resourced NGOs with good analytical capabilities, long-term engagement with this national standard-setting process should be a goal.

Another possibility is that the institutional arrangements that underpin TRIPS might be used by states to develop better macro-policy coordination than has existed in the past in relation to intellectual property standards. The connection between trade and intellectual property is hardly new. It has always been there. States have always kept a weather eye on the trade implications of intellectual property standards. They have always used intellectual property rules to play out 'beggar thy neighbour' trade games (Penrose, 1951, pp. 115–17).

Once states committed themselves to national intellectual property regimes, some form of international coordination to deal with the trade issues was necessary. International intellectual property regimes, TRIPS included, are means of coordinating national regimes, not a replacement for them. The need for such coordination has never been greater. Transnational companies in the global economy capable of moving investment resources into transformative technologies such as biotechnology may push states into races that might otherwise undermine the welfare benefits that intellectual property rights are capable of delivering to consumers. So, for example, national patent law generally imposes a requirement that the invention be useful. A patent office which relaxes this requirement may trigger a rush to the patent office seeking patents on information that may or not prove to be useful rather than useful products. It could be argued that this is exactly what has happened in the US with biotechnology inventions.[15] Other patent offices, worried about the investment implications of the rush for their domestic economies, may respond by also dropping their standards of usefulness. It is very much an open question as to whether this kind of regulatory competition is desirable. In these kinds of race those companies with the best lawyers do best, something that contributes nothing to efficient resource allocation. Consumers in all states bear the cost of patent protection without there being any corresponding gain in innovation.

The purpose of TRIPS is to eliminate distortions in international trade relating to intellectual property rights. Since these distortions are not just confined to a lack of standards of intellectual property protection, there is no reason in principle why the Council for TRIPS could not become a forum in which states began to address distortions that are occurring in global information markets because of either excessive intellectual property protection by one or more states or slippage in the application of intellectual property standards. The Council for TRIPS, as Article 68 makes clear, is there to be of service to all its members. The Council for TRIPS might prove to a good forum for this kind of international policy coordination because it is itself nested within a regime that recognises a diversity of principles such as sustainable development (see the WTO Agreement) and food security (see Agreement on Agriculture). It is a potentially a forum in which intellectual property might become an object of cross-cutting regulatory coordination. It is vital that this happen: intellectual property regimes like the patent system have for too long been allowed to operate as if hermetically sealed from other forms of social regulation.

TRIPS is an example of a much broader truth about the globalisation of business regulation: '[w]hen the US and EC can agree on which direction global regulatory change should take, that is usually the direction it does take' (Braithwaite and Drahos, 2000, p. 27). On intellectual property standards the US and Europe have generally taken hard lines. Europe like the US has been prepared to use coercion in the field of intellectual property. The European Community, despite its protestations about the use of 301 by the US, had in the same year as the US had reformed its trade law to accommodate intellectual property (1984) created its own version of 301 in the form of the 'new commercial policy instrument' to protect the Community's intellectual property interests.[16] It moved against Indonesia and Thailand for record piracy, as well as suspending Korea's GSP privileges for failing to provide satisfactory intellectual property protection for European companies. However, its use of its trade policy instrument did not match US bilateral activity, partly because the European Commission found it difficult to get consensus amongst it members as to which country it should be deployed against. The European Commission was also the quiet freerider on US aggression on intellectual property, sometimes sending in negotiators to conclude a bilateral agreement on intellectual property with a developing country after US negotiators had brought that country to the negotiating table using the 301 process.

The tough lines that have emerged from the metropoles of the West on the rules for the production and flows of knowledge suggest that developing countries will have to be very tightly organised on any future negotiations involving TRIPS. In particular they should give consideration to creating a developing country counterweight to the Quad. In the last round developing countries had no equivalent to the Quad, meaning that they had no counterweight to the agenda-setting powers of the Quad or its capacity to manage the crucial stages of a trade negotiation. The emergence of such a countervailing power would bring WTO negotiations closer to the ideal of democratic bargaining.

One possibility is that four developing-country leaders (for example, India, Brazil, Nigeria and China) could form a group that would represent developing-country interests in the hard or final stages of a multilateral trade negotiation. Each of these countries could chair a working group on some of the key negotiating issues of a given trade round. There could, for example, be a group on Services and Investment, a group on Intellectual Property and Biotechnology, a group on Agriculture and Goods and another on Competition, Environment and Labour (or whatever emerging issues there were in that trade round).[17] Other developing countries could join one of these four groups, perhaps with some taking responsibility for forming a working party on some aspect of the negotiations for which that group had overall responsibility (for example, an African country could take responsibility for forming a working group on intellectual property and biodiversity within the Intellectual Property and Biotechnology Group). One advantage of this structure would be that the expertise of developing countries would be pooled, thereby reducing the capacity problems that they faced in the last round.

As early as 1989 an OECD report observed that, because of OECD countries' advantages in biotechnology, developing countries, especially those heavily reliant upon agriculture, would 'bear the brunt of trade impacts for a long time to come' (OECD, 1989, p. 81). It follows that developing countries have also little to gain from a regimes like TRIPS that diminish the flow of biotechnological information to them as a public good. But developed states should also be questioning whether they ought to continue to support the rent-seeking agendas of big business on intellectual property rights. It is clear that much of the research that ends up in corporate intellectual property portfolios is public research in the first place. In biotechnology the dependence is striking with, for example, more than 70 per cent of scientific papers cited in biotechnology patents originating in solely public science institutions compared to 16.5 per cent originating in the private sector (McMillan *et al.*, 2000, p. 5). Strengthening global intellectual property standards imposes costs on consumers in developed countries as well as developing countries. It is just that some consumers in developed countries are better able to afford the price of patented or copyright protected technologies. There is also recognition in some developed countries that the impact of intellectual property standards on the rate and direction of innovation cannot be considered in isolation from environmental and health regulation as well as development issues. The negotiations that led to the Cartagena Protocol on Biosafety (2000) saw most states accept the need for a more integrated approach towards intellectual property standard-setting. The same might be said of the current negotiations on the International Undertaking on Plant Genetic Resources. One suspects that states which obstruct the pursuit of regulatory complementarities between intellectual property regimes on the one side and environmental, health and agricultural regimes on the other will in the long run find themselves isolated.

Conclusion

There are good reasons to think that democratic bargaining amongst states will increase the likelihood of obtaining efficient international intellectual property norms. Democratic bargaining minimally requires that the conditions of representation, full information and non-domination be met. In the past these conditions have not often been fulfilled. The international expansion of intellectual property regimes has been more a result of processes of colonisation and coercion than democratic bargaining. On the basis of the evidence it is also difficult to say that TRIPS itself was the product of democratic bargaining. This in turn raises questions about the efficiency of its norms and its legitimacy. Lying behind the current criticisms of TRIPS are also feelings of unfair treatment that will not easily disappear.

A future for TRIPS that sees it become more responsive to development and welfare goals lies with three distinct groups of actors – developed countries, developing countries and members of civil society. A summary of the prescriptions for action that this chapter has suggested for each of these groups is as follows:

- Members of civil society should continue to foster a more integrated approach to intellectual property standard-setting by linking intellectual property regimes to other regimes through webs of dialogue.
- Members of civil society should not ignore the importance of the national standard-setting process to the future evolution of TRIPS. They should seek representation on those national policy committees that advise governments on intellectual property standards.
- All states should be wary of further extensions to TRIPS standards in the absence of evidence that this contributes in some significant way to dynamic efficiency.
- All states should explore the possibility of turning the Council for TRIPS into a forum for the international coordination of a trade-based intellectual property system that has as its goal the global welfare of citizens.
- Developing countries will have to adopt a more coordinated approach to bargaining over intellectual property rights at the bilateral, regional and multilateral level. At the multilateral level they should give consideration to the formation of a counterweight to the Quad structured along the lines suggested by this chapter.

The future of TRIPS depends most heavily on the decisions of the US and the European Union. Whether these two states can transcend their past on intellectual property and shift WTO processes on intellectual property in the direction of improving welfare gains for all citizens is another matter.

Notes

1. See 'Industry that stalks the US corridors of power', *The Guardian*, Tuesday 13 February 2001, p. 3.

2. See s. 305 of the Trade and Tariff Act of 1984.
3. See 19 USC s. 2242.
4. See s. 505 of the Trade and Tariff Act of 1984.
5. The US brought 301 actions relating to intellectual property against Brazil in 1985 and 1987 and against India in 1991. Both were GSP beneficiaries. See Sell (1995).
6. The history of all s. 301 cases is available from the USTR website. See http://www.ustr.gov.
7. See, for example, Daniel Gervais, *The TRIPS Agreement: Drafting History and Analysis* (London: Sweet & Maxwell, 1998), p. 15; Jacques J. Gorlin, *An Analysis of the Pharmaceutical-Related Provisions of the WTO TRIPS (Intellectual Property Agreement)*; (Intellectual Property Institute, 1999), p. 2.
8. See 19 USC 2242(b)(1)(C).
9. The European Union is including intellectual property in the Euro-Mediterranean negotiations. These negotiations are part of an objective to create a free-trade area between 15 EU member states and 12 Mediterranean partners by 2010. Thus far Euro-Mediterranean Association Agreements have been concluded or are being negotiated with Algeria, Egypt, Israel, Jordan, Lebanon, Morocco, Palestinian Authority, Syria and Tunisia.
10. See Article 20 of TRIPS.
11. See 'Open Systems: The Need for a Balanced Copyright Regime in the European Union (EU)' available at http://www.sun.com/aboutsun/policy.
12. Braithwaite and Drahos define dialogic webs as follows (2000, p. 553):

    Dialogic webs are more fundamentally webs of persuasion than webs of control. They include dialogue in professional associations, self-regulatory dialogue in industry associations, auditors from one subsidiary of a TNC auditing the compliance with regulatory standards of auditors from another subsidiary, naming and shaming of irresponsible corporate practices by NGOs, discussions in intergovernmental organizations at the regional and international levels, plus any number of idiosyncratic strands of deliberation that occur within and across epistemic communities.

13. The review is available from the USTR website; see http://www.ustr.gov.
14. See *2000 Special 301 Report*, USTR website; see http://www.ustr.gov.
15. Significantly the USPTO has recently issued revised guidelines on the utility requirement: see 'PTO Final Examiner Guidelines on Utility Requirement' 66 Federal Register 1092, 29 December 2000.
16. See Council Regulation 2641/84.
17. I am indebted to a late night email conversation with John Braithwaite for helping me to think through this possibility.

References

Abbott, Frederick M. (1989) 'Protecting First World Assets in the Third World: Intellectual Property Negotiations in the GATT Multilateral Framework', *Vanderbilt Journal of Transnational Law*, vol. 22, p. 689.

Astudillo, Enrico B. (1999) 'Intellectual Property Regime of the Philippines', in Arthur Wineburg (ed.) *Intellectual Property Protection in Asia* (2nd edn) (Charlottesville, V.I.: Lexis Law Publishing).

Bain, J.S. (1956) *Barriers to New Competition* (Cambridge, Mass.: Harvard University Press).

Bradley, Jane, A. (1987) 'Intellectual Property Rights, Investment, and Trade in Services in the Uruguay Round: Laying the Foundations', *Stanford Journal of International Law*, vol. 23, p. 57.

Braithwaite, J. and P. Drahos (2000) *Global Business Regulation* (Cambridge: Cambridge University Press).

Cooter, R. and T. Ulen (1997) *Law and Economics* (Reading, Mass.: Addison-Wesley).

Easterbrook, F.H. (1981) 'Insider Trading, Secret Agents, Evidentiary Privileges, and the Production of Information', *The Supreme Court Review*, p. 309.

GATT (1979) *The Tokyo Round of Multilateral Trade Negotiations: Report by the Director-General of GATT* (Geneva).

Gereffi, G. (1983) *The Pharmaceutical Industry and Dependency in the Third World* (Princeton, New Jersey: Princeton University Press).

Gervais, D. (1998) *The TRIPS Agreement: Drafting History and Analysis* (London: Sweet & Maxwell).

Gorlin, Jacques J. (1999) *An Analysis of the Pharmaceutical-Related Provisions of the WTO TRIPS (Intellectual Property) Agreement* (London: Intellectual Property Institute).

Lazar, Alan, H. (1971) 'Developing Countries and Authors' Rights in International Copyright', in *Copyright Law Symposium*, vol. 19 (New York and London: Columbia University Press), p. 1.

McMillan, G.S., F. Narin and D.L. Deeds (2000) 'An Analysis of the Critical Role of Public Science in Innovation; the Case of Biotechnology', *Research Policy*, vol. 29, pp. 1–8.

Mills, D.M. (1985) 'Patents and the Exploitation of Technology Transferred to Developing Countries (in Particular, Those of Africa)', *Industrial Property*, vol. 24, p. 120.

North, Douglass, C. (1990) *Institutions, Institutional Change and Economic Performance* (Cambridge: Cambridge University Press).

OECD (1989) *Biotechnology: Economic and Wider Impacts* (Paris: OECD).

Olson, M. (1965) *The Logic of Collective Action* (Cambridge, Mass.: Harvard University Press).

Penrose, E. (1951) *The Economics of the International Patent System* (Baltimore: Johns Hopkins Press).

Report of Committee on Trade and Development (L/5913) (1984–85) *Basic Instruments and Selected Documents, General Agreement on Tariffs and Trade*, 32nd Supplement, 21.

Ricketson, S. (1987) *The Berne Convention for the Protection of Literary and Artistic Works: 1886–1986* (London: Centre for Commercial Law Studies).

Sell, Susan K. (1995) 'Intellectual Property Protection and Antitrust in the Developing World: Crisis, Coercion, and Choice', *International Organization*, vol. 49, pp. 315–49.

Subramanian, A. (1991) 'The International Economics of Intellectual Property Right Protection: a Welfare-Theoretic Trade Policy Analysis', *World Development*, vol. 19, pp. 945–56.

Tee, Khaw Lake (1994) *Copyright Law in Malaysia* (Malaysia: Butterworths Asia).

Vedaraman, S. (1972) 'The New Indian Patents Law', *International Review of Industrial Property and Copyright Law*, vol. 3, p. 39.

11
TRIPS and Developing Countries: How Level is the Playing Field?

Willem Pretorius[1]

The balance between producers and users of IP rights

The general complaint of the developing countries has been that the balance in the intellectual property (IP) debate has shifted too far in favour of technology producers. Negotiations over intellectual property rights (IPRs) have been influenced by vocal industry lobby groups; negotiations are being driven by concerns of trade liberalisation and international investment between developed countries; and the legitimate technological objectives of developing countries – predominantly technology users – are not being given due consideration. As stated by Professor Alan Fells in a speech given at the Asian and Oceanic Anti-Monopoly Conference:[2]

> Intellectual property laws have been captured by the interest of producers in countries which are net exporters of intellectual property ... In this part of the world we are losers.

The shift in favour of private interests has been helped along by a denial of the contingent nature of IPRs. IPRs are rights granted by the state as a means of meeting certain policy objectives – these rights are in no way inherent. Increasingly, however, certain interest groups are promoting IPRs as natural rights – rights that have a moral force that somehow elevates them above political challenge.[3] During the 1980s, for instance, the insistence of US industry and the US Government on the protection of IPRs began to take on a moral character (Weissman, 1996, p. 1086). The pharmaceutical industry was particularly vocal in this regard. Much of the rhetoric which helped construct US patent policy at this time used emotive terms such as 'piracy' and 'theft' when referring to developing countries' use of technology protected under US IPR laws. The arguments reflected an underlying assumption that a right granted over technology in one country could somehow be equated with a right of universal coverage. Yet this development denies the contingent nature of IPRs – legislatures could, after all, choose not to grant IPRs or to define them more narrowly.

The arguments were also embarrassingly in conflict with their own history as far as this form of protection is concerned (see also Chapter 14 by Sol Picciotto in this volume).

IP rights and developed countries – the history

France, Germany, Italy, Japan, Sweden and Switzerland, home of some of the most innovative pharmaceutical companies, persistently resisted providing pharmaceutical product patents until their industries had reached a certain degree of development. France introduced product patents in 1960, Germany in 1968, Japan in 1976, Switzerland in 1977, Italy and Sweden in 1978. During the first hundred years the US was still a relatively young and developing country and refused to respect international intellectual property rights on the grounds that it was freely entitled to copy foreign works in furtherance of its social and economic development. The UK, at that time the world leader in technology, attacked the US for not providing strong patent protection. These attacks and complaints had very little or no effect since the American firms wanted the freedom to imitate British innovations and put them on the market.

Notwithstanding this contradictory history, the developing world was left under no illusions about what to expect from developed countries on this issue when the Uruguay round trade negotiations commenced in 1986.

The Uruguay Round

Throughout the negotiations, developing countries vehemently contested the jurisdiction of the General Agreement on Tariffs and Trade (GATT) to deal with matters of intellectual property, insisting that the World Intellectual Property Organization (WIPO) was the appropriate forum for debate. Developed countries, on the other hand, were eager to move IP negotiations into GATT where their negotiating power was enhanced by the weaker developing country presence.

The developed countries got their way and IP rights were included in the agenda. After long and arduous negotiations the members of GATT signed the Final Act Embodying the Results of the Uruguay Round of Multi-lateral Trade Negotiations on the 15th of April 1994. The final document included the Agreement on Trade-Related Aspects of Intellectual Property Rights (TRIPS).

TRIPS was a triumph for the pharmaceutical community in particular, and for the intellectual property exporting countries generally. The developing countries, on the other hand, were clearly outgunned by the army of experts advising the negotiators of the developed countries and the end result for these countries was unsatisfactory, to say the least. First and foremost it removed the ability of these countries to balance their particular developmental need with the need for the protection of intellectual property rights. This fact requires no further elaboration. As the implementation of the agreement progressed, some other issues of concern crystallised. The two issues I will address are the following:

1. Although the IP rights of developed countries were well protected in TRIPS, the protection for traditional knowledge, emanating from developing countries, is totally inadequate.
2. It is also becoming increasingly clear that developed countries regard TRIPS, not as the final word on intellectual property protection, but rather as a solid foundation from where to extort greater degrees of protection from developing countries.

Traditional knowledge

Over the past decade or so, biotechnological, pharmaceutical and human healthcare industries have increased their interest in natural products as sources of new biochemical compounds for drug, chemical and agro products development (Reid *et al.*, 1993). The decade has also witnessed a resurgence of interest in traditional knowledge and medicine. This interest has been stimulated by the importance of traditional knowledge as a lead in new product development. Of the 199 drugs developed from higher plants which are available on the world market today, it is estimated that 74 per cent were discovered from a pool of traditional herbal medicine (Laird, 1994, pp. 145–9). One estimate suggests that in 1985 the value of plant-based medicines that were sold in developed countries, many of which were first used by indigenous people, amounted to US$43 billion (Posey and Dutfield, 1996, p. 34).

The search for these plants has been accompanied by an immoral appropriation of traditional knowledge. In the 1970s, for example, the National Cancer Institute (NCI) of the US invested in extensive collections of *Maytenus buchannii* from the Shimba Hills of Kenya. NCI was generally led by the knowledge of the Digo communities – indigenous to the Shimba Hills area – who have used the plant to treat cancerous conditions for many years. More than 27.2 tons of the shrub were collected by the NCI from a game reserve in the Shimba Hills for testing under a major screening programme (Juma, 1989). The plant yields maytansine, which was considered a potential treatment for pancreatic cancer. All the material collected was traded without the consent of the Digo, neither was there sufficient recognition of their knowledge of the plant and its medicinal properties.

The NCI has also collected *Homalanthus nutans* from the Samoan rainforests. The plant contains the anti-HIV compound prostratin. The collection was undertaken on the basis of traditional knowledge (Posey and Dutfield, 1996, p. 35). NCI has also benefited from traditional knowledge of local communities living around Korup Forest Reserve in Cameroon. The Institute has collected *Ancistrocladus korrupensis* from the reserve to screen for an anti-HIV ingredient, Michellamine B. This bio-prospecting effort has progressed into pre-clinical development.

Few, if any, benefits derived by the pharmaceutical industry from this important source accrue to the source countries and the traditional communities. In fact these communities are compensated for little more than their manual labour. According to Posey, less than 0.001 per cent of profits from drugs developed from natural products and traditional knowledge have accrued to traditional people who provided technical leads for the research (Posey, 1991).

There are, however, a few exceptions. These include Shaman Pharmaceuticals and The Body Shop.[4] Both Shaman and The Body Shop have developed mechanisms for returning some of the benefits from the commercialisation of medicinal plants and traditional knowledge to the indigenous people. The Body Shop also sponsors projects to assist local people in establishing enterprises for processing crude products.

Traditional knowledge plays a significant role in industry R&D programmes. It is currently supplied to commercial interests through databases, academic publications or field collections and it should be paid for in some form. We cannot simply rely upon the goodwill of companies and institutions, as The Body Shop and Shaman Pharmaceuticals are the exception not the rule. If something is not done now, mining the riches of indigenous knowledge will become the latest – and ultimate – neo-colonial form of exploitation of native peoples.

How does the TRIPS Agreement address this issue? I believe it is common cause that conventional patentability standards cannot be applied to traditional knowledge. A patentable invention must be new, which basically means that it must not have been put in the public domain by an act of some kind or through publication. Traditional knowledge is generally not new in the patent sense because it is created and passed on in ways that make it, from the point of view of patent law, part of the public domain. Once such knowledge is potentially accessible by others it loses novelty for patent purposes. Furthermore, the absence of financial and organisational competences of the indigenous and local people to monitor and enforce patents in modern economic space will inevitably lead to the use of their knowledge without due compensation.

TRIPS does not address the issue of the protection of traditional knowledge. It allows for the protection of plant varieties, either through patents or an 'efficient' *sui generis* system, or by a combination thereof. This provision is to be renegotiated four years after implementation of the WTO Agreement. This provision has serious limitations, however, both in its meaning and its effect. Its wording is unclear as it contains no definition of 'an effective' *sui generis* regime. There is a fear amongst developing country members that the norms on plant variety rights contained in the Act of the International Convention for the Protection of New Varieties of Plants 1991 will be forced upon them as the only acceptable norms to be applied (see Chapter 13 by Suman Sahai in this volume). This will again slant the issue in favour of the developed countries.

The more serious deficiency of this provision, however, relates to the limited relief it provides. Although a *sui generis* system may evolve as an important tool in the long-term protection of traditional knowledge, it requires the introduction and enforcement of complex legislation in individual countries. Traditional knowledge is often appropriated from communities that are not familiar with Western commercial practices and are geographically situated in the most remote areas. These communities will in all probability never benefit from the introduction of such a system. The only manner in which their rights can be protected is through multilateral recognition of their rights, preferably through TRIPS.

In my view, therefore, in addition to a *sui generis* system (should such a system be implemented in a particular country), TRIPS should provide further safeguards to ensure that this knowledge is not appropriated without compensation. The most efficient manner to achieve this is through the requirement of disclosure on registration of a patent. TRIPS should therefore contain a requirement that the enforcement of patent rights should be subject to the disclosure, at the time of registration, of the country of origin of biological materials and/or traditional knowledge. Registration in such instance should not take place unless the applicant proves that explicit consent for the use of these has been obtained. The application should further state whether compensation was paid and, if so, what the precise nature of the compensation was. The latter requirement will create transparency and may result, we hope, in the payment of *fair* compensation.

The developed countries – strengthening intellectual property protection

The USA and TRIPS plus

I now wish to turn to a topic which is far more controversial. Subject to Articles 27.2 and 27.3, Article 27.1 places a strict obligation on countries to provide patents for all inventions. It includes the obligatory registration of all patentable pharmaceutical products.

The obligation to grant patents to all qualifying pharmaceuticals inventions raises fundamental questions about life and survival and potentially conflicts with the enjoyment of basic human rights – in particular the right to health. It also raises important developmental issues. Prior to TRIPS, most IP systems, in both developed and developing countries, had refused, at some stage, to grant patents over pharmaceuticals in order to fulfil health and developmental objectives.

Developing countries were loath to forfeit this right to health. In the end, however, they were left with no choice as enormous pressure was brought to bear on them. This pressure took the form of the old stick-and-carrot method of negotiating from a position of strength. The stick was the threat of trade sanctions if they did not comply, and the carrot was 'favourable consideration' in relation to aid and preferential trade benefits in future bilateral trade agreements. The result was predictable: the developing countries fell in line.

Pharmaceutical industry pricing

Developing countries, and South Africa in particular, derived some comfort from the provisions of Article 6 of TRIPS, the specific footnote to Article 28 and the inclusion of Article 31. It was felt that compulsory licensing and parallel imports could do much to alleviate the harsh impact of Article 27.1 on their health and developmental concerns.

Contrary to what is generally understood, the problem the South African government has with the prices of pharmaceutical products is not limited to HIV/AIDS drugs. The problem lies far deeper. A study which compared the prices in relation to the thirty most prescribed patented drugs used in South Africa showed that, on average, the South African consumer pays 98 per cent more for such drugs than the best price available within the European Union.[5]

This inequitable pricing structure of pharmaceutical companies is not limited to South Africa. The price of Zantac (100 tablets) in fifteen developing countries and developed countries in Asia Pacific was found to range from US$3 to US$183. Australia and New Zealand, two advanced affluent countries, have recorded prices lower than those in eight developing countries. Mongolia, a least-developed country, has recorded prices almost nine times that of Australia and New Zealand. A critical examination of the retail prices of drugs in thirty-nine countries around the world, suggests that the guiding principle which the drug industry seems to adopt in fixing prices is to charge what the market can bear. In poor countries this may mean companies pursuing a high-price, low-volume strategy aimed at those classes that can afford the higher prices, whereas in rich countries it may well mean a lower-price, high-volume strategy aimed at the bulk of the population.

In confrontation on this issue, pharmaceutical firms insist that it is their right to charge prices taking into consideration the different demand curves for a particular product in various jurisdictions. Price discrimination, according to them, is beneficial as it allows more consumers to purchase the relevant product, and on the other hand continues to allow the manufacturer to recoup its costs and make a profit. Whether price discrimination makes the relevant product accessible to more consumers, especially poorer consumers, is affected by a number of factors including whether the company thinks it worthwhile chasing that part of the market.

Developing countries have two significant difficulties with this argument:

(1) In the first place demand in a particular jurisdiction is not taken into account. There are many pharmaceutical products for which a considerable demand exists in developing countries and for which products there is little or no demand in developed countries. The result is that there is no incentive for developed country manufacturers to meet the demand. Price discrimination never enters the picture. In any case, for the very poor in developing countries no

amount of price discrimination, short of zero cost, can bring needed drugs to them. There are, in other words, basic problems that the price discrimination argument simply does not address.

(2) The second difficulty relates to the contradiction in developed countries' attitude towards price discrimination when the result does not suit them. This much is clear from their attitude towards price discrimination in relation to dumping. Developed countries, generally, have anti-dumping legislation which is vigorously enforced. These laws prohibit price discrimination when products are imported and sold at a lower price in their jurisdiction than in the country of their origin. This form of price discrimination is also based on the demand curve faced by the manufacturer in a particular jurisdiction. It allows for cheaper prices in the importing country and contributes to the manufacturer's ability to maximise its profits. In this instance, however, political interests of the producers in developed countries overrides any economic justification, often to the detriment of the interest of producers in developing countries.

In any event, faced with these high prices for pharmaceuticals and the growing crisis of HIV/AIDS, tuberculosis and malaria, on 23 November 1997 the Government of South Africa adopted a controversial law, the South African Medicines and the Related Substances Control Amendment Act (Medicines Act). The provision that caused the controversy was s. 15(c), according to which the Ministry of Health may allow parallel importation of certain pharmaceutical products.

Let me reiterate: the issue is not about the importation of HIV/AIDS drugs but about the general right to parallel importation of pharmaceutical drugs as is permitted in TRIPS. That having been said, it must be emphasised that the HIV/AIDS issue is an extremely serious one. One in eight South Africans, one in seven Kenyans and one in four Zimbabweans has HIV/AIDS. US Surgeon General David Satcher has likened the HIV/AIDS epidemic in Africa to the plague that decimated Europe in the fourteenth century.

Existing treatments, which enable many people with HIV/AIDS in the US and other industrialised countries to live relatively healthy lives, are unavailable to all but a few people in Africa. Life-saving HIV/AIDS drug cocktails until recently cost about $12,000 a year in many African countries. This was vastly out of reach of all but a small handful of the growing African population with HIV/AIDS. As a result of the international public pressure generated by the global medicines campaign (see Chapter 15 by Ruth Mayne in this book) and competition from generic manufacturers price reductions began to take place. Some major companies dropped their prices to around $1000 to Sub-Saharan countries. However, the absolute poverty of many people in Africa still prevents them from privately purchasing medicines.

Irrespective of any other biases in the TRIPS Agreement, it is a fact that the TRIPS Agreement allows for parallel imports. Yet, despite the legality of these policy tools, multinational pharmaceutical companies object to parallel importation as they claim it unfairly curtails corporate profits. The US government has adopted a similar view, strongly opposing the efforts of the developing countries to undertake compulsory licensing, parallel imports or other similar measures for making HIV/AIDS drugs, as well as other life-saving drugs, more affordable and available in their countries.

The US government takes the view that it has the right to demand that countries do even more to protect intellectual property rights than required by the TRIPS Agreement – the so-called TRIPS Plus argument. The TRIPS Plus approach of the US is justified by it on the basis that if it grants a concession to a country in excess of its WTO obligations it is entitled to extract any trade concessions it wishes. This concession may require greater protection of patents than required by TRIPS.

This argument is clearly contrived. The issue is not about concessions in *bona fide* negotiations but about threats of withdrawal of benefits already agreed upon. Moreover, it ignores the fact that these benefits were indeed the carrot (or reward) for accepting the terms of the agreement at the time.

Nevertheless, the US has few qualms about the issue and has exerted extraordinary pressure on developing countries to prevent them from pursuing legitimate strategies such as parallel importation. In particular, the US government has undertaken a massive bullying effort to get South Africa to review provisions of its Medicines Act that would help the country make essential medicines more accessible and affordable.

The use of pressure tactics is borne out by a report from the State Department, which states:

> All relevant agencies of the US Government – the Department of State together with the Department of Commerce, its US Patent and Trade Mark office, the office of the United States Trade Representative, the National Security Council and the office of the Vice President – have been engaged in an assiduous, concerted campaign to persuade the government of South Africa to withdraw

or modify the Medicines Act provisions that give the government the authority to pursue compulsory licensing and parallel import policies.[6]

The State Department further explains how 'US government agencies have been engaged in a full court press with South African officials from the Department of Trade and Industry, Foreign Affairs and Health' in order to pressure them to change the law.

Examples of this 'full court press' are too many to fit into the confines of this chapter. I have thus selected, in the form of a timetable, a few of the more flagrant instances of unfair pressure by the US government in support of private pharmaceutical interests.

- Since mid-1997: according to the US Department of State, US Ambassador to South Africa, James Joseph, makes frequent public statements and multiple private démarches to high-ranking South African officials against the legitimisation of parallel imports.
- 4 October 1997: Ambassador James Joseph writes a letter to Dr Abe Nkomo of the Portfolio Committee stating, 'My government opposes a notion of parallel imports of patented products anywhere in the world. We argued for a prohibition of such parallel imports in the TRIPS Agreement. They are illegal in the United States.'
- 11 February 1998: The US Department of State tells USTR that the *New York Times* is researching an article on the South African trade dispute. Steven Fox from USTR tells Jay Ziegler in South Africa to use the following statement:

  We are very concerned about the implications of these amendments. We have conveyed our concerns to the government of South Africa in strong terms and are consulting closely with the affected US companies about appropriate action.

- 1 May 1998: USTR puts South Africa on the Special 301 watch list. USTR announcement focuses on the SA Medicines Act, including the authorisation for parallel imports.
- 30 June 1998: the White House announces that four items, for which South Africa had requested preferential tariff treatment under the Generalised System of Preferences (GSP) programme, will be held in abeyance pending adequate progress on intellectual property rights protection in South Africa.
- September 1998: Commerce Secretary Daley, during an official visit to South Africa, makes pharmaceutical patent protection a key item in discussions with South African Trade and Industry Minister Alec Erwin.

- 21 October 1998: HR 4328 is passed, and becomes PL 105–277. This omnibus appropriations law contains a provision inserted by Republican Rodney Frelinghuysen that cuts off aid to the government of South Africa pending a Department of State report outlining its efforts to 'negotiate the repeal, suspension, or termination of Section 15(c) of the South African Medicines Act'.
- 5 February 1999: the US Department of Trade sends a report to the US Congress, entitled 'US Government efforts to negotiate the repeal, termination or withdrawal of Article 15(c) of the South African Medicines and Related Substances Act of 1965'.
- 30 April 1999: USTR announces that South Africa is placed on the 'watch list' in its Special 301 Review, once again naming the issue of parallel imports.
- 21 July 1999: the House of Representatives, by a vote of 307 to 117, rejects the 'Sanders amendment.' The Sanders amendment would make it illegal for the Department of State to lobby Asian or African countries against access to essential medicines, if the country was TRIPS-compliant.

The European Union (EU) was not to be outdone. High-ranking officials such as Ambassador Fouere and Sir Leon Brittan, on a number of occasions, chastised the South African government for their policies in regard to compulsory licensing and parallel importation. They both neglected to state that parallel importation is allowed in the EU. The comments of Sir Leon Brittan were particularly galling as he has often been in conflict with pharmaceutical companies regarding his strong views on the importance of parallel importation as a tool to lower the cost of pharmaceutical products. The international moral outrage that developed around this kind of treatment of South Africa brought a change of behaviour. Under Commissioner Lamy the European Commission in particular went some way to supporting developing-country proposals for a pro-public health declaration on TRIPS.

In any event, in the US sympathy for the plight of Southern Africa slowly turned into general condemnation of the attitude of the United States government. US government officials, and particularly Vice-President Gore, were harassed at every opportunity. Eventually the United States government relented, by taking South Africa off their Special 301 watch list, and the following statement was issued by President Clinton:

> We were trying to discourage compulsory licensing in the area of health. We will not apply TRIPS Plus with respect to countries with medical emergencies.

This statement by the US government is once again somewhat of cold comfort. It is clearly not the intention of the US government to accept the parameters of the TRIPS Agreement as the last word on intellectual property rights. In fact, it is clearly nothing more than a desperate response to severe public condemnation of the callous attitude of the US government in regard to the issue of HIV/AIDS.

The EU and TRIPS Plus

The disregard for the provisions of TRIPS is not limited to the United States. Whereas TRIPS Plus, when referred to in the United States of America, relates mainly to additional protection for patents, this phrase in the European Union is normally used in relation to trademarks and geographical indications. The strategy is, however, the same. Notwithstanding strong indications of favourable bilateral trade benefits as *quid pro quo* for acceding to TRIPS, the EU followed the example of the US. It utilised bilateral trade negotiations to extort additional intellectual property protection. During these negotiations between South Africa and the EU, the EU, amongst other things, placed at issue certain so-called 'geographical indications', which included the names of various grape varieties as well as the names Ouzo, Grappa, Port and Sherry. I shall limit myself to the issue of Port and Sherry as the other indications are still the subject of some controversy.

The EU, relying on Article 22.3 of TRIPS, claimed that South African producers were not entitled to use the names 'port' and 'sherry' for their products. The South African government and the wine industry were adamant that the words 'port' and 'sherry' do not constitute geographical indications in South Africa, but constitute customary terms which have existed for some 200 years. It argued that the use of these names may even predate the use of the words by Portugal and Spain. 'Port' and 'sherry' are therefore customary terms as defined in Article 24.6 rather than geographical indications, and South Africa, as a member of TRIPS, was not obliged to cease use of these customary terms. The South African government also argued that if the WTO were to make a finding that the words 'port' and 'sherry' constitute geographical indications in the true sense of the phrase, then the fact that these terms have been used by South Africa for more than a century preceding TRIPS allowed South Africa to invoke the 10-year exception rule (see Article 24.4: allowing for the continuous use of a geographical indication used in a continuous manner for ten years).

It must be borne in mind that South Africa has since 1935 recognised geographical indications as a form of intellectual property and regulated the use thereof in respect of products originating in South Africa. It has prevented the use of 'champagne' and 'burgundy' and other 'genuine' geographical indications for more than sixty years. South Africa has thus been proactive in the protection of geographical indications long before the commencement of TRIPS negotiations. This made no difference to the EU, which chose to ignore both the South African record on the protection of geographical indications as well as the provisions of TRIPS. The attitude of the EU was similar to that of the US, in that it argued that TRIPS creates no more than a minimum standard for its members and that nothing prevents the EU from extracting more burdensome provisions in bilateral negotiations.

South Africa was forced to concede the issue, as smaller trading nations simply cannot resist the pressure of large economic communities to sell their 'birthright' for the metaphorical bowl of lentil soup.

There are a number of other issues of great concern to developing countries. The majority of these centre around the inability of developing countries to capitalise on their competitive advantage in respect of products where they hold such advantage. The biggest culprit in this instance is the EU and in particular its common agricultural policy. Various developing countries, including South Africa, can provide agricultural products to the EU at considerably cheaper prices than the price currently paid by European consumers. A good example of this is the use by European producers of beet sugar processes rather than importing cane sugar of the same or higher quality at prices 50 per cent below the protected price in Europe.

Agricultural subsidies in the US and standard specifications in the US and the EU are further constraints on the ability of developing countries to trade with the developed world. The relevance of these issues to TRIPS is that it was the anticipated success in agriculture by developing countries which was supposed to offset the increased costs to them of accepting TRIPS.

Conclusion

It is clear that there is a huge asymmetry in trade relations between the developed and developing members at the bilateral as well as the multilateral level. This asymmetry has led to enormous efforts by developing members to form a block based on certain agreed principles for negotiation and apply pressure on the developed countries for a further round of negotiations to address their issues of concern. The refusal by the developed countries to recognise these concerns must inevitably result in a world trade configuration where we will recognise only two types of country: developed countries and countries in need.

Notes

1. This chapter is written from the perspective of a competition lawyer. The views expressed herein are my own and do not purport to be the views of the South African government or any of its institutions.
2. 'Globalization and Competition Policy' – The Sydney Institute, Monday 23 April 2001.
3. Moral rights include the right of an author to be acknowledged as the source of a work and the right to the integrity of the work. These rights are part of the Continental authors' rights system. They are non-economic in character and in many jurisdictions they are inalienable.
4. These are pharmaceutical companies whose product development activities are largely based on traditional knowledge. They have established systems to recognise the value of traditional knowledge and to provide a certain measure of compensation to local people for the knowledge.
5. This study was conducted for the purpose of a South African Competition Board inquiry by one of the complainants in the matter, and was undisputed by the multinational defendant. Similar results have been reported to the South African Parliament by the Minister of Health (Dr Zuma at the time) on various occasions.
6. 5 February 1999 – The US Dept of State sends a report to the US Congress, entitled 'US Government efforts to negotiate the repeal, termination, or withdrawal of Article 15(c) of the South African Medicines and Related Substances Act of 1965'. (The report is available at http://www.cptech.org.)

References

Juma, C. (1989) *The Gene Hunters: Biotechnology and the Scramble for Seeds* (London and Princeton: Zed Books and Princeton University Press).
Laird, S. (1994) 'Natural Products and the Commercialization of Traditional Knowledge', in T. Greaves (ed.), *Intellectual Property Rights for Indigenous Peoples: A Sourcebook* (Oklahoma City, Okla.: Society for Applied Anthropology), pp. 145–9.
Posey, D. (1991) 'Intellectual Property Rights for Native Peoples: Challenges in Science, Business, and International Law', paper prepared for the International Symposium on Property Rights, Biotechnology and Genetic Resources, Nairobi, Kenya.
Posey, D. and Dutfield, G. (1996) *Beyond Intellectual Property* (Ottawa: International Development Research Centre).

Reid, W. *et al.* (1993) *Biodiversity Prospecting Using Genetic Resources for Sustainable Development* (Washington, DC: World Resources Institute (WRI)).

Weissman, R. (1996) 'A Long Strange TRIPS: The Pharmaceutical Industry Drive to Harmonize Global Intellectual Property Rules, and the Remaining WTO Legal Alternatives Available to Third World Countries', *University of Pennsylvania Journal of International Economic Law*, vol. 17, no. 4, pp. 1069–125.

Part IV

Ownership of Knowledge: Changing the Rules

12
Rethinking Intellectual Property Rights and TRIPS

Martin Khor

Introduction and summary

The Agreement on Trade-Related Aspects of Intellectual Property Rights (TRIPS) was established as part of the World Trade Organization (WTO) regime that came into operation on 1 January 1995. It established minimum standards for a set of intellectual property rights (IPRs) that WTO members have to institute through national legislation. Many developing countries had tried to resist the entrance of IPRs as a subject in the Uruguay Round, and then they tried to limit what they saw as the more damaging aspects of the proposals coming from developed countries. But at the end of the Round, the developed countries (and the companies and industries of the North that were the driving forces and lobbies behind the proposals and negotiations) succeeded in getting most of what they had hoped for on IPRs in TRIPS. TRIPS has been considered by some economics experts of developing countries as the WTO agreement that has the potential to cause the most damage to prospects for development.

In the six years since TRIPS was established, there has been increasing evidence of many social and economic problems (some of them quite dramatic and very serious) caused by the introduction of stricter laws on IPRs as a result of implementation of TRIPS. This is leading to increased public awareness around the world that the present IPR system is heavily tilted in favour of holders of IPRs and against the public interest. This awareness is giving rise to disenchantment with the IPRs regime and with TRIPS. In an increasing number of cases, this dissatisfaction has given rise to public outrage and street demonstrations.

Among the problems are:

- The jacking up of prices of consumer products (including some essential items such as medicines) by companies owning IPRs, reducing consumers' access and affecting their welfare, health and lives;
- The high cost to firms in developing countries which have to pay high royalties for use of technology, or are unable to get permission from IPR holders to use modern technologies, thus affecting the capacity of such countries to modernise; and
- The phenomenon of 'biopiracy' in which corporations (mainly of the North) have been able to patent biological resources and the knowledge of their use (most of which originate in the South).

In the first case, consumers in developed and developing countries lose out. In the second case, producers in developing countries are severely constrained from upgrading their technology. In the third case, farmers and indigenous people (especially in the South) have their knowledge appropriated and on top of that their ability to continue to use their resources and knowledge may be adversely affected. Consumers who depend on these groups also lose out. In all cases, the IPR holders, which are mainly large corporations of the North, are given the special privilege of monopoly rights which prevent competition from other or potential producers, thereby potentially allowing them to obtain global monopoly profits. This rentier income is at the expense of: consumers and the fulfilment of human needs; other producers; researchers and scientists who in many cases are prevented or constrained from making use of patented materials; economic development, as well as the environment.

As the imbalances and problems generated by TRIPS become more obvious, there is mounting public demand for change. The range of demands include the following:

- more time, flexibility and freedom to choose options for developing countries in the implementation of the agreement;
- restraint by developed countries and their corporations from taking action against developing countries;
- a review and revision of TRIPS to remove its problematic aspects and to enable the implementation of its positive aspects (such as provisions on technology transfer);
- the removal of TRIPS altogether from the WTO.

Some serious problems caused by IPRs and TRIPS

IPRs are not 'natural rights' but rather privileges granted to inventors and authors to reward them for inventions and works. This conferring of monopoly privileges is supposed to be an incentive for innovation, and to enable recovery of cost. Any IPR system has to balance the privilege given to inventors and corporations owning the IPRs with the public interest. The public interest includes consumer welfare, the right of other producers to use technology, the right to development, and environmental protection.

TRIPS has resulted in a very significant shift in the balance in the IPR regime away from the public interest towards the monopolistic privileges of IPR holders. TRIPS is a legally binding international framework enforceable in the WTO. The WTO has over 140 member states. TRIPS, therefore, has effectively globalised a 'one-size-fits-all' system of IPRs where the same standards are set for countries of differing levels of development. It is in the developing countries where the unsuitability and effects of many of its provisions are most adversely and acutely felt. Even in developed countries, consumers, the public and the scientific community in general also suffer adverse effects.

There follow some of the problems caused by TRIPS.

(a) Effects on consumer access to essential and other products

Consumers are becoming aware that prices of many IPR-protected products are jacked up, in some cases many times above the cost of production, because the corporations owning a patent or copyright can prevent competition from other or potential producers.

Pre-TRIPS countries were able to set their own IPR policies and legislation. Most developing countries exempted essential consumer items, especially pharmaceutical drugs, food products and biological materials (including seeds and plant varieties) from patentability. Under TRIPS most inventions are patentable if they meet the criteria of patentability (see Article 27.1). Inventions can only be excluded from patentability if they fall within a specified ground of exclusion. Drugs and food products are not explicitly mentioned as products that can be excluded. Some biological materials and processes appear to be included as patentable items and plant varieties must also be protected (although not necessarily by patents).

Prices of some consumer products are fixed by companies owning IPRs far above the levels that would prevail had there been free competition. The most obvious and outrageous example is pharmaceutical drugs, as shown dramatically in the recently highlighted case of AIDS medicines. The claim that but for the patent system the drugs would not exist is problematic. It ignores the vital role of the public-sector funding in producing many basic breakthroughs in medicine. Moreover, as Chapter 2 by Stuart Macdonald in this book shows, the patent system is fundamentally an anti-innovation system.

A year's supply of a combination of AIDS medicines costs US$10 000–15 000 in the USA. The price for a similar combination offered by an Indian generic drug producer is around US$300. The margin of profit for the branded product covered by patent seems high, even taking into account the costs of R&D. Under TRIPS standards, if a patent for a medicine has been registered in a developing country, other producers are not permitted to produce, import or sell the medicine (without the permission of the patent holder). Patients in developing countries will thus be even less able to afford medicines that are patented, as the AIDS drugs example shows.

TRIPS does allow for compulsory licensing, including in the field of pharmaceuticals, and it does not prescribe a rule for the exhaustion of intellectual property rights (see Chapter 5 by James Love). However, developing countries can be put under pressure not to take advantage of their rights under TRIPS (see Chapter 11 by Willem Pretorius). This kind of bullying has given TRIPS, which already has a bad name, an even worse image as it has become obvious that both the TNCs that own patents and the governments of some rich countries are adamant in putting the right to make monopoly profits above the right of patients to health and life.

When public outrage over this was expressed in South Africa and other developing countries, and echoed in developed countries through reports and actions by groups such as Médecins Sans Frontières, Oxfam, RAFI and GRAIN, and through the media, one of the drug firms announced it would supply a combination of two AIDS drugs at $600 to developing countries, a price level at which, it said, it would not make a profit. Clearly the profit margin from selling the drug at $10 000 and above was high. The reduction in the price for developing countries is read by some as an attempt by the company to limit the public outrage, save the patent system from a possible basic challenge, and remove the possibility of developing countries exercising their option of granting compulsory licences in relation to the patents on AIDS drugs.

In the case of another product, computer software, the prices are also usually far above the cost of production. If they have to purchase software products at developed country prices, most consumers in developing countries would be unable to afford them. This in turn would shut them out of an important part of the 'knowledge society' and be a major contribution to the global 'digital divide' (see Chapters 8 and 9 by Alan Story and Gary Lea in this volume). In many countries, consumers have obtained copies of software freely or cheaply. However, there is increasingly strict enforcement of copyright laws, made mandatory by TRIPS, in many countries, with raids by government enforcement agencies together with representatives of multinational software companies. As enforcement becomes more effective, the would-be users of software (individual consumers as well as companies, educational institutions and so on) will find their access shut off or significantly reduced.

(b) Adverse effects of TRIPS on development and industries in developing countries

Historically, technology transfer has played a key role in industrialisation. A large part of this transfer took place by firms imitating or copying the technologies used by others. Producers in developing countries will find it difficult or impossible to copy technology which is IPR-protected when TRIPS and associated national legislation take effect. Domestic firms that wish to make use of the technology will have to obtain permission from the holder of the relevant IPRs (who may or may not grant the permission, even if the applicant intends to pay the commercial rate) and pay expensive royalties. Many firms may not be able to afford the fees and those that can will find that the high cost reduces their ability to be competitive. The TRIPS IPR regime puts high barriers in the way of developing countries' efforts to upgrade their technology levels.

The one-size-fits-all, or rather one-standard-fits-all, approach of TRIPS is a great disservice to developing countries. Many of the present-day developed countries did not adopt IPR legislation or strict IPR standards when they were going through the stages of development that the developing countries of today are attempting to go through. In Switzerland a hundred years ago, as a rule, Swiss industrial inventions could be patented abroad where patent legislation was in effect but, as Switzerland had no patent laws, Swiss industries were free to copy foreign inventions without restrictions (Gerster, 1999). When most of the now-developed countries established their patent and other IPR laws in the nineteenth century, all of these IPR regimes were highly 'deficient' by the standards of today (Chang, 2001). Few of them allowed patents on chemical and pharmaceutical substances until the last decades of the twentieth century. Pharmaceutical products became patentable only in 1967 in West Germany and France, 1979 in Italy and 1992 in Spain. Similarly, chemical substances became patentable in 1967 in West Germany, 1968 in Nordic countries, 1976 in Japan, 1978 in Switzerland and 1992 in Spain (Chang, 2001).

If, at the same stage of their development, developed countries had had to adhere to the minimum standards set by TRIPS, it is most doubtful that many of them would have attained the levels of technology and industrialisation that they achieved. Yet the developing countries of today are asked to adhere to IPR standards that would effectively prevent them from taking the same technology path as the developed countries. It is hard to avoid the conclusion that TRIPS is a protectionist device designed not only to advance the monopoly privileges of global corporations but also to prevent developing countries from being successful competitors to developed countries.

As Correa (2000) concluded:

> The strengthening and expansion of IPRs are likely to adversely affect the conditions for access to and use of technology, and thereby the prospects for industrial and technological development in developing countries ... Under the TRIPS agreement, reverse engineering and other methods of imitative innovation – that industrialized countries extensively used during their own processes of industrialization – shall be increasingly restricted, thereby making technological catching-up more difficult than before. (pp. 18–19)

An example of difficulties facing local firms in developing countries is that of Indian industry attempting to adjust to India's implementation of its obligations under the Montreal Protocol, in which members have agreed to phase out their use of CFCs and other ozone-damaging substances by certain target dates. Indian-owned firms have been producing CFCs that are used in the manufacture of refrigerators and air-conditioners in India. The Indian CFC producers wanted to shift from making CFCs to an environmentally sound substitute, HFC 134a. A few companies in developed countries control the patents to HFC 134a. An Indian company seeking access to the technology of producing HFC 134a was quoted a very high price (US$25 million) by a transnational company (TNC) holding the patent. The TNC proposed to the Indian firm two alternatives to the sale, one being that it be allowed a majority share in a joint venture with the Indian firm and the other that the Indian firm agree to restrict its exports of HFC 134a produced in India.

Both options were unacceptable to the Indian firm. The initial quoted price was also far too high as it was estimated that the fee should at most have been US$2–8 million (Watal, 2000).

This case shows not only the difficulty for a developing country firm and industry to modernise its technology but also for a developing country to meet its commitments under a multilateral environment agreement (MEA). Even if a local firm is willing to pay the market rate to obtain permission to use patented technology, the patent holder can quote an unreasonably high price, or impose unacceptable conditions, or even refuse permission outright. Moreover, although some MEAs may have financial-assistance, technology-transfer and technology-assisting clauses supposedly to benefit developing countries, in practice developing countries are finding that developed countries may not fulfil their obligations on such assistance. This makes it harder for developing countries to fulfil their obligations under MEAs.

(c) IPRs, biological materials and biopiracy

Another major controversy is the way TRIPS has facilitated the patenting of life forms as well as 'biopiracy', or the exploitative appropriation by transnational companies of the biological resources and traditional knowledge of local communities based mainly in developing countries.

Before TRIPS, many developing countries did not permit the patenting of life forms, biological resources and knowledge about their use. This changed with TRIPS. Article 27.3(b) of TRIPS allows for the exclusion from patentability of plants and animals (but not micro-organisms) as well as the exclusion of essentially biological processes for the production of plants and animals (but not for non-biological and microbiological processes). Some scientists argue that there is no scientific basis for the patenting of life forms even if they are genetically modified. The patent system is an inappropriate method for rewarding innovations in the field of biological sciences or in relation to biological materials and processes (Shiva, 1995; Egziabher, 1999; Ho and Traavik, 1999). A fundamental critique of patents on life has been made by Tewolde Egziabher, the African scientist and General Manager of the Ethiopia Environment Authority, and Chair of the Africa Group in the negotiations surrounding the Convention on Biological Diversity (CBD). According to Tewolde Egziabher (1999), the patent system is inappropriate when applied to biological processes because living things are not invented. Furthermore, unlike mechanical things and processes, they reproduce themselves. This is also true of genetically modified organisms. He further argues that discoveries relating to life forms and living processes should also be rewarded, but not through the patent system:

> Distorting the meaning of patenting in order to make it applicable to life only serves to attract the rejection of the whole system. Who ever worried about the legitimacy of patenting before the 1990s, before it became known that the USA was allowing the patenting of living things? But now, opposition is growing all the time, opposition not only to the legitimacy, but also to the legality of patenting.

Article 27.3(b) also requires members to grant protection for plant varieties, either through patents, a *sui generis* system or a combination of both. Previously, few developing countries granted IPRs protection for plant breeding and plant varieties. TRIPS opens the road for either patenting or a system of plant breeders' rights that may restrict the right of farmers to save, exchange and use seed.

Many developing countries in the WTO have argued that Article 27.3(b) should be amended. The Africa group has proposed that the TRIPS review process should make it clear that plants, animals, micro-organisms and their parts, as well as natural processes, are unpatentable. It also proposed that the review of TRIPS under Article 27.3(b) clarify that, in implementing plant varieties protection, developing countries should be allowed to institute a *sui generis* law that protects the knowledge and innovations of indigenous and local farming communities and provides for the continuation of traditional farming practices, including the right to save, exchange, use seeds and sell harvest.

The signs are that TRIPS has opened the floodgates to the corporate patenting of life, and to biopiracy. The London-based *Guardian*'s special report on 'The Ethics of Genetics' (15 November 2000) found that, as of November 2000, patents are pending or have been granted by 40 patent authorities worldwide on over 500 000 genes and partial gene sequences in living organisms. Of these there are over 9000 patents pending or granted involving 161 195 whole or partial human genes.

Patents have been given on genes or natural compounds from plants that are traditionally grown in developing countries (including rice, cocoa, cassava) and on genes in staple food crops originating in developing countries (including maize, potato, soybean, wheat). Patents have also been granted on plants used for medicinal and other purposes (for example, as an insecticide) by people in developing countries. Examples include a US patent for the use of turmeric for healing wounds (this was successfully challenged by the Indian government on the ground that it has been traditionally used by Indian people for healing wounds) and the patenting by American scientists of a protein from Thai bitter gourd after Thai scientists found its compounds could be used against the AIDS virus.

The thousands of cases of life patents and the increasing evidence of biopiracy has aroused indignation among a wide range of people and institutions, including: governments of the South and their delegations at the CBD and WTO; organisations of farmers and indigenous people worldwide, particularly the South; development NGOs in the South and North; the environment community; and also the human rights community. The controversy has threatened the legitimacy and questioned the legality of the IPRs system and TRIPS.

(d) Questionable claims and unkept promises

Disenchantment over TRIPS and the IPRs regime has also arisen because some of the claims made on behalf of a strict IPR regime have not been borne out, whilst some promises of benefits have not been fulfilled. It has been claimed that a strict IPR regime is needed in order to promote innovation and research by providing incentives. However, there has been criticism from many quarters that in fact IPRs discourage or help to prevent scientific research (see Chapter 2 by Stuart Macdonald in this volume). In developing countries, most patents are held by foreigners, and local R&D can be stifled since the monopoly rights conferred by patents restrict the research by local researchers (Oh, 2000). There are also concerns that the changes to the IPRs policies in developing countries will adversely affect local research in the area of new plant varieties and genetically engineered plants. Researchers and librarians in the North are also concerned that current IPRs practices and trends in information technology will constrain and stifle the flow and use of information.

TRIPS has many references and provisions that deal with technology transfer. Article 7 on objectives states that IPRs should promote innovation and transfer technology. Article 66.2 on least-developed countries (LDCs) states that developed countries shall provide incentives to their enterprises and institutions to promote technology transfer to LDCs. However, little or nothing has been done by developed countries to provide either concessions or incentives to their enterprises to transfer technology to developing countries. Confidence in the sincerity and intentions of developed countries to fulfil all their obligations under TRIPS has been eroded.

Some conclusions and proposals

The IPR system under the influence of TRIPS has tilted the balance between owners and users of technology and knowledge much too far in the direction of holders of IPRs. Moreover, in the balance of rights and obligations of intellectual property owners, their privileges and rights have been overly protected whilst their obligations to the social and economic welfare of the public have been loosely defined. There are also asymmetries between North and South in the balance of benefits and costs. Developing countries are overwhelmingly dependent on innovations made in the North: patent applicants from developing countries constituted less than 2 per cent of all applicants in the US between 1977 and 1996. Developed countries dominate the trade in medium and high tech goods. Thus, the worldwide establishment of strict IPRs standards under TRIPS will result in benefits accruing overwhelmingly to the developed countries, paid for by the increased costs accruing to the developing countries. It is time to redress these imbalances and asymmetries.

The following are some proposals:

- Many developing countries are facing difficulties in implementing TRIPS at the national level. Taking this into account, the transition period for developing countries should be extended until a proper review of TRIPS is carried out and appropriate changes are made to the agreement.
- In implementing TRIPS through national legislation, developing countries must be allowed the flexibility to choose between different options, without any form of coercion or pressure being brought to bear on them. The various options, together with the advantages and disadvantages of each option, should be explained to developing countries.
- Within the scope and space enabled by the provisions of TRIPS, developing countries should make strong efforts to choose the options that are least damaging and that best protect national and public interests. (See TWN, 1998; Correa, 1998.)
- Pressures should not be put on developing countries through bilateral means, regional arrangements or the process of accession to WTO to get them to agree to implement IPR standards even higher than those in TRIPS. Such pressures have been and are being applied by some developed countries.
- Similarly, pressures must not be put on developing countries to give up the use of options available to them under TRIPS.

- The mandated review of Article 27.3(b) of TRIPS should resolve the artificial distinctions made between the patentability of some organisms and biological processes and not others. This may be resolved by following the proposal of the Africa Group in the WTO that the review should clarify that all living organisms and their parts and all living processes should not be patentable. Article 27.3(b) should be amended to reflect this goal of a prohibition on the patenting of life. The transition period for implementing Article 27.3(b) should be extended to five years after the review is completed.
- Plant varieties are part of living organisms. The exclusion of patentability should also apply to them. Countries should, however, be allowed to devise a suitable system of reward or incentive for plant breeders if they so desire. This should not be compulsory and should be left to each country to decide. Such a system should not compromise the rights and practices of local communities. Countries may also wish to institute policies and legislation that protect and promote traditional knowledge and the rights of local communities to their resources and their knowledge.
- In relation to medicines that are needed for serious and life-threatening ailments, countries should be allowed the flexibility to exclude these from patentability. Indeed, countries should be allowed to exempt pharmaceutical drugs in general and the drug industrial sector from being subjected to patent protection. This can be done through an amendment to TRIPS. (A proposal by developing countries, that 'the list of exceptions to patentability in Article 27.3(b) of TRIPS shall include the list of essential drugs of the WHO', is part of para. 21 of the Draft Seattle Ministerial Text of 19 October 1999 and is under active discussion on implementation issues currently before the WTO.)
- Countries should also be allowed to exempt environmentally sound technology from patentability.
- The transfer of technology provisions and the public welfare objectives of TRIPS (including Articles 7, 8 and 66.2) should be made legally obligatory and operationalised. Developed countries and their enterprises should be obliged to put into effect the transfer and dissemination of technology to developing countries.
- Developing countries should also be given the flexibility to exempt certain products and sectors from IPR protection on grounds of public welfare and the need to meet development objectives.
- Finally, WTO members should seriously reconsider whether TRIPS belongs in the WTO. IPRs are not a trade issue. Moreover, high IPRs standards constitute a form of protection that prevents or constrains the international transfer of technology. They constitute the

institutionalisation of monopoly privileges in the global trading system, an institutionalisation that results in rentier incomes, the restraint of competition and the promotion of anti-competitive behaviour. It is an aberration that TRIPS is located in a trade organisation whose main functions are supposed to be the promotion of trade liberalisation and conditions of market competition. The reality is that TRIPS was placed in the WTO because developed countries wished to make use of its dispute-settlement system in order to ensure effective enforcement of its disciplines on developing countries. Recently, there have been calls made to governments to transfer TRIPS out of the WTO. The joint NGO statement, 'WTO: Shrink or Sink', formulated in March 2000 and endorsed by a thousand NGOs worldwide, has called for the removal of TRIPS from the WTO.

Recently, in a letter to the *Financial Times* the free-trade economist, Jagdish Bhagwati, has argued that intellectual property protection does not belong in the WTO. He has declared support for the NGO statement 'asking for the IP leg of the WTO to be sawn off'. He also argues that the WTO must be about mutual gains in trade, whereas intellectual property protection is a tax on poor countries' use of knowledge, constituting a wealth transfer to the rich countries. 'We were turning the WTO, thanks to powerful lobbies, into a royalty-collection agency, by pretending, through continuous propaganda that our media bought into, that somehow the question was "trade related"', Bhagwati remarked. The review of TRIPS should therefore include on the agenda the question of its removal from the WTO so that the trade organisation can return to its mission of promoting balanced trade relations.

References

Chang, Ha-Joon (2001) 'Intellectual Property Rights and Economic Development: Historical Lessons and Emerging Issues', *Journal of Human Development*, vol. 2, p. 287.

Correa, Carlos (1998) *Implementing the TRIPS Agreement: General Context and Implications for Developing Countries* (Penang, Third World Network).

Correa, Carlos (2000) *Intellectual Property Rights, the WTO and Developing Countries* (Penang, Third World Network).

Egziabher, Tewolde (1999) 'Patenting Life is Owning Life', published in *Third World Resurgence*, June, no. 106, p. 11.

Gerster, Richard (1999) 'Patents and Development', published in the *Journal of World Intellectual Property*, July 1998, vol. 2.

Ho, Mae-Wan and Terje Traavik (1999) 'No Scientific Basis for Patenting under TRIPS Article 27.3b', published in *Third World Resurgence*, June, no. 106, p. 13.

Oh, Cecilia (2000) 'IPRs and Biological Resources: Implications for Developing Countries', Third World Network, Briefing Paper.

Shiva, Vandana (1995) 'Patents on Life Forms: Playing God?', published in *Third World Resurgence*, May.

Third World Network (TWN) (1998) *Options for Implementing the TRIPS Agreement in Developing Countries* (Penang, Third World Network).

Watal, Jayashree (2000) 'India: The Issue of Technology Transfer in the Context of the Montreal Protocol', in Jha Veena and Ulrich Hoffman (eds.), *Achieving Objectives of Multinational Environmental Agreements: A Package of Trade Measures and Positive Measures* (UNCTAD/ITCD/TED/6 April, United Nations), p. 63.

WTO (1999) Preparation for the 1999 Ministerial Conference: Ministerial Text Revised Draft (19 October).

13

India's Plant Variety Protection and Farmers' Rights Legislation

Suman Sahai

The Indian Parliament has finally passed the Plant Variety Protection and Farmers' Rights Act (2001). Its passage has ended a long and arduous struggle waged for the recognition of the rights of farmers in India's *sui generis* legislation. India has now put in place a law to grant plant breeders' rights on new varieties of seeds, for the very first time. It has simultaneously provided for farmers' rights.

A law granting plant breeders' rights was necessitated by the commitments that India made in the Agreement on Trade-Related Aspects of Intellectual Property Rights (TRIPS) when it ratified the Uruguay GATT Round in 1994. Article 27.3(b), which deals with the protection of new plant varieties, offers three options. Protection may be granted by a patent, an effective *sui generis* system or by a combination of the two. The *sui generis* system refers to the grant of plant breeders' rights. The precise type of system is not defined, except to say that it should be effective. India ultimately opted for the *sui generis* option but not without a determined struggle by civil society to stop seed patents.

What started as a Bill heavily loaded in favour of breeders and falling far short of protecting the rights of farmers has now got a reasonable section on farmers' rights. This is the result of a determined and sustained campaign by civil society groups, spearheaded by Gene Campaign. We have insisted since 1993, when the Uruguay Round was concluded, that if the status quo has to be changed in India and we have to grant plant breeders' rights, our legislation will also have to grant strong farmers' rights.

Gene Campaign's demand has been for a concept of farmers' rights that would allow the farming community to retain the same control over seed production and use that it has always had. As against the widely articulated demand that farmers' rights should constitute the

214

right to save seed from the harvest to sow the next crop (plant-back rights), Gene Campaign's position has been different. We have maintained that plant-back rights were no rights, only exemptions. Such exemptions, sometimes referred to as farmer's privilege, were allowed under the International Union for the Protection of New Varieties of Plants (1961) (commonly referred to as UPOV, its French acronym) and were limited to plant-back rights in varying degrees. In some UPOV member countries, France for example, limited exemptions were granted to farmers while in others, such as Greece, these were more generous. Exemptions for farmers were retained till the 1978 version of UPOV. They have been considerably diluted since. After the last amendment in 1991, exemptions for farmers are no longer a matter of course. They have been made optional and are subject to the consent of the breeder.

Gene Campaign has insisted that Indian law has to grant well-defined rights and not just provide beggarly exemptions to its farmers. These rights have to be recognised because of the past and present contributions made by the farming community to the conservation of agro-biodiversity and the role of farmers as dynamic breeders of new varieties which anchor the food security of the world.

To make certain the farmer does not get displaced by companies as a seed producer, the key element was to ensure that the farmer retained the right to sell seed to other farmers, even if the variety was protected by a breeder's right. This right to sell seed is crucial to maintaining the livelihood basis of the farming community and the nation's self-reliance in agriculture. This clause, the right to sell seed, was the most fiercely resisted and was till now the major bone of contention. In addition to this, as part of farmers' rights, we wanted payment for the use of farmer varieties and their informed consent to any use. We also wanted compensation for the farmer if poor-quality, spurious seeds led to crop failure.

A note on the campaign

The campaign for getting strong farmers' rights began at the conclusion of the Uruguay Round, as soon as the Indian government opted for the *sui generis* option under TRIPS. Gene Campaign worked with every new government that came, demanding a re-opening of the draft legislation and presenting our version of farmers' rights. The media campaign included writing articles in the English and vernacular press, exposing the official draft as bogus and detrimental to farmers, and explaining what kind of farmers' rights were needed in India and why.

We lobbied members of Parliament and State Assemblies, framed questions for MPs to raise in Parliament and prepared briefing documents for Joint Parliamentary Committees on the crucial need for farmers' rights. We mobilised public opinion by organising information meetings with rural people and local opinion-builders at the district and block levels.

In order to sustain the campaign, we produced very simple literature in regional languages. This was used by the roughly thirty-five Gene Campaign Core Groups in seventeen states, to educate rural people about their rights and to form the basis of their demonstrations, protests, memoranda and petitions to demand farmers' rights in a comprehensive form. These booklets and pamphlets were shared with other groups and unions. Campaign strategies included postcard and signature campaigns flooding the Agriculture Ministry. We held meetings in the constituencies of important MPs opposed to farmers' rights in order to apply the pressure of their voters on them. Seminars, workshops and discussions amongst farmers, scientists and policy makers were organised in many states. Gene Campaign Core Groups worked with many voluntary groups and some farmer unions in the states. Some of these are: the Abhinav Vikas Samiti in Bihar and Jharkhand; Kamraj Foundation and Sahitya Parishad in Kerala; Centre for Environmental Concerns, Andhra Pradesh; Centre for Environmental and Agricultural Development, Uttar Pradesh and Delhi; Vikas Manch in Karnataka; MS Swaminathan Research Foundation, Tamil Nadu; North Eastern Network in Assam, Meghalaya, Manipur and Nagaland. We worked with farmer organisations such as Kissan Morcha in Uttar Pradesh, Bihar and Rajasthan, Shetkari Sangathana in Wardha, Kissan Sabha in Haryana, and Punjab and the Sanyukta Kissan Sangh. Begun in 1994, we persevered with the campaign for seven years till we finally got a decent law on farmers' rights.

Importance of farmers' right to sell seed

The pivotal importance of the farmer having the right to sell (not save, not exchange, but sell) seed has to be seen in the context of seed production in India. In India, the farming community is the largest seed producer, providing about 85 per cent of the country's annual requirement of over 6 million tons. If the farmer were to be denied the right to sell, it would result in a substantial loss of income for him or her. But far more importantly, such a step would displace the farming community as the country's major seed provider. The only replacement, if this were to happen, would be the large life-science corporations. Budget cuts have seriously weakened the capacity and output of the other player in India, public research institutions. Globally, the agro-chemical giants turned life-science corporations are emerging as the largest seed producers in the industrialised nations. In Europe and the US, as also in Canada, Australia, New Zealand, Japan and, to a lesser extent, Korea and some Latin American countries, seed production is now in the hands of these corporations. Control over the seed sector was established by the simple expediency of buying up all the smaller seed companies. In India such a strategy cannot work because there are simply no seed companies of any significance or size that can be bought and that would transfer their market share to the multinational corporation (MNC) that bought it.

In India, a strategy to control seed production would have to rest on knocking the farmers out of the market by some other means. Since they are not organised in a company that can be purchased, this can only be done by legally taking away their right to sell seed. If the farmer can be stopped by law from selling seed (and by implication, producing seed), the market automatically becomes available to the next alternative, the MNC. This is precisely why the Farmers' Rights clause in the Indian plant variety protection legislation has been the subject of such a tussle between the seed industry and pro-farmer groups such as Gene Campaign.

Weak farmers' rights will allow seed corporations to dominate the seed market. Strong farmers' rights keep the farming community alive and well as viable competitors and an effective deterrent to a takeover of the seed market by the corporate sector. Control over seed production is central to self-reliance in food. The need for this self-reliance cannot be over-emphasised. Food security is at the forefront of national security. A nation that does not produce its own seed and its own food cannot be a secure nation. An analysis of the salient features of the legislation is given below.

Farmers' rights in the new law

The new law recognises the farmer not just as a cultivator but also as a conserver of the agricultural gene pool and a breeder who has bred several successful varieties. Farmers' Rights (s. 39, clause (iv)), in part reads as follows:

> The farmer ... shall be deemed to be entitled to save, use, sow, resow, exchange, share or sell his farm produce including seed of a variety

protected under this Act in the same manner as he was entitled before the coming into force of this Act.;

Provided that the farmer shall not be entitled to sell branded seed of a variety protected under this Act.

Explanation: for the purpose of clause (iii) branded seed means any seed put in a package or any other container and labelled in a manner indicating that such seed is of a variety protected under this Act.

This formulation allows the farmer to sell seed in the way he has always done, with the restriction that this seed cannot be branded with the breeder's registered name. In this way, both farmers' and breeders' rights are protected. The breeder is rewarded for his innovation, but without being able to threaten the farmer's ability independently to engage in his livelihood, and supporting the livelihood of other farmers.

Why will the farmer buy seeds of a variety under breeders' rights? The answer lies in the fact that the farming community is dynamic and constantly looks for better/different varieties of seeds to experiment with. Farmers will, if they can, try out new varieties being offered, procuring seed either from seed shops or from exhibitions organised by public research institutions. There is no reason why this will change. In India so far there has been no restriction on the movement of seed. Once bought, the seed belongs to the farmer, to do what he wants with. Since these conditions would have changed with the introduction of breeders' rights, it was important to secure legally the rights of farmers so that they can continue to experiment with new varieties without any threat to their self-reliance.

Other kinds of protection for the farmer

Apart from the right to sell the non-branded seed of protected varieties, the rights of farmers and local communities are protected in other ways as well. There are provisions for acknowledging the role of rural communities as contributors of land races and farmers' varieties in the breeding of new plant varieties. Breeders wanting to use farmers' varieties for creating Essentially Derived Varieties (EDVs) cannot do so without the express permission of the farmers involved in the conservation of such varieties. EDVs are those varieties which are more or less (essentially) the same as the parent variety except for very minor changes. For example, Bt cotton (an EDV) is a cotton variety identical to its parent except for the single difference of containing a bacterial gene from the Bacillus thuringensis.

Anyone is entitled to register a community's claim and have it duly recorded at a notified centre. The possibility of this kind of intervention enables the registration of farmers' varieties even if the farmers themselves do not register their varieties because of illiteracy or lack of awareness. If the claim on behalf of the community is found to be genuine, a procedure is initiated for benefit-sharing so that a share of profits made from the use of a farmers' variety in a new variety goes into a National Gene Fund.

Disclosure

Other details supportive of the rights of farmers are the explicit and detailed disclosure requirements in the passport data[1] required at the time of applying for a breeder's certificate. Concealment in the passport data will result in the breeder's certificate being cancelled.

GURT (terminator) forbidden

Breeders will have to submit an affidavit that their variety does not contain a Gene Use Restricting Technology (GURT) or terminator technology (varieties the subject of GURT have had a gene function switched off).

Exemption from fees

Farmers will be entitled to examine documents and papers or receive copies of rules and decisions made by the various authorities, without paying any fees. Such fees are payable by all other people.

Protection against innocent infringement

The legislation has also attempted to address a concern voiced in several quarters that when the new system of plant breeders' rights is imposed for the first time, there may be cases of innocent infringement of breeders' rights. Section 43 specifies that the farmer cannot be prosecuted for infringement of rights specified in the Act if he can prove in court that he was unaware of the existence of such a right.

Clauses that need improvement

Benefit-sharing

The use of farmers' varieties to breed new varieties will have to be paid for. Revenue will flow into a National Gene Fund. Despite its good intentions of protecting the interests of the farming community, the formulation of this section (s. 46.2(d)) is likely to create problems in implementation because the drafting is poor, even incomplete. The Gene Fund should be the recipient of all revenues payable to the farming community under various heads. Farming communities should collectively, rather than individually, access this money, except in clear cases where an identifiable farmer's variety has been used. Farmers should have the right to decide how this money, which they have earned, will be spent. The use of the money should not be restricted to conservation or for maintaining *ex-situ* collections.

The method for fixing and realising benefit-sharing should be made simpler and easier to implement. One approach to fixing benefit-sharing could be a system of lump-sum payments, based for example on (projected) volume of seed sale.

Protection against bad seed

In providing a liability clause in the section on farmers' rights, the farmer in principle is protected against the supply of spurious and/or poor-quality seed leading to crop failures. At present there is too much left to the discretion of the Plant Variety Authority which will fix the compensation. This will lead to arbitrary decisions and should be amended. If it is proven that the breeder has made false claims and that as a result the farmer has suffered a crop failure, then compensation should be awarded amounting to at least twice the projected harvest value of the crop. Compensation should be large enough to be a deterrent. In addition, a jail term should be provided if the breeder repeats the offence.

Breeders' rights

Breeders' rights over the varieties they have developed are more than adequately protected by the legislation. On registration, the breeder has rights of commercialisation for the registered variety either in his/her own person or through anyone he or she designates. These rights include the right to produce, sell, market, distribute, import or export a variety, in short, full control over the formal marketing of a variety. The strong protection granted to a plant breeder can be seen in the section dealing with infringement of a breeder's right where punishment in the form of substantial fines and jail terms has been prescribed for infringement.

Penalties for infringing breeders' rights

Violation of a breeder's right applies at several levels. It applies to the variety itself and also to its packaging. Legally, a similar-looking package to the breeder's will be considered as 'Passing Off' and so actionable.

Anyone other than the breeder naturally cannot use the registered name or denomination. The use of the same or similar name in any way, by action or even suggestion, will constitute a violation and is punishable.

Breeders' rights have been strengthened to the extent that if there is mere suspicion of violation or infringement, the onus of proving innocence is placed on the alleged violator. In any prosecution for falsely using a denomination, the burden of proof is reversed and it is incumbent on the alleged violator to prove that the consent of the breeder was obtained. This needs to be changed. The normal course in law is for the accuser to furnish proof for the accusation and there is no reason in this case to depart from this long-established principle of civil and criminal law.

Penalties range from Rs 50 000 to Rs 10 lakh as well as a jail term with a minimum of 3 months to a maximum of 2 years, depending on the severity of the damage caused. If the violator is actually selling, offering for sale or merely in the possession of a registered variety belonging to someone else, the jail term applicable will not be less than 6 months, going up to 2 years. If the offence is repeated, the minimum jail term prescribed is one year, extending to three years and the fine starts at Rs 1 lakh and may go up to Rs 20 lakh.

Rights of researchers

The Act contains provisions dealing with researchers' rights. These allow scientists and breeders to have free access to registered varieties for research and for creating other, new varieties. The breeder cannot intervene except when the registered variety needs to be used repeatedly as a parental line. In that case authorisation is required.

Protection of public interest

In the public interest, certain varieties may not be registered if it is believed that the prevention of commercial exploitation of such a variety is necessary to 'protect order or public morality or human, animal and plant life and health or to avoid serious prejudice to the environment'.

Compulsory licensing

The Act provides for the granting of a compulsory licence if it is shown that the reasonable requirements of the public for seeds have not been satisfied or that the seed of the variety is not available to the public at a reasonable price. The breeder is entitled to file an opposition but, should the charge be valid, the breeder may be ordered by the Authority to grant a compulsory licence under certain terms and conditions, including the payment of a reasonable licence fee. A compulsory licence, however, will not be awarded if the breeder can demonstrate reasonable grounds for his or her inability to produce the seed.

After plant-variety legislation, what next?

The next step is to decide through which international platform India will interact with other nations. The Indian government is a great votary of joining the UPOV system which is practically inimical to the needs of developing countries. It is likely that the new Indian law, with its reasonably strong farmers' rights, will raise issues of consistency with UPOV. UPOV does not acknowledge strong farmers' rights and granting the right to sell seed of a variety protected by a breeder's right will in all likelihood be inconsistent with UPOV standards.

Gene Campaign has been lobbying against India joining UPOV, pleading that developing countries need to craft their own platform in order to address their special needs, which are very different from the needs and requirements of industrialised countries for whom UPOV was developed.

CoFaB, a developing country alternative to UPOV

Along with the Centre for Environment and Agriculture Development, we have drafted an alternative treaty called the *Convention of Farmers and Breeders* (CoFaB). CoFaB has an agenda that is appropriate for developing countries. It reflects their strengths and their vulnerabilities and it seeks to secure their interests in agriculture and fulfil the food and nutritional security goals of their people.

Unlike the provisions of UPOV, CoFaB seeks to fulfil the following goals:

- Provide reliable, good-quality seeds to the small and large farmer;
- Maintain genetic diversity in the field;
- Provide breeders of new varieties with protection for their varieties in the market, without prejudice to the public interest;
- Acknowledge the enormous contribution of farmers to the identification, maintenance and refinement of germplasm;
- Acknowledge the role of farmers as creators of land races and traditional varieties which form the foundation of agriculture and modern plant breeding;

- Emphasise that the countries of the tropics are germplasm-owning countries and the primary source of agricultural varieties; and
- Develop a system wherein farmers and breeders have recognition and rights accruing from their respective contribution to the creation of new varieties.

Many of these features, like the role of the farmer as a breeder and a conserver, are part of the new Indian legislation, as is the farmer's right to share in the benefits derived from new varieties bred using farmers' varieties and land races. The farmer's right to reliable, good-quality seeds has been included in the law by providing a liability clause which will ensure compensation if the seed is of poor quality and fails to perform.

The UNDP Human Development Report (1999) has commended Gene Campaign's Convention of Farmers and Breeders as an alternative to UPOV. It describes CoFaB as a 'strong and coordinated international proposal which offers developing countries an alternative to following European legislation by focusing legislation on needs to protect farmers' rights to save and reuse seed and to fulfil the food and nutritional security goals of their people'.

Gene Campaign's purpose in drafting an alternative to UPOV was to provide the basis for a discussion on a non-UPOV platform for developing countries. Once there is a comprehensive analysis and critique of it and a consensus emerges among developing countries, it will not take long to come up with a final version of CoFaB.

India's Plant Variety Protection and Farmers' Rights Act provides rights to farmers and breeders and acknowledges the contributions of both. In India, as in all developing countries, many farmers are active breeders. Their innovation has to be respected and rewarded and provisions have been made in the new law to grant breeders' rights to farmer breeders. The new Indian law is far better adapted to the reality of developing country agriculture and more protective of its vulnerabilities than any version of UPOV. It is to be hoped that this law will prompt other developing countries to reject the UPOV model and develop their own *sui generis* system, one suited to their needs and requirements.

Note

1. The term passport data refers to information about a plant including its type, origin, history and ownership.

14

Defending the Public Interest in TRIPS and the WTO

Sol Picciotto

Should TRIPS stay in the WTO?

This chapter aims to discuss some of the defects of the World Trade Organization (WTO) as they affect the Agreement on Trade-Related Aspects of Intellectual Property Rights (TRIPS). The criticisms of TRIPS detailed in other chapters in this book demonstrate how it is potentially damaging to global public welfare. However, the alternatives to TRIPS could be even more harmful, since developing countries would be even more vulnerable to unilateral pressures and sanctions, and coerced bilateral agreements.

The central concern for any multilateral framework for intellectual property rights (IPRs) is that it should enable the scope of IPR protection to be defined by public welfare criteria. I suggest that it is from this perspective that we should consider whether TRIPS should remain in the WTO, and under what conditions. I suggest that this requires at a minimum some significant reforms of the WTO, particularly to rescue TRIPS and the WTO from the damaging effects of their capture by private interests.

Justifying IPRs: is a global public welfare standard possible?

IPRs are a very peculiar institution. They are a grant by the state of an exclusive right over intellectual creations, which creates a monopoly over intangible assets. This artificially created scarcity is in many ways inappropriate for knowledge-based assets, since they do not deplete when shared. In fact, both new technology and artistic and literary works provide the greatest social benefits by being widely diffused. Public availability enhances both pleasure and profit, since diffusion also reduces the marginal costs of further innovation. This is also true from the viewpoint of the originator, who rarely has an interest in concealing her or his creations. Originators also have other concerns, which can be protected in various ways, such as obtaining recognition for their contribution, and safeguarding the integrity of their creations (sometimes referred to as 'moral' rights).

Economists have therefore always had difficulty finding adequate justifications for these exclusive rights (Plant, 1934; Drahos, 1999). The common rationale refers to the need for an economic incentive to encourage innovation. However, closer examination of the socioeconomic processes of innovation and creativity shows that many of the justifications for IPRs are weak at best (see Stuart MacDonald, Chapter 2 in this book). The main spur to innovation is the 'first-mover' advantage, which ensures a higher rate of profit for leading-edge firms until the innovation becomes generalised. This does not require the artificial creation of monopoly rights. It is therefore paradoxical that the WTO, which is supposedly geared to stimulating economic efficiency through open markets, should establish obligations aiming at high levels of protection of monopoly rights. Furthermore, successful innovation depends on collective effort, much of which needs to be publicly funded or supported and to take place through an open exchange of ideas.

Thus, any valid justification for IPRs is much more limited, as a right of appropriation giving the originator sufficient protection to allow and encourage commercialisation. It is therefore vital that the extent of the monopoly should be limited, and balanced by obligations to ensure the optimum social benefit from diffusion. It is especially important to ensure such a balance since IPRs are generally exploited not by authors or inventors, whose creativity they are supposed to reward, but by large information-based corporations.

The balance between the rights of appropriation and obligations to ensure diffusion should be determined by public welfare criteria. This is not easy, since the super-profits which result from monopoly rights have always made the process of legislating on IPRs subject to intensive lobbying by private interests. It is even more difficult to strike this balance for global public welfare, given the very big differences in socioeconomic conditions between countries. When the modern systems of IPRs emerged during the early nineteenth century in the main capitalist countries, they generally required only national criteria of origination. This in effect encouraged the free importation of foreign inventions and books, which today is denounced as piracy. Only gradually did the main developed countries agree reciprocal recognition, culminating in the multilateral agreements establishing the Paris Industrial Property Union of 1883 (Plasseraud and Savignon, 1983), and the Berne Copyright Convention of 1886 (Ricketson, 1987). Nevertheless, the USA, which has now appointed itself the main global policeman of IPRs, refused copyright protection for foreign works until 1891, to protect local low-cost publishing (Barnes, 1974), and did not become a Party to the Berne Convention until 1989, at the same time that it placed the issue of IPRs on the agenda of the Uruguay Round. It seems that the late converts may be the most fervent apostles.

WTO: market access, regulation and the rule of law

The aim of inserting IPRs into the broader multilateral framework of the WTO was to overcome the difficulties of reaching consensus within a single-focus organisation such as WIPO, because of lack of reciprocity between countries which are mainly importers and those which are mainly exporters of information-based products and services (Ryan, 1998). This information gap exists mainly between developed and developing countries. Developing countries only reluctantly accepted the Uruguay Round package of trade-offs between improved market access for traded goods (textiles and agricultural products) and IPR protection. The danger is that they will be obliged to grant rights which facilitate TNCs' control over new knowledge-based industries, while their access to markets for old-industry products remains restricted.

TRIPs has placed IPRs firmly within the WTO's machinery, which is geared towards imposing 'disciplines' on national state regulation to ensure 'market access'. Advocates of neo-liberalism claim that these obligations do not restrict a state's right to regulate, provided it does not discriminate in favour of domestic firms. However, the experience under GATT has been that *any* regulatory differences are seen as an obstacle by foreign firms seeking access to a market, and the validity of national regulations has to be justified by stringent criteria, in particular the 'least-trade-restrictive' test. Even where GATT recognises a specific exception, as it does for IPRs in Article XX(d), it is hard to reconcile the conflict between the National Treatment obligations of Article III and the right to regulate under Article XX (Evans, 1996). For example, it could be argued that a requirement for local working of patents is neutral, but foreign patent owners would argue it discriminates against them and is protectionist of local industry.

Thus, the WTO agreements also entail a shift towards international harmonisation of regulation, by requiring states to adopt internal regulations based on international standards. It is not surprising that this has made the WTO the focus of debates and conflicts about globalisation. This raises three main issues for the WTO as an institution:

(i) the 'linkages' between the WTO and related regulatory regimes (especially standard-setting bodies);
(ii) the tension between uniformity and appropriate diversity inherent in the slippery concept of harmonisation; and
(iii) the accountability, transparency and responsibility of the WTO as a public institution.

The 'linkages' issue has been mainly associated with the debate about the 'social clause', in which it has been widely asserted that the ILO, not the WTO, is the appropriate body for labour standards. Equally, one of the criticisms of TRIPS is that WIPO should be the relevant body for IPRs. It can also be said that the Codex Alimentarius Commission is the relevant body for food safety standards, and the ISO and other bodies for technical standards. In practice, the WTO does not replace these other organisations, but the problem is that it has been placed in a powerful position towards them. A key issue for the future role of the WTO in global governance is whether it can develop truly cooperative relationships with such related organisations, rather than assuming that international trade should dominate all other concerns.

Perhaps the key element of the power of the WTO is that it can authorise the application of trade sanctions for breach of any of its agreements, under the procedures laid down in its Dispute-Settlement Understanding (DSU). This innocuous-sounding arrangement, developed as a form of political-diplomatic mediation and arbitration under the GATT, has become a world economic court in all but name (Weiler, 2000). It is also central to the legitimation of the WTO. As its new Director-General, Mike Moore has put it,

At the WTO, governments decide, not us... We do not lay down the law. We uphold the rule of law. The alternative is the law of the jungle, where might makes right, and the little guy doesn't get a look in. (Moore, 2000)

However, to paraphrase Clausewitz, law may be the pursuit of trade politics by other means. The rules governing the global economy are in fact laid down at the WTO, and in practice its complex systems of agreements and regulations are made and administered by unelected technocrats, whose activities are occasionally given political approval by semi-informed Trade Ministers. The WTO can't claim legitimacy merely because it acts through law, if the processes for making and applying those laws lack transparency, responsibility and accountability to the public (Picciotto, 2001). Further, when law is used to define and enforce economic rights, it can reinforce the rights of the economically strong, the haves against the have-nots. It also gives considerable power both to those who make the rules and to those who interpret them, the adjudicators.

The two issues, linkages and the legitimacy of WTO law, are powerfully combined in the important provisions on 'cross-retaliation' in the DSU. These govern the circumstances in which trade sanctions can be applied for a violation of any of the WTO's rules. The inclusion of TRIPS in the WTO will leave developing countries open to trade sanctions if they are found deficient in implementing any provision of TRIPS. The converse is also possible, and a developing country may be allowed to withdraw protection for IPRs of a developed country which is found to have violated trading rules.[1] In principle, 'cross-retaliation' under the DSU is only allowed if sanctions in the 'same sector' would be 'impracticable or ineffective'.[2] Thus, a state which fails to rectify measures found to be in breach of the patent provisions of TRIPS should, in principle, be subject to sanctions in respect of patent rights. However, cross-retaliation against a developing country's trade exports is likely to be approved under WTO rules, since withdrawal of IPR protection would be considered ineffective, precisely because few IPRs are owned by people or institutions in developing countries.

Furthermore, a developed country complaining of breach of TRIPS is likely to be able to show some hindrance also to a potential market in goods. This is enough to give the complaining state complete freedom to apply sanctions entirely to imports of goods, without even the need for approval as cross-retaliation, under the WTO rules as they were interpreted in the *Bananas* dispute. Following that decision, the US was able to retaliate against the EU's Bananas regime entirely against imports of goods from the EU, even though its complaint mainly concerned trade in services.[3] In contrast, Ecuador had to justify cross-retaliation by suspension of its obligations towards the EU under TRIPS, and this was permitted only to the extent that suspension of concessions in traded goods and wholesale trade services would be insufficient.[4]

These inequities show that the rules concerning cross-retaliation, and the freedom given to the complaining state to select sectors against which to retaliate, should be reconsidered in the review of WTO dispute settlement.

Private rights or public interests?

The WTO is especially unsuited to the evaluation of the desirable scope of IPR protection because of its domination by private interests. Defenders of the WTO argue that national state regulation tends to be protectionist because it is the product of the 'capture' of states by special interests. For example:

> Free trade and democratic government face a common obstacle – the influence of concentrated interest groups ... The WTO and the trade agreements it administers act to restrain protectionist interest groups, thereby promoting free trade and democracy. (McGinnis and Movesian, 2000, p. 515)

However, a far bigger danger is the converse: the deployment of free-trade rhetoric to secure the capture of the WTO by private interests, and thus to restrict the regulatory powers of democratic states. This pattern originated in US trade policy, with the establishment of the office of US Trade Representative (USTR), and the development of its powers and duties to open foreign markets for US firms under the provisions of the now-notorious s. 301 of the Trade Act.[5] This was extended to intellectual property in 1984 and strengthened by introducing the 'Special 301' annual review procedures in 1988.[6] It has been well documented that the capture of US trade policy by the pharmaceutical and media firms obtained the deployment of s. 301 of the Trade Act in support of strong intellectual property protection, and the insertion of TRIPS in the WTO (Ryan, 1998).

In principle, the WTO multilateral framework provides some defence, for WTO member states, against purely unilateral actions. However, the rejection of the EC complaint against s. 301 allows the US to continue to use it, based on US undertakings that the WTO dispute-settlement procedures will be complied with where they are relevant. This effectively allows the US (and for that matter the EU) to put pressure on states on IPR issues beyond the scope of TRIPS, provided they don't involve breaches of WTO obligations. Developing countries should adopt a common stand to resist bilateral pressures and insist that TRIPS be treated as a maximum and not a minimum.

In any case, the EC complaint did not tackle the pernicious way in which the s. 301 procedure in effect makes the USTR an agent for business firms in bringing WTO complaints. The procedure allows any 'interested person' to petition the USTR, and although the USTR has discretion in deciding whether to investigate, it is unlikely to refuse a petition by an important US firm. If an investigation finds a violation of US rights under a trade agreement or international law, the USTR is required to take action. Where a WTO agreement is involved, this means a WTO complaint must be filed.

Moreover, the mercantilist character of WTO bargaining, and the adversarial nature of its dispute-settlement procedures, induce a tit-for-tat mentality in governments. They tend to see their role as being to support 'their' firms and industries, although in the guise of upholding the law. Thus, the European Commission followed the US in introducing procedures encouraging business interests to bring complaints, which further strengthens their power to dictate the agenda of trade policy. In 1984 the EC adopted its version of s. 301, the New Commercial Policy Instrument (NCPI: see Zoller, 1985), which was replaced after the Uruguay Round from 1995 by the Trade Barriers Regulation (TBR: EC 3286/94).

The European authorities point out that unlike s. 301, the TBR aims only at enforcing rights under international agreements, and does not allow actions which are unilateral or aimed at forcing new concessions (van Eeckhaute, 1999, p. 200 fn. 4). Nevertheless, it is advertised as providing a means for private parties to trigger trade complaints, and was a key element of the Market Access Strategy launched by Leon Brittan in 1996, aiming to take the offensive in response to the spate of WTO complaints launched by the USA.[7] In practice, the main procedure used for trade complaints has been that under Article 133 of the EC Treaty.[8] However, the TBR procedure allows a firm (if supported by the Commission) to override political opposition by a blocking minority of member states in the Article 133 Committee.[9] Thus, a complaint by German aircraft manufacturer Dornier, against Brazil's export financing scheme as applied to aircraft, was brought under the TBR, since the Commission could see that there would be opposition in the Article 133 Committee from member states with firms acting as suppliers to the Brazilian aircraft producers (van Eeckhaute, 1999, p. 211).

The encouragement that these provisions give to firms to articulate their commercial interests in terms of market access rights has undoubtedly contributed to the rapid growth of complaints under the DSU. Even under TRIPS, although transition periods delayed its coming into force, there has been a high level of disputes. In its first 6 years, 23 complaints have involved TRIPS (out of 231 in total), 5 Panel reports (out of 53), and 1 Appellate Body report (out of 32).[10] In effect, all have been initiated by either the USA or the EU,[11] and most complaints so far have been between developed countries, since they had the shortest transition periods for implementing TRIPS. However, important cases have been brought against India and Brazil to enforce the special protections during the transitional period, and the US was quick to initiate complaints against Argentina and Brazil once their transitional periods expired.

The WTO's DS mechanism is supposed to help states resolve trade disputes amicably, but converting private interests into public claims seems to have exacerbated economic conflict, especially between the two major trading blocs, the USA and the EU. There is little evidence that governments are heeding the admonition of s. 3.7 of the DSU that 'Before bringing a case, a Member shall exercise its judgement as to whether action under these procedures would be fruitful.' Since these are governmental acts, brought in the public interest, the decision to initiate a complaint should be subject to democratic scrutiny. Instead, it is treated as an executive decision, usually taken by officials, with the support of politicians.[12] This again shows the lack of transparency and accountability of the procedures for regulating international economic relations.

However, effective democratic evaluation of whether a trade complaint should be initiated is hindered by the view that this simply involves enforcement of private legal rights. Indeed, some argue that the WTO's market access obligations should be treated as rights directly enforceable by private parties in domestic courts (Petersmann, 1998). This could occur as a matter of domestic constitutional law of any member state, if the WTO agreements could be considered as 'self-executing' or having direct effect. Until now this has not generally been the case, in particular in the EU where the European Court of Justice has over the years rejected claims that either GATT or the WTO agreements have direct effect in EC law.[13] However, in a recent case involving an alleged trademark violation, the ECJ's Advocate General accepted the claimant's argument that Article 50 of TRIPS (specifying provisional measures for IPR enforcement) should be regarded as having direct effect within national law, thus overriding any conflicting provision (in this case, in Dutch law). The ECJ itself refused to go so far, although it did suggest that national laws should as far as possible be interpreted to comply with WTO obligations.[14]

Property rights v. human rights

The view that private rights should be legally entrenched is also put forward by some who argue for the 'constitutionalisation' of the global trading system. One version, put forward by Ernst-Ulrich Petersmann, espouses a neo-liberal constitutionalism, which would enshrine the 'freedom to trade' as a fundamental right of individuals, legally enforceable through national constitutions in national courts (Petersmann, 1993). In this perspective, 'equal rights of the citizens may offer the most effective strategy for compensating the "democratic deficit" of international organizations' (Petersmann, 1998, p. 28). Petersmann puts forward an explicitly neo-Kantian liberal view, which asserts that a new era of world peace and prosperity can best be assured by the unrestricted pursuit of economic benefits through trade, under an umbrella of principles embodying individual cosmopolitan rights.

This ultra-liberal view assumes that the pursuit of individual self-interest, especially through economic exchange, is ultimately beneficial to all. Hence, the development of principles embodying individual rights, and the adjudication of conflicting rights-claims, would be sufficient to ensure universal consent and legitimacy. This would therefore justify even the entrenchment of internationally agreed principles so as to override national parliamentary supremacy, to secure the 'effective judicial protection of the transnational exercise of individual rights' (Petersmann, 1998, p. 26).

Petersmann responds to the challenge of Seattle by accepting that freedom of trade should also be accompanied by other human rights, which should all be enshrined in the WTO 'constitution' (Petersmann, 2000). In his view, however, 'Most human rights guarantees are about individual freedom, non-discrimination, equal opportunities, and rule of law', and a difficulty of applying them in trade law is their neglect of "economic liberties"'. His emphasis, however, is on rights of private property and market freedoms. Thus, he points to the protection of intellectual property rights in the TRIPS agreement (although, to his regret, it does not refer to human rights law), and advocates in addition the protection of competition and of the rights of 'the general citizen in maximizing consumer welfare through liberal trade' (*ibid.* 21–3).

The constitutionalisation of the WTO and other international economic institutions by the introduction of human rights is also advocated by some NGOs and others in the human rights community (Mehra, 2000). They also regret that human rights, as they have developed historically, have been most strongly articulated in the 'first generation' civil and political rights, while the 'second generation' economic, social and cultural rights are often considered to be aspirations at best; and 'third generation' collective rights such as self-determination and sustainable development are hard to operationalise as enforceable rights.

However, this view of economic rights is very different from Petersmann's. It is significant that the right to property has been considered a civil rather than an economic right, and that this is the only positive economic right recognised by Petersmann, the remainder are 'liberties'. This ignores the rather fundamental economic questions of access to land and natural resources, shelter, food and work, let alone cultural rights. It is these that are generally treated as aspirational or unenforceable rights, which of course are those of the have-nots. Thus, a view of human rights based on the right to property and market freedoms would simply have the effect of legitimising socioeconomic inequalities.

Nevertheless, a serious effort is being made to counterbalance neo-liberal globalisation by the assertion of universal human rights norms. This entails counterposing the neo-liberal view of human rights with one based on the broader concepts of economic, social and cultural rights developed in the past few decades through the UN and other bodies. This suggests that substantive issues in international economic regulation should be viewed in the light of human rights norms (Oloka-Onyango and Udagama, 2000). In relation to TRIPS agreement, for example, the Sub-Commission on the Promotion and Protection of Human Rights of the UN Commission on Human Rights, approved a Resolution in August 2000 (UN Commission, 2000), affirming that:

> the implementation of TRIPS Agreement does not adequately reflect the fundamental nature and indivisibility of all human rights, including the right of everyone to enjoy the benefits of scientific progress and its applications, the right to health, the right to food, and the right to self-determination, there are apparent conflicts between the intellectual property rights regime embodied in TRIPS Agreement, on the one hand, and international human rights law, on the other;

and consequently urging governments and international organisations to integrate into their legislation, policies and practices:

> provisions, in accordance with international human rights obligations and principles, that protect the social function of intellectual property.

This certainly helps to provide another perspective on the ways in which international economic regulations are formulated, interpreted and implemented into legal obligations.

However, it is also clear that 'human rights' are contestable, not immutable concepts. They may therefore open up space for debate about conflicting values underlying different rights-claims. In particular, property rights entail a balance between private rights of control and public interests in the 'commons'. Ultimately, how the balance is struck between different conflicting rights-claims must be decided by democratic political means. Thus, a recourse to human rights does not resolve issues about the substantive content of international economic rules, it merely shifts the debate to a different ground. Indeed, if human rights norms are limited to liberal concepts of protection of private property and individual liberty, they may inhibit important public policy concerns such as the alleviation of poverty, disease and hunger.

This is well illustrated by the constitutional challenge brought by pharmaceutical firms against South Africa's new medicine laws. Strikingly, this case was based on claims of human rights violations, especially the deprivation of property without compensation.[15] Certainly, strong counter-arguments could be made,[16] especially since the South African constitution is in some respects post-liberal and recognises rights to housing (Article 26), as well as healthcare, food, water and social security (Article 27). These provisions place an obligation on the government to take 'reasonable legislative and other measures, within its available resources, to achieve the progressive realisation of each of these rights'. Few other constitutions provide such a basis to balance vested property rights against the rights of the dispossessed. Even so, the collapse of the case owed much to the global attention attracted by the access to the medicines campaign, and the possibility of building international support around the issue of HIV-AIDS. In other contexts, the defence of public policy against private interests will be much more difficult.

WTO rules and national sovereignty

A different approach would aim to ensure that WTO rules allow national states sufficient scope to make their own judgements about the public interest. This would resist pressures for economic globalisation to override national and local political judgements about public welfare. Thus, it has been stressed, especially by developing countries, that TRIPS should be interpreted with flexibility, to avoid imposing a 'one-size-fits-all' model for IPRs. On the other hand, supporters of IPRs have stressed that TRIPS must establish a 'high level' of protection.

Certainly, as suggested above, what is meant by 'harmonisation' is a central issue for the WTO. In general, the WTO Agreements establish standards against which national regulation should be evaluated, rather than detailed rules for implementation into national law. Even TRIPS, which is in many respects very specific about what national laws must contain, leaves considerable leeway for states to tailor national laws and policies to suit their own circumstances. It should be recalled that TRIPS contains two kinds of obligation requiring national IP laws to comply with international standards. First, it requires WTO members to apply the main provisions of several multilateral treaties, in particular the Berne and the Paris Conventions. In addition, the TRIPS Agreement itself contains a number of minimum requirements for IP protection, for example requiring copyright protection for computer programs (Article 10), and patent protection for microbiological processes (Article 27.3(b)).

Significantly, however, TRIPS is non-prescriptive on the conditions for the granting of private rights, but much more specific and detailed about the procedures for enforcing those rights, and on the permissible limits to private rights to safeguard the public interest. This is particularly important in relation to patents. The basic provisions on patentability in TRIPS Article 27 owe much to the draft Patent Harmonisation Treaty, which was abandoned in 1991 after six years' work in WIPO.[17] However, TRIPS drafters essentially selected those provisions favouring patent owners, many of which were actually strengthened compared to the 1991 WIPO draft. Thus, TRIPS chose the more stringent options in the WIPO draft on the 20-year minimum term, the requirement of product patents and the reversal of the burden of proof for process patents; and the power for states to limit patentability was somewhat more narrowly drawn, in particular by specifying that it does not extend to micro-organisms or to non-biological or microbiological processes. On the other hand, although TRIPS specifies the three basic conditions of patentability (novelty, inventive step and industrial applicability/utility), these are not defined. Nor does TRIPS make any attempt to clarify the all-important distinction between a discovery and an invention. It is this laxity that has allowed patent offices in some countries, notably the USA, to grant 'patents on life', and to encourage biopiracy and the privatisation and commodification of community knowledge and techniques. In this respect, there is a need for greater specificity and less flexibility in TRIPS.[18] As presently worded, the failure by a state to allow patenting of micro-organisms and microbiological processes could result in a complaint under TRIPS, whereas there is no basis for complaint about over-broad protection that is due to lax interpretation of patentability requirements.

Where flexibility is important is in the interpretation of the limits on the protection of private property rights to safeguard the public interest in access to new technologies and knowledge. The difficulty is that, while the criteria for granting private rights are widely drawn, the scope for states to limit these rights for public purposes is defined quite specifically in TRIPS. This allows WTO review of any public-interest limits on IPRs enacted at national level. Indeed, the first two decisions on the substantive provisions of TRIPS have done precisely that. In the EC complaint, *Canada Pharmaceuticals* (WT/DS114/1), the Panel ruled that the 'limited' exceptions allowed under Article 30 did not justify the 'stockpiling' provisions which allowed generic drugs manufacturers to begin production before the end of the 20-year patent term, although the 'regulatory review' exception is permissible. Similarly, in relation to copyright, the Panel struck down the US provisions allowing music broadcasting without payment by small businesses, although it accepted that the 'homestyle' exception could be regarded as one of the 'special cases which do not conflict with a normal exploitation of the work' permitted by TRIPS Article 13.[19]

It is important that the WTO's DS bodies should clarify their proper role in these situations. It would be inappropriate for them to become in effect an appeals court against decisions by national bodies, whether legislatures, courts, or officials such as patent examiners. Their task is to apply the principles of WTO agreements such as TRIPS to review the adequacy of national rules for trade purposes. Thus, interpreting whether national provisions 'do not conflict with a normal exploitation of the work and do not unreasonably prejudice the legitimate interests of the rights-holder', should not entail substitution of a WTO view of the public interest for that of accountable national public bodies. Its task rather is to review whether national provisions fall within a range of possibilities that can be considered 'normal' or 'reasonable'. In so doing, it is vital to be sensitive to the role of national bodies in striking the appropriate balance between protection of rights holders and the public interest in free diffusion. In practice, it could be said that the decisions in the *US Copyright* and *Canada Pharmaceuticals* cases did offer a pragmatic compromise, in permitting some and invalidating other exceptions.

However, some commentators have argued that the legitimacy of the WTO DS system would be enhanced by the explicit acknowledgement that it is not an appeals but a review process, and an articulation of its standard of review. Thus, Robert Howse puts forward a principle of 'institutional sensitivity' in relation to other bodies which may have a particular expertise or particular stake in the laws and policies which come under WTO review (Howse, 2000, p. 62). Lawrence Helfer goes further, and proposes that WTO adjudication could usefully adopt the principle of 'margin of appreciation' developed in the human rights context by the European Court of Human Rights (Helfer, 1998, 1999). This suggests that the 'appropriate scope of supervisory review' of an international adjudicatory body should be 'to review public decisions for their conformity to certain standards and to grant a remedy if it finds that there has been an unjustifiable breach of those standards' (Macdonald, 1993, p. 84).

More broadly, the 'margin of appreciation' principle has been justified as an expression of elements, which could be described as basic to international institutions engaged in the tasks of 'managed interdependence'.[20]

- *Interpretation of international standards* – International agreements between states, especially those establishing regulatory standards, are necessarily formulated in general terms, leaving considerable leeway for interpretive choices which may involve important issues of values.
- *Subsidiarity and diversity* – As far as possible, internationally agreed standards should be interpreted to give the primary responsibility for choices involving values to the national or local levels of government, which are closest and most responsive to the people affected.
- *Democracy* – Decisions taken by public bodies which are democratically accountable should not lightly be overturned by less accountable bodies such as tribunals or committees of experts.

Developing global welfare standards

As suggested in the previous section, a fundamental problem with TRIPS is the assumption that its aim is to establish a 'high level of protection', which is taken to mean strong exclusivity rights. Indeed, the amendment of TRIPS to include any 'higher level' of protection which might be adopted in other treaties to which all WTO members are party is envisaged in both TRIPS (Article 71.2) and the WTO Agreement itself (Article IX.6). This seems to assume that a 'high level' treaty is one that gives maximum scope for private rights of owners, rather than the broader social interest of encouraging diffusion.

It is important, therefore, to oppose the essentially neo-liberal view that international legal obligations should entrench private rights, including property rights, as a check on any regulatory requirements embodying public interests that may be established at national level by states. We should remember that the so-called 'private' rights in this context are in practice those of large corporations, the TNCs. In reality, these are institutionalised bureaucracies whose power over immense concentrations of assets and activities requires that they be publicly accountable. Thus, it is misleading to consider these as 'private' rights, since they are not personal rights of individuals.

Further, IPRs are not 'natural' rights but, as explained in the first section, state-enforced monopolies which artificially create a scarcity. Thus, a consideration of the public welfare impact must enter into the definition and interpretation of the scope of such rights. It would be inappropriate and ineffective to entrench IPRs as private rights at the international level, subject to possible limits in the public interest determined only at national level. This has been made clear by the recent debates about the impact of TRIPS on access to drugs. These have highlighted issues (discussed in other chapters in this volume) such as the appropriate scope for parallel imports, which can only be effectively evaluated against global public welfare standards.

Thus, there is an inescapable need to develop global welfare standards against which to evaluate the definition and scope of international economic rights and obligations, such as those in TRIPS. Indeed, the TRIPS Agreement itself contains firm statements of such standards, in Articles 7 and 8, which are worth recalling here.

Article 7: Objectives

The protection and enforcement of intellectual property rights should contribute to the promotion of technological innovation and to the transfer and dissemination of technology, to the mutual advantage of producers and users of technological knowledge and in a manner conducive to social and economic welfare, and to a balance of rights and obligations.

Article 8: Principles

1. Members may, in formulating or amending their laws and regulations, adopt measures necessary to protect public health and nutrition, and to promote the public interest in sectors of vital importance to their socioeconomic and technological development, provided that such measures are consistent with the provisions of this Agreement.

2. Appropriate measures, provided that they are consistent with the provisions of this Agreement, may be needed to prevent the abuse of intellectual property rights by right holders or the resort to practices which unreasonably restrain trade or adversely affect the international transfer of technology.

It is not surprising that in the important June 2001 debates in the TRIPS Council, the importance of evaluating TRIPS provisions in the light of these principles has been stressed.

Clearly, the development of such global welfare standards, and the evaluation of TRIPS provisions in light of them, requires wide-ranging public discussions. The campaigns over the impact of TRIPS on access to pharmaceutical drugs has enabled such a debate to be begun. The way has been cleared for this by the withdrawal of the US complaint against Brazil's local working requirement, and the collapse of the legal challenge to the South African medicine laws. Although these claims for the protection of private rights have been suspended, we are still only in at the initial stages of the debate over the framing of an international IPR regime that can adequately reflect global welfare standards.

Notes

1. It has been argued that such retaliation may be effective for developing countries, whose small domestic markets and relatively few tariff bindings may make trade sanctions ineffective; but that suspension of concessions under TRIPS might best take the form of compulsory licensing rather than forfeiture of vested IPRs, which might amount to expropriation (Subramaniam and Watal, 2000).
2. Under the DSU, sanctions (compensation) are only lawful if a WTO complaint has been upheld, and the offending measures have not been withdrawn. A successful complainant should first seek compensation in the same sector where a violation has been found, and Article 22.3 defines sectors as goods, the relevant service sector, or each category of IPRs. The complainant has the initiative: unless it accepts an offer from the losing state, it may propose the level and type of sanction it wishes to the DSB, which may only reject them by consensus, so in practice the DSB is a rubber-stamp. Although the losing state may request arbitration (by the original Panel if available), the arbitrator can review only the level of the compensation sought, and its compatibility with the relevant WTO agreement (including the cross-retaliation provisions of DSU 22.3). Complainant states are generally careful to target retaliatory sanctions to damage only the purely domestic firms of the target states, rather than industries in which their own TNCs may have investments. There is no check on this, since the arbitrator cannot review the 'nature' of the suspension sought.
3. The US exports virtually no bananas, so the real economic injury was for loss of market access by firms such as Dole, for breach of EU commitments under the General Agreement on Trade in Services (GATS) for wholesaling and distribution services. However, GATT law has been interpreted to protect trade expectations and not actual trade volume, so that hindering even the very small potential for US banana exports to the EU amounted to a violation of its rights under GATT as well as GATS. So the Arbitrators held that the US decision to apply sanctions entirely to imports of goods did not involve

cross-retaliation under DSU Article 22 ('the United States has the right to request the suspension of concessions in either of these two sectors, or in both, up to the overall level of nullification or impairment suffered', para. 3.10 of the Decision of the Arbitrators, WT/DS27/ARB, 9 April 1999).

4. Ecuador's request for suspension of concessions was referred to the Arbitrators, who found that the damage it had suffered amounted to US$201.6m, and that *to the extent that suspension of concessions in traded goods and wholesale trade services would be insufficient*, Ecuador could seek DSB permission to suspend concessions under TRIPS.

5. Sections 301–10 of the Trade Act 1974 (as amended) establish procedures for US firms and industry associations to file petitions which must be followed up by the USTR. Under s. 301(a), the USTR is *required* to take action if it finds a breach of a trade agreement or of 'the international legal rights of the US'; under s. 301(b) USTR has a *discretion* to act against acts or policies of a foreign state it finds to be 'unreasonable or discriminatory' and a burden or restriction on US commerce.

6. In 1984 lack of adequate intellectual property protection was added to the 'unfair trade practices' provisions of s. 301 of the 1974 Trade Act. In 1988 the Omnibus Trade and Competitiveness Act enacted 'Special 301', mandating the US Trade Representative (USTR) to identify countries with inadequate IP protection, explicitly to support US negotiating objectives in the Uruguay Round.

7. This section has particularly benefited from discussions with Gregory Shaffer of University of Madison Law School, and access to his unpublished paper, based on interviews with trade officials (Shaffer, 2000).

8. Under the NCPI, 7 complaints were filed and five cases opened over ten years (van Eeckhaute, 1999, p. 200 fn. 5); under the TBR, sixteen procedures have been initiated in a little over five years, three of which related to TRIPS (European Commission, 2000); of these, six have led to WTO complaints, of a total of fifty-four initiated by the EC. However, the Commission channels many of the cases resulting from representations by firms or business associations through the Article 133 procedure.

9. Under Article 133 (formerly 113) of the EC Treaty, the Commission conducts negotiations for trade agreements under an authorisation from the Council and in consultation with a special committee appointed by the Council; it was amended by the Amsterdam Treaty (1997) to allow the Council (acting unanimously) to include services and IPRs, although this does not give the EC legislative competence in these areas. The Nice Treaty (2001) proposes further amendments, including allowing the authority to be given by a qualified majority, except in relation to topics for which unanimity is required for the adoption of internal rules or where the Community has not yet adopted internal rules.

10. Data derived from Overview of the State of Play of WTO Disputes as at 2 May 2001, http://www.wto.org, accessed 15 May 2001.

11. The only exception is the complaint by Brazil against the US (WT/DS224/1), brought essentially in retaliation.

12. Although s. 301 was enacted by the Congress, its effect is to mandate action by the executive branch, and this was delegated in 1988 from the President to the USTR, an unelected official (Bhagwati and Patrick, 1990, pp. 50–7).

13. See most recently *Portugal v. EC*, Case C-149/96, ECR [1999], p. I-8395.
14. *Hermès International v. FHT Marketing Choice BV*, Case C-53/96, ECR [1998] p. I-3603; discussed in Mavroidis and Zdouc (1998), pp. 410–13. However, in *Portugal v. EC*, para. 49, the Court limited this to the interpretation of EC measures intended to implement WTO obligations.
15. See Notice of Motion in the High Court of South Africa, Case number: 4183/98, 42 applicants, against the Government of South Africa (10 respondents). Article 25 of the constitution prohibits the taking of property except in terms of a law of general application, for a public purpose and with the provision of compensation. Heinz Klug gives an excellent account of the struggles over the drafting of the property clause, in the key context of land rights (Klug, 2000, pp. 124–36).
16. As in the Amicus Curiae brief by the Treatment Action Campaign, available from http://www/tac/org/za, accessed 10 June 2001.
17. The draft text as presented to a Diplomatic Conference at The Hague in June 1991 has recently been republished as WIPO document SCP/4/3. Following the successful conclusion in 2000 of the Patent Law Treaty, which mainly governs procedural matters, WIPO's Standing Committee on Patents has renewed work on harmonising substantive aspects of patent law. In preparation, the WIPO Bureau identified six 'basic issues underlying the grant of patents which are of particular importance to the further development of the patent system', viz., 'the definitions of prior art, novelty, inventive step (non-obviousness) and industrial applicability (utility); sufficiency of disclosure; and the structure and interpretation of claims': WIPO (2000), para. 9.
18. As suggested in the Communication from Kenya on behalf of the African group, 6 August 1999, WT/GC/W/302, paras 19–21.
19. Interestingly, the likelihood of a WTO review was raised during the debates in the US Congress on the Fairness in Music Licensing Act (McCluggage, 2000).
20. My version is adapted from Mahoney (1998), p. 2.

References

Barnes, J.J. (1974) *Authors, Publishers and Politicians. The Quest for an Anglo-American Copyright Agreement 1815–1854* (London: RKP).
Bhagwati, J. and H.T. Patrick (eds) (1990) *Aggressive Unilateralism. America's 301 Trade Policy and the World Trading System* (Ann Arbor: University of Michigan Press).
Drahos, P. (ed.) (1999) *Intellectual Property*, International Library of Essays in Law and Legal Theory (Aldershot, Ashgate-Dartmouth).
European Commission (2000) 'Trade Barriers Regulation: the First Five Years', conference on The Challenge of Globalisation: the European Union's Market Access Strategy, Brussels.
Evans, G. (1996) 'The Principle of National Treatment and the International Protection of Industrial Property', *European Intellectual Property Review*, vol. 18, no. 3, pp. 149–60.
Helfer, L.R. (1998) 'Adjudicating Copyright Claims under TRIPS Agreement. The Case for a European Human Rights Analogy', *Harvard International Law Journal*, vol. 39, no. 2, p. 357.

Helfer, L.R. (1999) 'A European Human Rights Analogy for Adjudicating Copyright Claims under TRIPS', *European Intellectual Property Review*, vol. 21, no. 1, pp. 8–16.

Howse, R. (2000) 'Adjudicative Legitimacy and Treaty Interpretation in International Trade Law: the Early Years of WTO Jurispudence', in J.H.H. Weiler (ed.), *The EU, the WTO, and the NAFTA. Towards a Common Law of International Trade?* (Oxford: OUP), pp. 35–69.

Klug, H. (2000) *Constituting Democracy. Law, Globalism and South Africa's Political Reconstruction* (Cambridge: CUP).

McCluggage, L.A. (2000) 'Section 110(5) and the Fairness in Music Licensing Act: Will the WTO Decide the United States Must Pay to Play?' *Idea: The Journal of Law and Technology*, vol. 40, pp. 1–47.

Macdonald, R.S.J. (1993) 'The Margin of Appreciation', in R. S. J. Macdonald, F. Matscher and H. Petzold (eds), *The European System for the Protection of Human Rights* (Dordrecht: Nijhoff), pp. 83–124.

McGinnis, J.O. and M.L. Movesian (2000) 'The World Trade Constitution', *Harvard Law Review*, vol. 114, pp. 512–605.

Mahoney, P. (1998) 'Marvellous Richness of Diversity or Invidious Cultural Relativism?', *Human Rights Law Journal* (Special Issue on The Doctrine of Margin of Appreciation under the European Convention on Human Rights: its Legitimacy in Theory and Application in Practice), vol. 19, no. 1, pp. 1–6.

Mavroidis, P.C. and W. Zdouc (1998) 'Legal Means to Protect Private Parties' Interests in the WTO', *Journal of International Economic Law*, vol. 1, pp. 407–32.

Mehra, M. (2000) *Human Rights and the WTO: Time to Take on the Challenge*, published on the WTOwatch website at http://www.wtowatch.org.

Moore, M. (2000) 'The Backlash against Globalization?', speech delivered in Ottawa, 26 October (published on the WTO website www.wto.org, accessed 27 January 2001).

Oloka-Onyango, J. and D. Udagama (2000) *Preliminary Report on Globalization and its Impact on the Full Enjoyment of Human Rights to the Sub-Commission on the Promotion and Protection of Human Rights of the UN Commission on Human Rights* (E/CN.4/Sub.2/2000/13).

Petersmann, E.-U. (1993) 'National Constitutions and International Economic Law', in M. Hilf and E.-U. Petersmann (eds), *National Constitutions and International Economic Law* (Deventer: Kluwer), pp. 3–53.

Petersmann, Ernst-Ulrich (1998) 'How to Constitutionalize International Law and Foreign Policy for the Benefit of Civil Society?', *Michigan Journal of International Law* vol. 20, p. 1.

Petersmann, E.-U. (2000) 'The WTO Constitution and Human Rights', *Journal of International Economic Law*, vol. 3, no. 1, pp. 19–25.

Picciotto, Sol (2001) 'Democratizing Globalism', in D. Drache (ed.), *The Market on the Public Domain?* (London: Routledge), pp. 335–59.

Plant, A. (1934) 'The Economic Theory Concerning Patents for Inventions.' *Economica*, n.s. 1(February), p. 45.

Plasseraud, Y. and F. Savignon (1983) [Paris 1883] *Genèse du Droit Unioniste des Brevets* (Paris: Librairies techniques).

Ricketson, S. (1987) *The Berne Convention for the Protection of Literary and Artistic Works* (Deventer: Kluwer & London, Centre for Commercial Law Studies, Queen Mary College).

Ryan, M.P. (1998) *Knowledge Diplomacy. Global Competition and the Politics of Intellectual Property* (Washington, DC: Brookings Institution Press).

Shaffer, Gregory (2000) 'The Law-in-Action of International Trade Litigation in the US and Europe: The Melding of the Public and Private', unpublished paper, draft of 24 May.

Subramaniam, A. and J. Watal (2000). 'Can TRIPS Serve as an Enforcement Device for Developing Countries in the WTO?', *Journal of International Economic Law*, vol. 3, no. 3, pp. 403–16.

UN Commission on Human Rights (2000) *Intellectual Property Rights and Human Rights. Geneva, Sub-Commission on the Promotion and Protection of Human Rights*, E/CN.4/Sub.2/2000/7.

Van Eeckhaute, J.C. (1999) 'Private Complaints Against Unfair Trade Practices. The EC's Trade Barriers Regulation', *Journal of World Trade*, vol. 33, no. 6, pp. 199–213.

Weiler, J.H.H. (2000) *The Rule of Lawyers and the Ethos of Diplomats: Reflections on the Internal and External Legitimacy of WTO Dispute Settlement* (Harvard Law School, Harvard Jean Monnet Working Paper 09/00).

WIPO (2000) 'Suggestions for the Further Development of International Patent Law'. Document SCP/4/2, 25 September.

Zoller, E. (1985) 'Remedies for Unfair Trade: European and United States Views', *Cornell International Law Journal*, vol. 18, p. 227.

15

The Global Campaign on Patents and Access to Medicines: An Oxfam Perspective

Ruth Mayne

Introduction

Not so long ago, intellectual property was an esoteric issue confined to patent offices, intellectual property specialists and company lawyers. But the global campaign on access to medicines helped change all that. By the time Oxfam joined the campaign in early 2001, the issue of patents and medicine was already rising rapidly up the public and policy agenda.

Nevertheless, although there was growing awareness of the need to improve access to vital medicines in poor countries, the major pharmaceutical companies and key northern governments denied that WTO patent rules were contributing to the problem. They said that other factors – poverty, poor health infrastructures, and lack of political will of governments – were more important. NGOs agreed that all these factors were important, indeed many had campaigned for years on these very issues, but they insisted that patents were also a key problem. They argued that helping lower the prices of key medicines by making patent rules on health more flexible was a vital step towards combating the health crisis in poor countries.

In the space of a few short months between February 2001 and November 2002, a remarkable series of events occurred that meant that industrialised countries were no longer able to ignore the impact of WTO patent rules on health. These events included the attempts of 39 pharmaceutical companies to sue the South African government over the terms of its Medicine Act, the US trade dispute with Brazil over its patent law, a unified developing-country strategy to obtain a pro-public health interpretation of the TRIPS Agreement, and the consideration given by the Canadian and US governments to use compulsory licensing to gain access to adequate supplies of cheap anti-anthrax medicines.

Despite their earlier denials, rich country ministers found themselves agreeing to a pro-public health clarification of the Agreement on Trade-Related Aspects of Intellectual Property Rights (TRIPS) at the 4th WTO Ministerial in Doha in November 2001. While the clarification will not solve all the public-health problems arising from TRIPS, it is an important step forward in the struggle for affordable medicines, and a victory for developing countries at the WTO.

The global public concern generated around these events also contributed to a number of other advances: the company climb-down over South Africa and the US decision to drop its trade dispute with Brazil widened the political space for poor countries to implement pro-public health patent policies; the pharmaceutical giants further cut the prices of some vital patented medicines in some poorer countries; and a global health fund for drug purchases had been set up (albeit inadequately funded).

This chapter offers an Oxfam perspective on these events, and on the role that the global patents and medicines campaign has played in bringing about these changes. Unfortunately, in such a short chapter it is impossible to do justice to all the individuals and organisations involved in the campaign.

The global campaign on access to medicines

The global campaign on access to medicines grew in response to the major health crisis in the developing world. While public health is being transformed by medical advances in rich countries, 14 million people die every year of treatable diseases in poor countries. HIV/AIDS is compounding the problems of infectious tropical diseases, and ravaging not only the poorest countries in Africa, but also middle-income countries such as South Africa and Thailand. Yet those most in need are the least able to afford treatment. Around one third of the world's population do not have regular access to essential medicines, and tropical diseases account for less than 1 per cent of the global health-research budget.

Campaigning groups contended that WTO patent rules were set to further reduce poor people's access to vital medicines. By introducing global rules that shield powerful companies from cheaper generic competition, they argued that TRIPS would raise prices for newly patented medicines. The negative impact of patents on access to medicines has been dramatically illustrated in the case of HIV/AIDS medicines that were initially priced far beyond the reach of most poor countries. But the problem extends beyond HIV/AIDS to the new drugs needed to treat drug-resistant strains of old killers such as tuberculosis and malaria.

Moreover, TRIPS is unlikely to address the massive market failure in research and development relating to neglected diseases. The markets of poor people in developing countries are simply too small to influence the R&D decisions of large companies. While 75 per cent of the world's population live in developing countries, they account for only around 10 per cent of global pharmaceutical medicine sales. Strengthened patent protection in poor countries will not change the basic market reality. Large injections of public funds, and public–private partnerships are needed.

By the time Oxfam joined the global campaign on access to medicines, other organisations had already succeeded in getting these issues on to the policy and public agenda. In 1996, Health Action International (HAI), a network of public-health workers with members in more than seventy countries, organised two important international meetings, which brought together health activists from around the world, and formed the basis of the international coalition on patents and medicines.

This network drew on the research conducted by WHO on the important role of generic medicines, as well as analysis by individuals such as Dr Kumariah Balasubramaniam, a pharmaceutical adviser to Consumer International's Health and Pharmaceutical Programme in Asia and the Pacific, and intellectual property experts such as Carlos Correa. Jamie Love, Director of Ralph Nader's Consumer Project on Technology (CPT), played a pivotal role with his knowledge of drug development costs, intellectual property and trade agreements, and technology transfer issues.

Médecins Sans Frontières (MSF) joined the coalition with the launch of its own campaign in September 1999, and quickly became a major player. In March 2000, MSF, HAI and CPT held a conference in Geneva on TRIPS in the run-up to the WHO World Health Assembly. The meeting helped generate support for the WHO's revised drug strategy, agreed at its General Assembly in May 2000, and which mandated the organisation to assess the public-health implications of trade agreements. This was followed by two other seminars aimed at influencing policy makers on research and development into tropical diseases and the TRIPS

Agreement. Meanwhile organisations such as the South Centre, Third World Network, and the Quaker United Nations Office, Geneva were providing technical and legal support to developing countries' missions in Geneva to further develop their own analysis and strategies.

The international alliance built on and supported campaigns at the national level. NGOs in countries such as South Africa, Brazil and Thailand were active on the issue (see below). In the US, campaigning by AIDS activists and health groups such as ACT-UP Philadelphia and the Health GAP Coalition helped pressurise President Clinton into issuing an Executive Order in May 2000. This stated that the USA would no longer threaten sanctions against Sub-Saharan African countries if they were using TRIPS safeguards to gain access to HIV/AIDS medicines.

The expertise of these pressure groups meant that they were able to exercise influence on governments through insider-lobbying. But the sheer scale of the humanitarian crisis, combined with the adverse impact of patent rules on people in poor countries, also enabled them to generate a large amount of press interest globally. This in turn began to force governments to take the health crisis and the problems posed by global patent rules more seriously.

Oxfam International's campaign

Oxfam's decision to launch its own campaign was influenced by a number of factors. Because of its overseas development and emergency work, Oxfam was already acutely aware of the health crisis facing developing countries, in particular in Africa. A large part of Oxfam's work focuses on public-health for those affected by conflict and natural disasters, and it also seeks to improve people's health through support for long-term development and health projects. Oxfam also has a long history of campaigning for debt-relief and increased international finance targeted on health and education budgets, and has lobbied the World Bank against the introduction of user fees for health services in poor countries.

Through its trade campaign, Oxfam was increasingly aware of how WTO patent rules were set to deepen the existing health crisis. This issue lent itself particularly well to popular campaigning, as it provided a powerful human illustration of how unjust global trade rules work against people in poor countries. The strong role of Northern governments and companies in shaping global patent rules meant that Oxfam International, an international alliance of NGOs based principally in Northern countries, could explain and seek the involvement of its approximately 1 500 000 supporters to bring about change.

In short, Oxfam's Cut the Cost campaign seeks to improve poor people's access to medicines by cutting the cost of vital medicines. The campaign's objectives are to reform global patent rules in favour of public-health; to stop the US and TNCs intimidating poor countries that seek to use the existing TRIPS safeguards to gain access to the cheapest possible medicines; to obtain systematic price reductions for key medicines; and to establish a global fund to finance research and development into neglected diseases and help developing-country governments purchase vital drugs. The campaign strategies focus on influencing the policy and practice of Northern governments and companies, and involve building alliances with other campaign groups, developing-country governments, sympathetic individuals in government and opinion-formers, medical and health professionals, and socially responsible scientists. Media work and popular campaigning are both vital elements of the campaign strategy.

Oxfam also seeks to bring a broader development perspective to the access to medicines campaigns, and has raised other health-related issues of concern to developing countries and Southern NGOs, such as the biopiracy of medicinal plants and knowledge from developing countries, and the lack of efforts to protect traditional knowledge and promote locally based research and development. It also raises questions about the broader development-costs of TRIPS, working in alliance with groups such as the influential Third World Network.

Campaign gains

South Africa

In March 2001, shortly following the launch of the campaign, there was immense media coverage of the attempt by thirty-nine global drug companies to sue the South African government. The companies claimed that South Africa's 1997 Medicine Act, which allowed the government to import cheap versions of patented medicines, undermined their patent rights. It was an extraordinary public-relations blunder, which revealed a misplaced sense of omnipotence in an industry used to getting its own way.

The court case was extensively reported by media around the world. In large part the press slated the industry for putting profits before lives in a country where around 4.5 million people are infected by HIV/AIDS. The *Financial Times* described the companies as 'bone-headed'. The subsequent climb-down was also greeted with astonishment. The *Wall*

Street Journal described the industry as 'reeling from an unprecedented wave of public scorn', and *The Economist* asked 'how did the industry get itself in such a mess?'

The South African government's decision to fight the case was a critical factor in generating global media interest. The presiding judge noted that it was a landmark case with implications far beyond South Africa. Treatment Action Campaign (TAC), a local voluntary network campaigning for affordable treatment for people with HIV/AIDS, played a key role in supporting the South African government's defence case. In spite of the fact that the Pharmaceutical Manufacturers Association (PMA) of South Africa had hired most of the local legal talent, TAC was able to generate vital legal analysis which seriously challenged the industry case, and helped underpin media coverage and international campaigning. It also collected testimonies from people living with HIV/AIDS that illustrated the human cost of patented medicines.

The global NGO campaign added to the global pressure on the industry to withdraw from the court case. International agencies such as MSF and Oxfam helped ensure the story was transmitted around the world. Oxfam's campaign launch, for example, had already received extensive global coverage, so when it launched its press briefings on the South African case in Pretoria, Bangkok, Brasilia, Delhi, Brussels, Washington and London, these helped spread the story.

International NGOs also helped to organise campaign actions and lobbying, petitions, and letters to governments and industry, calling on the companies to withdraw from the case. Company directors were publicly named and shamed in press briefings. Oxfam organised a publicity stunt outside the South African court in which people dressed as company directors were put in a dock with their names hung around their necks; the photographs were transmitted around the world. MSF presented a petition with 250 000 signatures to the South African PMA press conference. Oxfam invited Glenys Kinnock, MEP, and the actress Michelle Collins to South Africa, the latter helping to ensure television and tabloid press coverage in the UK. Ministers and parliaments of various European Union countries and the European Parliament, called on the companies to withdraw.

The South African court case was so significant because it did more than any other previous event to raise public awareness about the impact of global patent rules. Campaigners hope that the strong public condemnation, followed by the company climb-down, will encourage other developing-country governments to implement TRIPS in a way that favours public-health.

The international concern generated around the court case also intensified the price war on anti-retroviral drugs, both between the pharmaceutical giants, and between them and the generic drug companies. Large companies cut drug prices in an attempt to recoup some public support, to blunt the offers from generic drug companies, and to stave off a growing public backlash against global patent rules. Raymond Gilmartin, Merck's Chairman and Chief Executive, was reported as saying 'if we don't solve the drug access problem then our intellectual property is at risk'.

Prices of key HIV/AIDS medicines for triple therapy set by global drug companies continued to fall, from the original patented price in the US of around $10 000 per patient per year, to the discounted prices offered to African countries of around US$900 by March 2001. Yet even these offers did not match those from Indian-based generic companies, the lowest of which had reached US$289 (from Auribindo) by August 2001. All this testifies to the importance of public pressure and generic competition in bringing down prices. However, the discounts from global drug companies are not sufficient to bring the medicines fully into the reach of African governments. This will require the flexible use of compulsory licensing, so that African countries can produce or import cheap generics, combined with massively increased international aid.

That said, the international pharmaceutical industry continues to operate to a long-term game plan. Companies have argued that their stance will be vindicated further down the road, when it becomes clear that access to HIV/AIDS medicines in South Africa has still failed to improve, despite the withdrawal of the industry from the court case. This will show that lack of political will and inadequate health infrastructures are the key barriers to ill health, rather than alleged constraints imposed by patent rules.

NGOs agree that a range of factors are responsible for ill health and continue to pressure governments to do more, and campaign for more finance for cash-strapped health services. TAC, for example, recently took the South African government to court in an attempt to get it to provide nevirapine to cut mother-to-child transmission of HIV. Then in January 2002, TAC and MSF ignored patent rules and imported Brazilian generic versions of key anti-retrovirals into South Africa for use in an AIDS treatment programme. Zachie Achmat of TAC, in a joint press release with MSF and Oxfam, said that 'Central to the success of Brazil's AIDS programme is the manufacturing of generic drugs. The South African government should pursue compulsory licensing to ensure that generic anti-retrovirals can be produced or imported in South Africa.'[1]

The corporate sector

Part of Oxfam's campaign was directed at British-based Glaxo Smith Kline (GSK), which as an industry leader was seen as potentially capable of bringing change in the industry. At the launch of its campaign Oxfam had released a detailed report on the company that received widespread press coverage. It called for changes in both its pricing and patent policy, and in lobbying practice. Specifically, Oxfam challenged GSK to respect national health policies, to develop equitable pricing schemes to widen access to its medicines in poor countries, to provide funds to a global international research fund created under the auspices of the WHO which would operate without IP conditionality, and to ensure that the lobbying positions of PhRMA and other industry interest groups respect public-health needs.

Shortly after the launch of Oxfam's campaign, socially responsible investment teams of five city investment houses decided to host a closed meeting with GSK and Oxfam to discuss the issues raised by Oxfam's report. The investors expressed concern that a bad public image on this issue could damage GSK's long-term share price. One investor said, 'investors want the company to have something that looks more like a coherent strategy towards access to medicines. They have to raise their game in understanding how seriously the public takes this issue and how seriously investors take it.'[2] Subsequently, the social investment teams of many of these investment houses began to ask pharmaceutical companies to report on their policies for promoting access to medicines in poor countries. At the meeting, GSK promised to present a new policy framework outlining its stance on its pricing and patent policies.

In order to keep up the pressure on the company, Oxfam supporters wrote to GSK's Chief Executive, held protests outside its AGM in May 2001 and asked questions inside the meeting. In June 2001 the company issued a statement in which it extended its offer of cheap AIDS drugs to sixty-three countries. It also promised to make cheap anti-malarials available, to continue research into diseases that afflict poor countries and to establish a corporate social-responsibility committee. Oxfam welcomed these policies, but reiterated that potentially reversible price reductions by individual companies could not substitute for reforms to patent rules which would allow vital cheap generic competition to bring down prices in a more sustained manner. It also urged companies to help develop a global systematic and transparent system of tiered pricing. Oxfam subsequently produced a public report on

Pfizer, one of the key drivers behind the TRIPS agreement. Yet the pharmaceutical industry continues to downplay the important social function of generic drugs companies in providing low-cost, life-saving drugs to poor people, and in generating employment and foreign-exchange savings in poor countries.

Brazil

The next major campaign effort was over Brazil, where a similar pattern of commercial and political pressures was playing itself out. International pharmaceutical companies had threatened to withdraw investments, and had persuaded the US to request a WTO dispute-settlement board over Brazil's alleged violations of TRIPS. The industry and the US government saw Brazil's patent law as a protectionist measure aimed at fostering domestic industry, whereas the Brazilian government claimed it was vital to its flagship HIV/AIDS programme. The Brazilian government decided to stand up to the US, and because of the success of its AIDS programme gained strong support from AIDS activists and NGOs both in Brazil and globally. After several months of a tense stand-off, another victory was achieved when the US backed down and withdrew the case. The US did not concede the point but indicated that in the current climate it was better to deal with the issue bilaterally, and Brazil agreed to consult with it over possible future use of the contested article in its patent law. The withdrawal came shortly after the June WTO TRIPS special session on patents and access to medicine, in which the US found itself isolated in its rigid stance on TRIPS. Once again, NGOs had played an important role in raising public awareness. Brazilian NGOs mobilised in defence of the government HIV/AIDS programme and patent law, and Oxfam, AIDS activists and others in the North helped to generate international concern and exert pressure on governments.

Anthrax

In November 2001, the consideration given by the US and Canadian governments to use compulsory licensing in order to obtain adequate supplies of anti-anthrax antibiotics brought the story of WTO patent rules into the living rooms of millions more people. In an astonishing display of double standards, the US government raised the possibility of licensing or importing generic drugs if Bayer didn't reduce prices and step up supplies of its anti-anthrax antibiotics. Bayer quickly dropped the price of ciprofloxacin by half. Shortly prior to this, the Canadian Health Ministry had decided to override Bayer's patent until they realised that this left them open to charges of hypocrisy.

These were precisely the kind of tactics used by the Brazilian government that the US had opposed earlier in the year. But the hypocrisy extended even further, because at precisely the same time that the US and Canadian governments were using compulsory licensing as a negotiating tool with companies, they were also actively blocking proposals to clarify WTO rules which would allow developing countries to use compulsory licensing in a similar way. It is salutary to note that anthrax has fortunately killed only a handful of Americans so far, whereas infectious diseases kill 14 million people every year, and HIV/AIDS has killed 23 million people.

The remaining battle over TRIPS

An important element of the patents and access to medicines campaign has been the growing and unprecedented collaboration between developing country trade missions in Geneva and NGOs to shift TRIPS in favour of public health. Emboldened by NGO campaigns and public condemnation over the South African case, developing countries proposed in April 2001 that the WTO hold a special session on patents and access to medicines, to discuss the impact of patents on medicines and to clarify the existing flexibilities in TRIPS. This was an extremely astute move, as it would finally force the international community to discuss an issue that had been consistently ducked elsewhere because of industry pressure. Even the US agreed to this, possibly seeing it as an opportunity to convince developing countries of the importance of patents.

The first TRIPS Council discussion was held in June 2001, followed by an informal session in July. Developing countries presented strong collective statements expressing their concerns about the public-health impact of TRIPS. They also argued that a strong pro-public health clarification of the rules was needed so that they could use the existing safeguards without fear of legal bullying or trade sanctions. At the September 2001 TRIPS Council meeting, despite opposition from the US, Switzerland, Japan and Canada, the Africa group on behalf of more than fifty developing countries seized the initiative and presented a draft declaration on TRIPS and public health for adoption at the forthcoming 4th WTO Ministerial.

In November 2001, just before the Ministerial Summit, the Chair of the WTO General Council issued a considerably watered-down draft declaration, which was supposed to provide a compromise solution. Developing countries were angry that it contained US proposals that had not been discussed with them. The draft text largely lacked the brackets that are used to signify the fact that the matter is yet to be negotiated. The US proposals diluted the key developing-country demand 'that nothing in the Agreement shall prevent governments from taking measures to promote public health and gain access to affordable medicines'. It also tried to restrict key clauses in the declaration to HIV/AIDS and other pandemics, which would mean governments would have to wait until millions of people were dying before safely using the TRIPS safeguards, rather than using them for preventive or contingency action.

Developing countries were worried that the US proposal, with its offers of extended transition periods for least-developed countries, might tempt the poorest countries to agree to a weak proposal. They made it clear that they would rather have no declaration than a weakened one. Meanwhile, NGOs publicised and promoted the developing-country proposal in Northern countries. The European Commission had shifted its position in favour of developing countries on some issues, and said it was working to broker a consensus among the WTO member states, although some critics suspected that in reality the EC was just fence-sitting. While some European governments, such as the Dutch, had provided backing to developing-country proposals, others such as the UK and Germany were reportedly holding back progress.

In the event, the issue dominated much of the discussions at Doha and WTO Ministers finally approved a text stating that 'the TRIPS Agreement does not and should not prevent governments from taking measures to protect public health and ... to promote access to medicines for all'. Although this wording was not as strong as the text in the original developing-country proposal, it clearly affirms the primacy of public health over intellectual property rights.

The Declaration went on to clarify some of the key contested areas of TRIPS. It affirmed that governments have the right to grant compulsory licences and the freedom to determine the grounds upon which such licences are granted. The declaration also confirms that governments are free to determine what constitutes a national emergency or other circumstance of extreme urgency – including public-health crises – which allows them to use a fast-track procedure for issuing compulsory licences. It also confirmed that governments are free to determine their own policies for exhaustion of intellectual property rights – parallel imports – without challenge. The declaration also grants least-developed countries an extra ten years – until 2016 instead of 2006 – before they must implement the obligation to provide pharmaceutical patent protection. However, in order to benefit from this extension least-developed-countries will need to be encouraged to amend their existing legislation as all but two African countries have already implemented pharmaceutical patenting.

Commentators indicate that these clarifications will have interpretive value in the case of future dispute-settlement procedures. This, along with the huge profile given to the issue, should give developing countries the confidence to make full use of the existing safeguards, and make it more difficult for the US or drug companies to bully them over pro-health patent policies. The Declaration also provides developing countries with a useful yardstick for negotiating bilateral trade agreements and ensuring appropriate technical assistance.

One serious public-health problem that remained unresolved at Doha is the way TRIPS restricts countries from exporting cheap generic medicines to poor countries. Most poor countries can't afford expensive patented medicines and most do not have the capacity to make affordable generic medicines themselves. They therefore need to be able to import cheap generics from other countries. Currently, poor countries can still issue, or threaten to issue, a compulsory licence to import them from large developing-country generic producers such as India. But when these generic-producing countries comply with TRIPS, which they must do by 2005 at the latest, this source will gradually dry up. Not only does TRIPS require countries to restrict third parties from making, and selling cheaper generic versions of the product (Article 28), it also says that compulsory licences to override patents can only be granted predominantly for the supply of the domestic market (Article 31(f)). This represents a major imbalance in TRIPS as it means poor countries without sufficient manufacturing capacity will be unable to make effective use of the compulsory licence provisions in order to gain access to affordable medicines.

The Doha Declaration on TRIPS and Public Health went some way to recognising this problem. It said, 'We recognise that WTO members with insufficient or no manufacturing capacities in the pharmaceutical sector could face difficulties in making effective use of compulsory licensing under the TRIPS Agreement. We instruct the Council for TRIPS to find an expeditious solution to this problem and report to the General Council before the end of 2002.' Many developing countries and NGOs, including Oxfam, have proposed that the simplest and most effective way of ensuring that poor importing countries can gain access to affordable medicines would be to lift TRIPS restrictions on export. Under Article 30, the TRIPS Agreement allows governments to make limited exceptions to the exclusive rights conferred by a patent. WTO Ministers could therefore simply agree that Article 30 can be used by countries to allow exports of medicines and other health products to countries with unmet health needs.

The US and much of industry have opposed this approach in favour of the weakest possible solution: a waiver or moratorium on disputes relating to compulsory licensing for export. Most NGOs reject a waiver as it would only offer a temporary measure, would have to be reviewed annually, and would waste a unique political opportunity to get a permanent solution. The European Community was initially open to an Article 30 solution, but at the June 2002 TRIPS Council it expressed its preference for an amendment to the compulsory licensing provisions in TRIPS to allow generic producing countries to issue a compulsory licence for export of pharmaceutical products. The problem with this option is that both the importing and exporting countries would have to issue a compulsory licence. This would leave importing countries heavily dependent on decisions in other countries, and would create uncertainties for governments and companies as both licenses would be open to legal challenge from companies. Neither would this solution eradicate inequality in the use of the safeguards, which was the intent of paragraph 6 of the Declaration.

There is also industry pressure on the US and EC to restrict solutions to the poorest countries, to only HIV/AIDs, tuberculosis and malaria, to emergency situations, or to narrow definitions of manufacturing capacity. Such restrictions would be unacceptable on health grounds and would run counter to the intent of the Doha Declaration which affirmed members' rights to use measures to protect public health and to promote access to medicines to all.

A solution based on an Article 30 approach could result in significant health gains. However, even this would not fully solve the public-health problems caused by TRIPS. The deeper problem is that the production of cheap generic versions of patented medicines is likely to become increasingly dependent on a complicated system of compulsory licensing and exceptions that will be a nightmare for generic firms in poor countries, but a dream come true for lawyers. Nor will it stem the growing demands for reform of TRIPS rules. As the other chapters in this book illustrate, the concerns over TRIPS go further than health, and relate to its broader development impact on poor countries, and the way it can restrict poor people's access to knowledge-rich goods such as seeds, education materials and computer software.

Achieving substantive reforms to global patent rules, whether to TRIPS or to the increasing number of bilateral intellectual property agreements, remains a major challenge. Unsurprisingly, the international pharmaceutical industry remains hard line in its defence of the TRIPS Agreement, from which as other chapters in this book show, it gains so much. And the large pharmaceutical companies, some of the most globalised in the world, wield a heavy influence over Northern governments. Nevertheless, it is remarkable to look back over the last year and see how the terms of the debate have shifted. As recent policy debates and press coverage, including recent debates at the World Economic Forum, indicate, the question of TRIPS reform has now moved to the mainstream.

Conclusion

The gains outlined in this chapter were possible in part because of the sheer injustice of a situation in which sufferers in Northern countries have access to the latest vital life-saving medicines, whereas those in poor countries do not. The combination of effective global campaigning by NGOs, and the widespread media coverage of the issue, created a reputational risk for the pharmaceutical companies that they could not ignore. For developing countries, the knowledge that there was growing public concern within Northern countries, a decisive factor in influencing government policy, emboldened them to take a strong unified stance at the WTO. Moreover, the fact that developing-country governments such as those in South Africa and Brazil stood up to the US and powerful drug companies in their own countries was also critical in attracting public interest. But international condemnation would not have been so strong without the public-relations errors of the pharmaceutical companies, and the reprehensible actions of the US government.

To date, the NGO campaign has been effective because it combined: strong public campaigning messages and actions based on powerful human illustrations that helped generate public outrage and high media coverage across TV, radio and print; global and cross-sectoral alliances of NGOs that supported and built on strong national campaigns, and shared analysis through the Internet; a growing alliance between developing countries and NGOs at the WTO; partially successful attempts to find supporters among rich countries; informed insider face-to-face lobbying at the highest level based on plausible analysis and evidence; and the strategic targeting of companies and governments at different times. Nevertheless, there is still much to be done in the battle for cheap medicine, adequate healthcare and reform of global patent rules.

Notes

1. Joint press release of MSF, TAC, Oxfam and COSATU, 29 January 2002, Johannesburg.
2. *Financial Times*, 16 February 2001, GSK to review drug pricing policy.

Index

Note: f = figure, n = endnote/footnote, t = table.